# Six Weeks To Marketing Excellence

Hodder & Stoughton

A MEMBER OF THE HODDER HEADLINE GROUP

Orders: please contact Bookpoint Ltd, 130 Milton Park, Abingdon, Oxon
OX14 4SB. Telephone: (44) 01235 827720. Fax: (44) 01235 400454. Lines are
open from 9.00–6.00, Monday to Saturday, with a 24 hour message
answering service.
Email address: orders@bookpoint.co.uk

*British Library Cataloguing in Publication Data*
A catalogue record for this title is available from The British Library

ISBN 0 340 812613

First Published 2003
Impression number   10 9 8 7 6 5 4 3 2 1
Year                2007 2006 2005 2004 2003

Copyright © 2003 Ros Jay, Andrew Whitaker, Richard Perry, Pete Laver, Dee
Twomey, Guy Clapperton, Sue Cave.

All rights reserved. No part of this publication may be reproduced or
transmitted in any form or by any means, electronic or mechanical, including
photocopy, recording, or any information storage and retrieval system,
without permission in writing from the publisher or under licence from the
Copyright Licensing Agency Limited. Further details of such licences (for
reprographic reproduction) may be obtained from the Copyright Licensing
Agency Limited, of 90 Tottenham Court Road, London W1P 9HE.

Typeset by SX Composing DTP, Rayleigh, Essex.
Printed in Great Britain for Hodder & Stoughton Educational, a division of
Hodder Headline Plc, 338 Euston Road, London NW1 3BH by
Cox & Wyman, Reading, Berkshire.

**chartered**
**management**
**institute**

*inspiring leaders*

## The leading organisation for professional management

As the champion of management, the Chartered Management Institute shapes and supports the managers of tomorrow. By sharing intelligent insights and setting standards in management development, the Institute helps to deliver results in a dynamic world.

## Setting and raising standards

The Institute is a nationally accredited organisation, responsible for setting standards in management and recognising excellence through the award of professional qualifications.

## Encouraging development, improving performance

The Institute has a vast range of development programmes, qualifications, information resources and career guidance to help managers and their organisations meet new challenges in a fast-changing environment.

## Shaping opinion

With in-depth research and regular policy surveys of its 91,000 individual members and 520 corporate members, the Chartered Management Institute has a deep understanding of the key issues. Its view is informed, intelligent and respected.

For more information call 01536 204222 or visit www.managers.org.uk

# C O N T E N T S

## Week One: Marketing Plans

| | | |
|---|---|---|
| **Introduction** | | 11 |
| **Sunday** | What is a marketing plan? | 12 |
| **Monday** | Asking questions | 21 |
| **Tuesday** | Researching the answers | 36 |
| **Wednesday** | The objectives | 49 |
| **Thursday** | Converting objectives into action plans | 62 |
| **Friday** | Putting the plan together | 73 |
| **Saturday** | Using the marketing plan | 85 |

## Week Two: Viral Marketing

| | | |
|---|---|---|
| **Introduction** | | 102 |
| **Sunday** | Get the basics right | 103 |
| **Monday** | Vital viral ingredients | 121 |
| **Tuesday** | Guiding content principles | 133 |
| **Wednesday** | Viral hosts, vehicles and characteristics | 142 |
| **Thursday** | Keep it simple | 157 |
| **Friday** | Start on the right foot | 167 |
| **Saturday** | Get going | 183 |

# CONTENTS

## Week Three: Building a Brand

| | | |
|---|---|---|
| **Introduction** | | 195 |
| **Sunday** | From products to brands | 197 |
| **Monday** | What have we got? | 212 |
| **Tuesday** | Completing the audit | 229 |
| **Wednesday** | Positioning | 243 |
| **Thursday** | Bringing the brand to life | 252 |
| **Friday** | When the brand speaks | 265 |
| **Saturday** | Managing the plan | 279 |

## Week Four: Direct Marketing

| | | |
|---|---|---|
| **Introduction** | | 291 |
| **Sunday** | Customers, competitors and capability | 292 |
| **Monday** | Planning your strategy and setting objectives | 304 |
| **Tuesday** | Finding and keeping the right customers | 315 |
| **Wednesday** | Building and using your marketing database | 329 |
| **Thursday** | Selecting the right media | 343 |
| **Friday** | Creating and executing campaigns | 355 |
| **Saturday** | Measurement and management of success | 366 |

# C O N T E N T S

# Week Five: Free Publicity for your Business

| **Introduction** | | 383 |
|---|---|---|
| **Sunday** | Getting started | 384 |
| **Monday** | Structuring your press release | 397 |
| **Tuesday** | Who does what in a magazine? | 410 |
| **Wednesday** | Following up your press release | 422 |
| **Thursday** | Sustaining relations with the press | 436 |
| **Friday** | Non-press PR | 446 |
| **Saturday** | Conclusions and coping with problems | 456 |

# Week Six: Consumer Behaviour

| **Introduction** | | 471 |
|---|---|---|
| **Sunday** | Basic psychological processes | 472 |
| **Monday** | Attitudes to money | 486 |
| **Tuesday** | Purchasing | 499 |
| **Wednesday** | Different types of consumer | 513 |
| **Thursday** | Product advertising | 528 |
| **Friday** | Product retailing | 535 |
| **Saturday** | Negative effects and implications | 547 |

# ABOUT THE AUTHORS

## Susan Cave

Susan Cave has worked as an occupational psychologist and is presently employed in education at the University of Kent. She is an experienced lecturer and examiner in psychology at all levels and has published texts on environmental psychology and therapeutic approaches in psychology, as well as a range of material for teachers.

## Guy Clapperton

Guy Clapperton has been a journalist for many years. He is now freelance and regularly contributes to *The Guardian* Business Solutions Section, *The Observer*, *The Financial Times*, *The Evening Standard* and *Director* magazine.

## Ros Jay

Ros Jay is a freelance business writer and editor. She has written a number of books on marketing topics and also advises small businesses on corporate image and marketing.

## Pete Laver

Pete Laver is one of the UK's leading brand specialists. He currently provides consultancy and training services to blue-chip businesses such as Heinz, Sainsbury's and Centrica. His brand and communication courses are held worldwide and he is a trainer for the Chartered Institute of Marketing. He is also a visiting lecturer for Greenwich University's Masters Degree programme.

# ABOUT THE AUTHORS

## Richard Perry

Richard Perry develops global branding programmes and integrated marketing initiatives for international organisations. He is the General Manager of Gyrogroup UK.

## Dee Twomey

Dee Twomey is a Chartered Marketer and Managing Director of Marketing Zone. She has a business degree and diplomas in direct marketing, market research, sales promotion and marketing. Dee has created commercial success for leading businesses. Visit www.marketingzone.co.uk or e-mail dee@marketingzone.co.uk.

## Andrew Whitaker

Andrew Whitaker is a Director of the online marketing specialists DS.Emotion, developing integrated programmes which give a sustainable competitive advantage and demonstrate real return on investment for both business and consumer brands.

# Marketing Plans

**ROS JAY**

**WEEK ONE**

# CONTENTS

## Week One

| | | |
|---|---|---|
| **Introduction** | | 11 |
| **Sunday** | What is a marketing plan? | 12 |
| **Monday** | Asking questions | 21 |
| **Tuesday** | Researching the answers | 36 |
| **Wednesday** | The objectives | 49 |
| **Thursday** | Converting objectives into action plans | 62 |
| **Friday** | Putting the plan together | 73 |
| **Saturday** | Using the marketing plan | 85 |

Week One
# INTRODUCTION

Marketing is the lifeblood of any business. You may have a great product, loads of technical know-how and years of experience in financial management. But if you want your business to thrive – let alone grow – you need good, sound marketing. And the first and most crucial step towards that is the marketing plan.

Many business people think they can get away without a marketing plan. Many others try not to think about it at all, because secretly they haven't really got a clue what it is or how to put one together.

But the best and most successful businesses have a clear and thorough plan. What's more, it doesn't live buried somewhere at the bottom of a filing cabinet; it's one of their most useful tools and they refer to it frequently. A really good marketing plan will make it far easier for you to run your business smoothly and effectively.

Some businesses may fail to recognise the value of marketing planning, but the banks and financial institutions don't make the same mistake. A business that tries to apply for a loan or a grant without a good marketing plan is unlikely to get very far.

# What is a marketing plan?

So what exactly is a marketing plan? What goes into it? What does it look like? How long does it take to put one together?

We'll spend today answering all these practical questions, so that once we start drawing up the plan, you'll know what you're trying to achieve.

Essentially, a marketing plan is like a route map for your business. And it should cover three basic areas:

- where you are
- where you are going
- how you are going to get there

## Where you are

If you're working out a route on a route map, you have to know where you're starting from before you can work out the best way to reach your destination. So the first stage of drawing up the marketing plan involves establishing precisely where your business is now.

Week One

# S U N D A Y

It doesn't matter whether you're just starting up a business or whether you've been in business for a while. You need a marketing plan that starts from *now*.

The first part of the marketing plan establishes your current position. There are certain things that it needs to include:

- information about your product or service
- information about your customers and prospects
- information about your competitors
- information about your business

This is a very useful exercise for you to go through. You might imagine that since you obviously know where you are, it's rather pointless to waste time writing it down. But this isn't the case.

You'll be surprised how many things you don't know that you will have to go and find out – we'll be looking at this in more detail on Monday and Tuesday. What's more, going through this process helps you to home in on certain aspects of your marketing operation that you might not have given attention to otherwise. It brings weaknesses and opportunities into sharp focus.

You also need to establish at the start of your marketing plan precisely where you are because other people may want to know. The bank manager for a start, anyone you apply to for a loan or go to for advice, a new business partner, and so on. Having the information set out in black and white will turn out to be useful for all sorts of reasons.

# Week One
## SUNDAY

This process of taking stock of your position before you start to think about your goals will help prevent mistakes later on. And mistakes can sometimes be expensive. Here's an example:

> One of the things you will do when you establish where your business is now, is to analyse your weaknesses. Perhaps you will discover that apart from the directors or most senior managers, no one else in the business is very good at taking on important responsibilities.
>
> Now suppose that a customer places a huge order. You accept it eagerly, but it's far too big to handle without delegating a lot of the work and responsibility to someone more junior. But hang on – you haven't got anyone you can confidently delegate it to.
>
> This kind of situation can create huge muddle and expense to put right. If only you'd started training up your staff a year ago, ready to handle large orders by themselves if need be.

You might think that it would have been obvious from the start that there was no one in the company to whom you could delegate this sort of order. But in fact, this is the kind of mistake that companies often make, unfortunately.

Of course it was obvious from the start, *if* you thought about it. But all too often, you don't think about it. The process of drawing up a marketing plan helps you to focus on exactly this sort of potential mistake in time to avert trouble.

# SUNDAY

Week One

You'll see on Monday and Tuesday that the way you go about putting together this section of the marketing plan is to ask yourself lots of questions – we'll be looking at how you find out which questions to ask.

And then you go and find the answers – it's as simple as that. Once again, we'll be going into more detail about where and how to find the answers.

## Where you are going

We've already established that you can't work out your route if you don't know where you're starting from. It's equally difficult if you don't know where you're going. So this section of the marketing plan sets out where you are trying to get to. There are three main stages in this part of the process:

- identify your critical success factors
- set your objectives
- draw up a sales forecast

Week One

# SUNDAY

### *Identifying your critical success factors*

First, you need to establish the factors which are critical to your success. Which things have you absolutely got to get right in order to succeed and grow? It may not be the end of the world, in some lines of business, if your prices are not particularly competitive – for example if you sell top of the range designer clothing. But if you run an office stationery business and you can't match your competitors' prices, you could go out of business as a result. So you will need to work out which aspects of your business or service are critical.

### *Establishing your marketing objectives*

This is where you state your objectives. You will need to draw heavily on the first part of your plan to do this, which is yet another reason for having put down where you are now in black and white.

For example, the first part of your plan may have drawn your attention to a new type of product you could add to your range. So your objectives may include developing this product. Or the first section of the plan may have highlighted weaknesses that you want to eliminate – this would then be one of your objectives.

Objectives can be both large and small. The examples above might be relatively small things. You might also have objectives for expanding the business, which you will need to set out. Are you planning to open three new branches next year? Or franchise out the operation? Or employ your own sales force instead of using agents? These are all large objectives that need to be stated in your marketing plan.

## SUNDAY

You will also need to refer to your critical success factors to establish some of these objectives. If you're running an office stationery business, it may be a crucial objective to be able to match your competitors' prices on all frequently ordered products.

*Sales forecast*
This is the part of your marketing plan where you need to include your sales forecast. A lot of people find this bit somewhat unnerving, since they don't really know how to forecast sales. They feel they are plucking numbers from the air.

However, there are techniques, which we will examine on Wednesday, for removing a lot of the guesswork from this process. Of course there are still some gaps that you will have to fill in with educated guesses, but you can go a long way towards an accurate forecast once you know how.

## How you are going to get there

You have established where you are, and you've identified where you want to get to. This final section of the marketing plan explains how you plan to get from A to B. In other words, it states how you plan to achieve your objectives. This section is, in essence, your marketing strategy. In other words, it is the bit of the marketing plan which contains precise tasks and specific targets.

At this stage, it sounds to most people like an insurmountable challenge to draw up a marketing strategy. But by Thursday, you'll have collected all the information you need to do it. Then it's just a matter of sitting down and working through it. Honest.

# SUNDAY

By the time you come to draw up the marketing strategy, you'll know how to achieve your objectives in considerable detail. Which is a good thing, because a marketing strategy is not something to be woolly about. You need to be very specific about how you will achieve each objective, and to consider:

- precisely what you will do to reach each objective
- how often you will do it
- what it will cost
- the results you expect from this action

As you can see, this is the action plan part of the document. The rest is crucial, especially if you want information, or if something is going wrong and you want to know why. But this final section of the plan is the part you will need to work from on an everyday basis.

## The practicalities

So that's the information that goes into your marketing plan: where you are now, where you are going, and how you are going to get there. So what does the document actually look like? And how long will it take to write?

We'll spend Friday answering this sort of question more fully. But in general, it will probably take you a solid week or two to put the plan together from scratch. This will be reduced, of course, if you have done some of the work already, or if there is more than one of you working on it. In any case this is only a rough guide.

## SUNDAY

At the end of this, you will have a neat, clear document, smart but simply laid out, which will probably be between about ten and 25 pages long. It may be more if your business is very complex – if, for example, you sell into several very different markets.

## What is the marketing plan for?

We've already seen a lot of the benefits of a marketing plan:

- It tells you things you didn't know before.
- It helps you focus on areas you might otherwise miss.
- It helps prevent mistakes.
- It enables you to determine your critical factors for success.
- It enables you to set clear marketing objectives.
- It means you can work out how to achieve these objectives.

# Week One
## SUNDAY

These benefits should be enough in themselves to make the process of drawing up the plan worthwhile. But what are you supposed to use it for once you've finished putting it together?

For a start, you may find you need to show it to people outside the business – bank managers, potential investors, advisors, accountants, prospective business partners and so on. But you should also use it regularly as one of your most helpful business tools. You should review it regularly (we'll look at this in detail on Saturday) and it will tell you how your marketing operations are going. It will also help you spot why things have gone wrong, and enable you to put them right.

## What is the difference between a marketing plan and a business plan?

One of the things that people frequently want to know is what the difference is between a marketing plan and a business plan. The answer to this is very simple. The marketing plan is part of the overall business plan. A business plan will also include a financial plan, details of administration systems, manufacturing and stock control forecasts, and so on.

## Summary

Today, we've outlined what a marketing plan is, so that once you start to put it together you know what you're aiming towards.

# MONDAY

Week One

## Asking questions

We've already seen that the first thing you have to do to draw up your marketing plan is to establish where you are now. There are two stages to this: asking the right questions, and finding out the answers. Today, we're going to concentrate on the questions.

*Questions to establish where you are now*

- questions about your product or service
- questions about your customers and prospects
- questions about your competitors
- questions about your business

YOU ASK THE QUESTIONS

Obviously, in order to get the most out of this exercise, you're going to have to know precisely which questions to ask. So that's what we're going to look at now.

Week One

# MONDAY

## Your product or service

What exactly is it that you're marketing? You need to describe your product or service range, and every variable that it has.

No, this isn't as pointless as it may sound. We already know that outsiders (such as the bank manager) may want this information, but you may need it too. In fact, you should write it down for the very reason that it seems you shouldn't: there is a strong inclination to take it for granted.

Most companies never question the basic range they offer. But one of the strengths of a marketing plan is that everything in it is open to question whenever you review it. And often – very often – the problem with small companies that are trying to turn into large companies is that their original product range is holding them back. But they don't see it.

> *Example*
>
> Suppose you manage an organisation that runs training seminars and invites companies to send delegates along. As time goes by, more and more companies ask you to go along to their site and run in-house seminars for them – that's the way the trend is going.
>
> After a while, it gets harder and harder to fill your open seminars. They start to lose you money. But you think 'We're a company that organises open seminars, we always have been. We must invest more in this side of the business so that it becomes profitable again'.

## MONDAY

*Week One*

This is a mistake that companies frequently make. Perhaps you should try harder to sell your seminars. On the other hand, perhaps the market has dried up and you're pouring money into a bottomless pit. The only way you'll find out which is the case is from your marketing plan. But your marketing plan only contains the answers to the questions you asked it.

That's why you must ask every possible question. Including every possible question about your product. That way, you can be sure that if anything ever needs to change, it will show up at your marketing plan review sessions.

All right, so what are these questions you're supposed to be asking about your product or service?

*Questions about the product or service range*

- *What is the product or service?* What is the range? What does it look like? Does it come in a choice of colours or sizes? Are there customised options? Do you sell accessories and add-ons?

Week One

# MONDAY

- *Where do the raw materials come from?* You might think this is a manufacturing question, and you'd be right, of course. But it's also a marketing question. Are the supplies good enough quality for your customers? Are they delivered fast enough to fulfil orders on time?
- *What is the packaging like?* Once again, this question has a marketing dimension. If your product looks basic, it won't be easy to charge a premium price for it, whatever its performance is like. And the packaging may influence the distribution, making the product too large or too heavy for certain distribution methods.

*Questions about selling the product or service*

- *How is the product transported?* Is transportation a problem because of cost, weight, fragility, size or anything else?
- *Where is it sold?* Direct through the post? From your own premises? Through a retailer?
- *In what form does it reach the customer?* Is it ready to use, or does it need to be assembled, painted, programmed or whatever?
- *Does it need explaining?* Will the customer understand it, or does it need instructions to go with it?
- *Is it easy to use?* Are there any integral problems that the customers might find irritating? Does it take ages to warm up, or need recharging three times a week?
- *How easy is it to increase production if sales go up?* Will you get caught out having to pay overtime you can't afford? Or sub-contracting? Or will you simply fail to deliver on time? (You can often get round these problems if they occur, but usually at a cost. That's why you need to plan for them.)

# MONDAY

Week One

As you can see, not all these questions apply to every product or service. And there may be others that are particularly pertinent to yours. But this is a good general guide, and you should add other questions if you think of them.

Remember that you will be reviewing and updating your marketing plan regularly, so you can always add information later. But try to cover everything you can from the start.

## Your customers and prospects

If you are just setting up a new business, or launching a product for a new market, you still have to ask these questions. It's just that in your case all your customers will be potential at the moment. Don't worry; tomorrow we'll find out how to get the answers to these questions even if you don't have a single customer yet.

*Questions about the customers*

- *Who are they?* What age? Male or female? Business or private? Where do they live? What is their income?
- *What are their buying trends?* Do they buy more or less than they used to? What about the overall market trend? Do they buy more or less if they hit hard times?
- *How much will they pay?* Would they buy more if it were cheaper? Would they pay more if it were better quality?
- *How do they know about the product or service?* Do they see it in a shop? Is it advertised? Is it reviewed in the press? Do you exhibit at trade shows?

## Week One
# MONDAY

- *Where do they buy it?* In a shop? What kind of shop? By mail order? By phone?

*Questions about the customers' attitudes to the product or service*

- *What do they like about your product or service?* What are the features they go for? Is it price? Accessories? After-sales service? Does the product have status value?
- *What do they dislike about it?* There must be some people who don't buy from you but from someone else. What would they say was wrong with your product or service?
- *What do they like about this type of product or service?* What are the general benefits that your product shares with the competition? (To give you an example, all people who buy electric egg whisks do so because they are faster and easier than the alternatives.)

> - *What do they dislike about this type of product or service?*
> - *Why do your existing customers choose your product or service rather than your competitors'?* In other words, what makes you unique?

Once again, these questions are not exhaustive, but they should give you a pretty good idea of the kind of thing you need to include in your marketing plan.

It's terribly important that you also ask the questions you might not like the answers to, such as 'what do your customers like least about your product or service?' And when it comes to finding the answers, you must be brutally honest. If your competitors are better than you in certain areas, you must acknowledge the fact. These will be some of the areas where you can generate the most improvement, but only if you recognise your shortcomings.

## Your competitors

Your customers are going to judge you against your competitors constantly – and be ready to switch allegiance any time it seems worthwhile. So you had better know what they know.

This part of the plan will obviously need revising as competitors change, but for the moment you want to start with a snapshot of what the competition is up to at the moment.

Week One

# MONDAY

Again, it's extremely important that you also ask yourself all the questions you think you might not want to hear the answers to, such as what your competitors are particularly good at. These are precisely the questions you *need* to know the answers to. Far too many business people fail because they convince themselves that they are wonderful and the competition is hopeless.

> *Questions about the competition*
>
> - *What product or service are your prospects using at the moment?* If they aren't buying from you yet, are they buying from someone else? Making do without? Using an alternative product? For example, if you sell electric egg whisks, do your prospects buy from a competitor, use a rotary whisk, use a fork, or not eat beaten eggs at all? What proportion of them use each of these options?
> - *Who are your competitors?*
> - *Do they offer anything beyond a basic service or product?* If so, what? Does their product come with extra features? Do they offer a choice of service levels?
> - *What has each of your competitors got that you haven't?*

There's another useful exercise to go through when it comes to asking questions about your competitors. Draw up a table like the one on the next page. Allow as many columns as you have main competitors, plus a column for yourself. Allow enough space to fill in each section with the necessary information.

Week One

# MONDAY

|  | Your product/service | (competitor) | (competitor) |
|---|---|---|---|
| **Product or service** (what is the range?) | | | |
| **Price** (standard item for comparison) | | | |
| **Special offers** (what are they?) | | | |
| **Quality** (marks out of 10) | | | |
| **Customer-care skills** (marks out of 10) | | | |
| **Reputation** (marks out of 10) | | | |
| **Delivery** (marks out of 10) | | | |
| **After-sales service** (marks out of 10) | | | |
| **Location** (local, regional, national etc.) | | | |
| **Advertising** (what and where?) | | | |

Week One

# MONDAY

## Your business

The final list of questions you need to draw up is about the business itself. These questions are, of course, to do with marketing, but in the broadest terms. They are questions about things that are integral to the whole business. The best way to compile this list is by using SWOT analysis.

If you haven't come across this before, it sounds horribly technical. But in fact SWOT is simply an acronym for:

- strengths
- weaknesses
- opportunities
- threats

The process of SWOT analysis involves asking yourself to describe these four factors as they apply to your business. Not how you would like them to be, but how they actually are. So let's take a look at how to do it.

The accepted way to do a SWOT analysis of your business is to draw yourself a table like the one below, and then fill in each section with a list of the appropriate points.

| Strengths | Weaknesses |
|---|---|
| | |
| Opportunities | Threats |
| | |

Week One

## MONDAY

We'd better go through the four categories and explain what kind of answers you're going to need to fill in.

*Strengths*

The strengths and weaknesses are all to do with internal factors related to the business. You cannot have every strength there is. Being a large company can be a huge strength because it gives you a degree of financial clout that a small business can never have. On the other hand, a small company can have great speed of response and flexibility in customer handling that a multinational can't hope to achieve. You may have a broad customer base or a highly targeted customer list; you are unlikely to have both, and yet both could be strengths. So don't expect everything. Just concentrate on listing what strengths you have now.

You should list *all* your plus points in this quarter of the table – low costs, good technical knowledge or whatever.

Week One

# MONDAY

> *Examples of strengths*
>
> - low costs
> - low overheads
> - good location
> - flexibility
> - good internal communications
> - well-motivated staff
> - highly skilled staff
> - good product expertise
> - good market knowledge
> - broad customer base
> - good reputation
> - sound finances
> - up-to-date product/service range
> - up-to-date equipment
> - sophisticated computer system

Not all of these strengths will be relevant to you, and you may have others. Every business is different. But these examples should have given you a pretty good idea of the kind of things you're looking for. You'll see from this list that even if yours is a new business you may already have a number of strengths you can list.

*Weaknesses*
When it comes to weaknesses, you must be absolutely honest with yourself. You may think you *ought* to have a highly skilled workforce, but if you don't you must list this fact as a weakness. Otherwise it won't get on to the list of things to improve.

## MONDAY

You will probably notice that the weaknesses are usually the other side of the 'strengths' coins. So if low costs are a strength, for example, high costs would be a weakness.

*Examples of weaknesses*

- high costs
- high overheads
- poor location
- lack of flexibility
- poor internal communications
- poorly motivated staff
- poorly skilled staff
- overdependence on one or two key staff
- limited product expertise
- poor market knowledge
- small customer base
- weak reputation

- financially weak
- out-of-date product/service range
- out-of-date equipment/machinery
- computer system that needs upgrading or replacing

## Opportunities

Opportunities and threats are external market forces that impinge on your business in some way. These factors can come from all kinds of sources: customers, competitors, suppliers, EC regulations, government legislation and so on. They can even come from the media; look at the effect the BSE scandal had on the beef and dairy industries, largely because of the media interest that surrounded it.

### Examples of opportunities

- weak competition (at least in some areas)
- competitor going out of business or moving away
- expanding market
- new legislation in pipeline that will be good for the market
- grants available
- good new source of raw materials available
- useful exhibition coming up
- new, skilled staff joining the company

## Threats

As with strengths and weaknesses, threats are often the flip-side of opportunities. Only you can know exactly which areas to look at, because each business is so different. Your particular market may have special threats or opportunities that don't affect other businesses. But once again, here are some ideas.

# M O N D A Y

### Examples of threats

- strong competition
- competitor giving special offers or discounts
- shrinking market
- new legislation in pipeline that will be bad for the market
- grants available to competitors
- important supplier going out of business/raw materials going up in price
- good staff leaving the company
- expensive legal action pending

## Summary

We've looked at the questions you need to ask as soon as you start to put your marketing plan together and at how you can find out about the business itself using SWOT analysis. You may already know the answers to some of the questions we've asked. Tomorrow we'll find out how to go about answering the rest of them.

Week One

# TUESDAY

## Researching the answers

Now you have a very long list of questions with no answers to them – as yet. Today is all about researching the answers to the questions we asked yesterday. Some of these are very easy to answer, while others take much longer. The important thing is not to guess at any of the answers but to do everything you can to be sure that your answers are accurate.

There are three places you can go to for answers to your questions, and we'll look at each one in turn:

- off-the-shelf information
- your customers – or potential customers, if you're just starting out in business
- other people

## Off-the-shelf information

The first place to find ready-made information is inside your head. So the first thing to do is to go through the list of questions you drew up and write down the answers to everything you are sure you know the answer to.

## TUESDAY

This may be less than you think. Do you really know that your customers appreciate your fast delivery times? Have they ever said so? Have you ever asked them? Or read someone else's research into what matters to customers in your particular market? If not, you are only assuming the information, and you shouldn't write anything down just yet. You may well be right about how your customers feel, but we're not writing down guesses and assumptions, we're only writing down known facts.

However, you probably will know the answers to the questions about what your product range is, and about your competitors, and you'll know a lot of the answers to the SWOT analysis.

Once you've written down the answers that you are sure of at this stage, your list of questions should already be starting to look a little more manageable. There are now several places you can go to find off-the-shelf information which will give you the answers to an enormous number of questions.

*Your own records*
This is one of the best places to start, and one of the many reasons for keeping thorough customer records.

Assuming you're already in business, and have decent customer records, you should be able to extract all sorts of information that you hadn't realised before. For example, if you look at how your customers responded when you introduced an express delivery service – how many used it regularly, how many used it occasionally, and so on – you can start to answer the questions about delivery times.

Week One

# TUESDAY

Now you know what information you're looking for, you should be able to work out how to extract it from your records. What's more, these records of the way your customers really behave are far more reliable than anything your customers *say* they will do if, for example, you raise your prices, or introduce a fast delivery option.

Incidentally, this is also a good way to establish whether the quality of your customer records is a strength or a weakness. You can now enter that on your SWOT analysis.

*Libraries*
There are plenty of useful publications that any main library should have. There are also several good business libraries around the country, which your local library should be able to direct you to. Here are some of the most useful publications to look out for:

- *Yellow Pages* and *Thomson Directories,* which should give you plenty of information about potential customers, competitors and so on. Some large libraries will stock a complete set.
- *Kompass* directory lists British companies by industry, name, product and location.
- *The Source Book* organises marketing information by services and industry sectors. It will also tell you about directories, trade associations and so on.
- *Directory of British Associations* will point you towards any trade associations or societies that could help you.

# TUESDAY

- *Marketsearch* publishes around 20,000 market research reports. One of them could be just what you need.
- *BRAD (British Rate and Data)* lists every newspaper and magazine, from the trade press to local freesheets, in Britain. It gives you their distribution figures, advertising rates and so on, and will answer several of your questions about advertising.
- *Municipal Year Book* gives you a listing of local authorities including contact names.
- *The Retail Directory* lists large retail and department stores and gives the names of buyers.

*Trade associations and regulatory bodies*
You can often get useful information from these organisations, who publish annual reports and industry information. Some of them may charge you for this information, but if it's your own industry or a major industry for you to sell into, it could still be well worth it.

Regulatory bodies, such as the Law Society and the British Medical Association, are often good sources of information, along with trade associations. These should all be listed in some of the publications above.

*Trade press*
BRAD will give you listings of every trade and specialist magazine or newspaper you can imagine. Ring up the ones that are relevant to your business and ask for a copy – the advertising department will often let you have one free along with a rate card. It will be packed with information that is useful to you.

# Week One
## TUESDAY

You could even ask one of the editorial staff to answer the odd question if you're really stuck and need someone with industry knowledge. They're far too busy to answer long lists of questions, but this can be a handy last resort.

*Government departments*
If you contact the Central Statistical Office in central London they will send you a list of government publications. You can get census reports, overseas trade information, social trends and so on. If you need information about exporting, contact your local Department of Trade and Industry office, who give very helpful advice and information.

*Your local enterprise agency*
This will be listed in the *Yellow Pages* under 'Business Enterprise Agencies'. Each enterprise agency is different, but they all give a wealth of advice to new and existing businesses – and it's often free. They can probably tell you about exporting, grants and loans for which you are eligible, EC legislation and plenty more.

## Your customers

If you want to know what your customers and prospects think, the simplest way is to ask them. You can talk to them face-to-face, you can phone them, or you can write to them. There are three categories of customers you can talk to:

- existing customers, to find out why they buy from you
- potential customers, to find out what would persuade them to buy from you
- ex-customers, to find out why they stopped buying from you

Week One

# TUESDAY

Overlaying this, you might have more than one group of customers if you sell into more than one market.

*Talking to your customers face-to-face*
The easiest way to do this is simply to chat to your customers informally when you are doing business with them. You could say, for example, 'We're doing a bit of research at the moment to find out how our customers feel about our delivery service. Could you tell me what you think?'

This is a cost-effective and time-effective way to research your customers, and it often generates some very useful ideas and suggestions.

On the down side, however, it's hard to build up a large sample of customers, or a long list of questions – your customers won't want to answer more than one or two off the cuff. Also, people are less likely to be honest face-to-face if their views are negative.

Week One
# TUESDAY

Overall, this is a good approach if you're only after the answers to one or two questions, or if you're looking for suggestions.

*Telephoning your customers*
You can always phone up customers. Tell them what you want and ask them if they can spare the time: 'Hello Mr Smith. It's Kim Jones here from ABC Ltd. We're trying to find out more about how we can improve our service to customers. I was wondering if you could spare me about five or ten minutes to answer a few questions?'

This has the advantage that you can ask more questions than you could do face-to-face, and you can make sure you ask everyone the same questions. However, it can be both expensive and time consuming if you want to research a large sample of your customers.

Generally speaking, you should use this approach when you only need to speak to a few customers, but want to ask several questions and want to be able to quantify the results.

*Writing to your customers*
The other option is to ask your customers to fill out a questionnaire. You can hand it out if you meet your customers regularly, or you can send it out with deliveries or bills (in which case you are only surveying customers who place orders). Alternatively, of course, you can post it.

The benefit here is that you can survey a lot of customers relatively cheaply, and you can quantify the results because you have asked them all the same questions. You can also give customers the option of remaining anonymous, which can lead to more honest replies.

# TUESDAY

*General guidelines for research*

There are certain fundamental mistakes that novice researchers – understandably – are inclined to make. Research is something that everyone gets better at with practice. Once you find that certain questionnaire answers aren't at all helpful, you'll learn what type of questions not to ask. So here are a few tips to help you avoid the classic pitfalls.

- *Keep your questions neutral.* If you say 'Are you happy with our delivery service?', most customers will go for the easy option and say yes. Instead ask them, for example, 'What do you think of our delivery service?'
- *Don't be ambiguous.* If you ask someone 'Do you change your car frequently?', they may think once every five years is frequently, or once every six months isn't. So ask them 'How often do you change your car?'
- *Be consistent if you want to add up the answers.* This applies if you're talking to customers face-to-face or over the phone. If you ask each customer a slightly different question, you won't be able to add up the answers properly.
- *Don't ask the customer to give up more than five or ten minutes of their time.* This applies to both telephone surveys and written questionnaires. If you have a long list of questions you want answered, you can ask one group of customers one set of questions and another group a different set. Choose the groups in a way which will divide them randomly, such as selecting them alphabetically, rather than dividing them according to location or ordering frequency.

Week One
# TUESDAY

- *Use multiple choice questions on written questionnaires.* These are much easier to analyse when you get them back. You can always mix them with other questions if you feel it would be helpful.
- *Don't expect an overwhelming response to postal questionnaires.* Somewhere between 5% and 20%, if you're mailing existing customers, is very respectable.

## Other people

If you still have unanswered questions after looking up off-the-shelf information and talking to your customers, don't worry. There are still a few other people you can talk to.

*Suppliers*
Your suppliers can tell you plenty about your raw materials and other supplies. They are also often experts in their own field, which could be very useful to you.

Week One
# TUESDAY

They can tell you something about what your competitors are up to if they also supply them. Don't expect them to give away any confidences though; you wouldn't want them to tell your competitors confidential information about you. But they can probably tell you whether you get more or fewer complaints relating to their supplies, and so on.

*Competitors*
No, you're not expected to knock at the door and ask to go through their confidential customer records. But you can visit their shop, exhibition display stand or whatever and pick up a brochure. Or reply to their advertisements in the press.

Ring them up and ask for a copy of their annual report. If your address gives you away, use a different one. This may seem unethical, but it's normal business practice – you're only asking for publicly available material. And they're probably doing the same thing to you if they have any sense. Make a note of how fast they answer your call and send you their mailpack, and what their attitude is like on the phone.

*Non-competing businesses*
You can offer to swap useful information with other businesses who sell to the same market. If you sell display stands to shops, talk to someone who sells tills. You both have the same customers. If your business is local, you could phone up someone running exactly the same type of business 250 miles away, and offer to swap research information.

*Advisors*
Take all the advice you can, from bank managers and accountants to enterprise agencies. A lot of them are experts and can tell you a lot of what you need to know.

Week One

# TUESDAY

## Filling in the blanks

You should by now have answered virtually all the questions on your original list. But there are probably a few left that you still don't have answers for. What are you supposed to do about them?

Well, if you really can't come up with an answer at the moment, you'll have to guess. At least by now you have probably reached the stage where it will be a pretty informed guess. But make it clear that it's a guess by writing 'estimate' after it in brackets or something like that. That will stop you forgetting later that the answer may not be totally accurate. You must also make yourself a note to find out the accurate answer as soon as you can.

*Researching under time or budget limitations*
Ideally, you should always allow yourself a few weeks at least to put together a marketing plan. We established earlier that it is likely to take a week or two, but this will probably need to be spread over several weeks.

Week One

# ■ T U E S D A Y ■

However, if you've just picked this book up because you have to produce a marketing plan by the end of this month, you probably don't want to hear this. If this is the case, you'll have to put the time available into answering the questions which fall into one of two categories:

- questions which are very important
- questions to which you can't even hazard an answer

For a new business, you should change the schedule to give yourself time to put together the fullest possible marketing plan – it's that important. But if you are producing a marketing plan for an existing business, you may find that there are a few things that it will take you a while to

# Week One
## TUESDAY

establish, or cost more to find out quickly than you can afford. In this case make a good guess and then start researching the answer so you can fill it in accurately as soon as possible.

Suppose you assume that your fast delivery time is important to your customers. Write that down for the time being (noting that it is 'to be confirmed'), and then start asking each customer you deal with whenever you get the chance. In a short while, you'll have enough researched answers to be able to fill in the answer properly.

And you can schedule in some time in a couple of months for doing fuller research on the other areas that need answers. Put aside time for making phone calls or drawing up a questionnaire.

## Summary

You should now have written down answers to all the questions you listed on Monday and have all the information you need to put together the marketing plan. You may have had to make educated guesses at the last few questions, but most of them will be well-researched, accurate answers arrived at by using the three main sources of information.

Week One

# WEDNESDAY

# The objectives

You have spent the last couple of days establishing where you are now. So it's time to consider where you are going with your business. That's what we'll be doing today. There are three stages in this process:

- identify your critical success factors
- set your objectives
- draw up your sales forecast

This is the part many people regard as the heart of the marketing plan. In fact, the rest is just as crucial, but it's true that this section gives you direction and tells you where you should focus. Once the plan is complete, this is the part that helps you keep your eye on the ball.

You've already made things massively easier for yourself by working out where you are now, so don't be daunted by phrases like 'critical success factors' and 'sales forecast'. It's really not difficult, as we're about to find out.

Week One
# WEDNESDAY

## Your critical success factors

These are the things you absolutely *must* do well in order for your business to be successful. They are your priorities. They could mean you have to improve your performance in any number of areas, such as:

- reducing costs
- improving customer service
- speeding up lead times or delivery times
- developing new products
- improving quality
- increasing the size of your customer base
- improving after-sales service

These are just a few examples of the categories in which you might have to improve your performance. This should give you a broad picture; the specific improvement will probably be narrower than this. For example, when it comes to reducing costs, the thing that is critical to your success will probably be to reduce delivery costs, or sales costs, or whatever. You're looking for fairly precise factors.

So how do you identify your own critical success factors? You'll find all through today that you can only decide where you are going by referring to the work you've done already. And that process starts here.

On Monday, we drew up a table comparing your product and service with your main competitors' which you should have filled in by now. You are going to need to refer to this table in order to work out your critical success factors.

Week One
# WEDNESDAY

When you study the table, you'll see where your performance is falling significantly below your competitors'. You'll also see where everyone is scoring high or performing well – these are usually the areas that are crucial in your line of business. Perhaps everyone's prices are low, or everyone repairs faults within four hours. Have a look at this sample section from the table.

|  | Your product/ service | (competitor) | (competitor) |
|---|---|---|---|
| Delivery | 8 | 6 | 7 |
| After-sales service | 3 | 4 | 2 |
| Quality | 4 | 7 | 8 |

Everybody is clearly putting a high priority on delivery, and you compare well with the rest of them. After-sales service is poor, but so is everyone else's. Perhaps this isn't too important to your customers. When it comes to quality, however, your marks are below the rest of the opposition's. They are giving it high priority – they presumably think it's important – but you don't seem to be competing well at all.

This suggests that quality is a critical success factor that you need to work on. It also suggests that delivery is a critical success factor, but in this case one that you are doing well at.

*Double-check your facts*
You can't rely on this table alone. But that's okay. You've done enough work already so that you don't have to. For one thing, you might know something the table doesn't –

# WEDNESDAY

perhaps you have a successful strategy of operating at a low quality and therefore a lower price than anyone else. If you know this works, that overrides anything the table is telling you.

You can also check this information against your customer research, from your sales records as well as from talking to customers or reading other people's research. It should confirm that quality is (or isn't) a critical factor. It should also tell you whether delivery is as important to your customers as you and your competitors seem to think. And are you all correct in thinking that after-sales service isn't important? Perhaps this is one area where you can get ahead of the field.

More often than not, your other research will bear out your competitor comparison table. But sometimes there will be differences, so it's always important to double check.

*List the critical success factors*
Remember that you're focusing on the *critical* factors at the moment – not all the areas where there's scope for improvement, but the ones you rely on to keep your competitive edge. List these on a separate piece of paper, because you're about to need them in order to set your objectives.

Incidentally, if you're just starting out in business you can work out the critical factors by looking at your competitors' performance alone; you should still go through this process, just leave your own performance out of the equation for now.

Week One

# WEDNESDAY

## Your objectives

These are your statements of what you are aiming to achieve. Clearly, the critical success factors you have just listed will be top priority. These are not optional, by definition. If a factor is critical to your success, you must address it. Otherwise you can't succeed.

After that, you can go through the rest of the facts you have collected, and establish what other objectives to set yourself.

The answers to your questions about your products or services may highlight areas where you need to make improvements, such as sourcing raw materials, or packaging design.

The information about your customers should tell you whether you are missing openings in the market that you should explore, or whether there are aspects of your product design that your customers would like to see improved.

Week One
# WEDNESDAY

You should have established plenty of information about your competitors other than the table we've just looked at. This too will tell you which factors, while not actually critical to success, nevertheless leave room for improvement. Perhaps they have a cheaper source of raw materials than you, or lower labour costs, enabling them to keep prices down.

And your SWOT analysis will identify strengths and opportunities to exploit and weaknesses and threats to overcome.

*Timescale*
How far ahead are these objectives supposed to be set? Are we talking next week's plans or next year's? It varies from one business to the next, but generally speaking you should be looking a year ahead. In some businesses it will need to be longer. If you build and sell cruise liners that can take years to build, you should be looking much further ahead.

Start with a one-year plan, unless there's an obvious reason not to, and revise this if it becomes preferable to. You will be reviewing your plan regularly, as we'll see on Saturday, but every so often it will need a full update.

If you have a slack period in the year, this is a very good time to hold a regular update. This means that just before your annual update, your plan won't be looking very far ahead at all. If you need to work a year ahead all the time, update every couple of months so you have a constantly rolling marketing plan.

# WEDNESDAY

Week One

*How to express your objectives*

You need to be realistic with your objectives, but challenge yourself. You also need to be specific about what you're going to achieve.

> **Example**
>
> Suppose your delivery isn't as fast as the competition's. You need to improve it. Your objective should not simply state: 'To speed up delivery'.
>
> You need to state exactly what you will aim for: 'To deliver 95% of orders within four working hours, and the remainder within six hours'.

*Setting priorities*

Some of your objectives can be achieved without investment. But some cannot, and you won't necessarily be able to afford to make all the necessary investments straight away. So you need to prioritise.

We've already seen that the objectives related to your critical success factors have to be addressed at once. But what about the rest of them?

Not all your objectives will relate directly to your products or services, but many of them will. If you have a fairly broad product range, you may need to decide which products to invest in first. If you get this right, you should realise a sufficient return on investment to be able to fund the next phase of objectives.

# WEDNESDAY

There is a very simple matrix that can help you to work out which of your products or services are most worthwhile.

|  | High market share | Low market share |
|---|---|---|
| **High growth** | Top priority | Average priority |
| **Low growth** | Average priority | Low priority |

Allocate each of your products or services to one of these categories, according to its growth rate and its share of the market. If your company is local, this means your share of the local market for the product. As you can see, top priority should go to fast growing products with a high share of the market.

As far as your priorities for your other objectives are concerned, estimate for each one the cost of achieving it, and the potential revenue as a result of achieving it. Then grade them according to their potential profit (i.e. revenue minus cost). If you need to estimate the potential revenue you could gain by improving, say, an aspect of your after-sales service, do this on the basis of the extra sales it will earn you (or the value of the customers you now lose that you won't once the improvement is made).

## Your sales forecast

The sales forecast is not the place to set yourself impossible tasks. You are supposed to be forecasting what you expect your sales to be, not what you would like them to be.

# WEDNESDAY

*Weekly or monthly?*
Most businesses forecast monthly sales, and find this sufficient. But if you're in a fast-moving market, where you have to respond quickly to new trends, you may need to forecast on a weekly basis. If you only find out once a month whether you're on target, you might have lost valuable time learning that you're behind target – time that you could have spent making changes.

*What does a sales forecast look like?*
A sales forecast can be just about as simple or as fancy as you like. Let's concentrate on the simple version to begin with. All you have to do is to draw up a table with the next 12 months (or 52 weeks) across the top. Down the side you list each of your products or services.

Now you simply fill in each square with the amount of sales revenue you expect from each product in that month. As you can see from the example, this allows you to add up rows or columns to calculate the total sales revenue each month, or the total revenue from each product or service over the year.

That's the basic format (as shown opposite). But there are other things that some businesses find it helpful to add. If you think they would be useful for you, add them in, or add another table to show them.

Week One

# WEDNESDAY

| Product | \| 1 | 2 | 3 | 4 | 5 | 6 Month | 7 | 8 | 9 | 10 | 11 | 12 | Total |
|---|---|---|---|---|---|---|---|---|---|---|---|---|---|
| A | | | | | | | | | | | | | |
| B | | | | | | | | | | | | | |
| C | | | | | | | | | | | | | |
| D | | | | | | | | | | | | | |
| E | | | | | | | | | | | | | |
| F | | | | | | | | | | | | | |
| G | | | | | | | | | | | | | |
| H | | | | | | | | | | | | | |
| Total income | | | | | | | | | | | | | |

# WEDNESDAY

> **Additional information for sales forecasts**
> - The number of units of each product you expect to sell.
> - At what (average) price you expect to sell each unit.
> - Income earned and cash due as separate entries, especially where payment may be slow or delayed.
> - Sales of each product to each customer type, where you are selling into more than one market.
> - Sales by geographical location.

For sales by product, location or anything other than month or week, it's best to draw up a separate forecast for each month. You can view this alongside your overall basic forecast for the year.

## Summary

Not only do we know where we are at the moment, but now we know where we're going as well.

The important thing is to work out what needs to be done, concentrating especially on those things that are absolutely essential for success.

Then you have to determine where you are going. Set yourself challenges, but make them realistic ones, and draw up a sales forecast based on what you expect your sales to look like, not some fantasy of what you would like them to be.

Once you've done all that, you're ready to go on to the last stage of preparation – working out how to get from where you are to where you're going.

Week One

# THURSDAY

## Converting objectives into action plans

The final stage of preparation, before you finally commit your plan to paper, is to work out how you're going to get from where you are to where you're going – your route map.

There are three steps you have to go through to convert each of your objectives (from yesterday) into a marketing strategy, or action plan:

- look at the options
- consider the practicalities
- select the best route

You've already established that your objectives are achievable – if challenging – so you know it's all possible. Every one of your objectives can generate a workable action plan. So let's look at the best way to do it.

Week One

# THURSDAY

## Look at the options

You should have a list of your objectives, and you need to go through each one in turn. Treat each one separately, and go through the process in this chapter to put together a mini action plan for each one. When you've finished, all these action plans together will make up your marketing strategy.

For most of the objectives you have set, you'll find there are a number of ways you might achieve them. Let's take the example that you're trying to reduce your delivery times to under four working hours. There are several (feasible) ways you might do this:

- Contract out all your deliveries to someone else.
- Change your working system so orders are processed faster, drivers check in more frequently, and so on.
- Employ more drivers.

You might well come up with more options if you're in this situation. For the moment, simply write down the possibilities. We'll worry about how to pick the right one in a minute.

The important thing is to think as freely as possible to make sure you consider everything that might be useful. This is a process in which imaginative thinking and open-minded approach are valuable. Try to brainstorm ideas for this with other people if you can; it's an excellent way to generate ideas.

Week One

# THURSDAY

There are more methods than can possibly be listed here for improving every aspect of your marketing. But it is possible to give you an idea of the kinds of activities to think about. These can be broadly divided into five main marketing areas. Most of your objectives will fall into one of these categories:

> *Five key areas of marketing*
>
> - increase awareness of your company and your products/services
> - increase existing customers' loyalty
> - secure sales
> - generate higher turnover
> - increase your knowledge of your market

We can take each of these in turn and list the type of options you should be considering. However, don't be tempted to think that these lists are exhaustive. Be open to thinking up other approaches for achieving your objectives as well.

> *Increase awareness of your company and your products/services*
>
> - advertising – local and national press, trade press, radio, TV
> - press releases – in the local, national or trade press
> - direct mail – using your own mailing list, bought list, rented lists
> - exhibitions
> - sales promotions
> - telephone selling

# THURSDAY
*Week One*

- personal sales visits
- customer/prospect newsletter
- special events
- sponsorship

*Increase existing customers' loyalty*

- improve customer care
- make more contacts with customers
- give customers a single point of contact
- improve delivery
- improve product quality
- improve after-sales service
- improve accuracy of billing

*Secure sales*

- close the sale on a higher percentage of visits/phone calls
- improve quality/range of brochures and other sales literature
- get customer's signature on contract/deposit earlier in process
- improve sales training for staff

*Generate higher turnover*

- increase sales on certain products and services
- launch new products and services
- increase prices
- concentrate on the most profitable product lines
- employ more sales staff

# Week One
## THURSDAY

- use sales agents
- open new branches
- enter new markets
- sell regionally as well as locally, or nationally as well as regionally
- start exporting, or expand your exporting operations

*Increase your knowledge of your market*

- run customer surveys
- hold customer forums
- subscribe to trade journals
- conduct your own research
- commission market research
- buy in ready-made research
- talk to suppliers
- research competitors
- form partnerships with non-competing businesses

Not every one of these approaches will work for every option, of course. But you will usually find there's more than one way to achieve your objectives.

*Making it more specific*

These are only broad approaches, of course. They are not the whole story. Each one of them still begs several questions which need answering. Let's look at a few examples.

# THURSDAY

- *Exhibiting.* This is one way to increase awareness, but your objective will have been more specific. It will have said, for example, 'To increase awareness of our products among business customers in the tourism industry'. So your options for achieving it must be more specific too. You'll need to suggest which exhibitions you should attend, what stand you should use, which staff should attend and so on.
- *Commissioning market research.* Again, this will increase your market knowledge, but you'll need to be more specific. What sort of research will you commission? Questionnaires in the post? People with clipboards on street corners? Who do you intend to survey? What sort of information are you aiming to get from it? From whom will you commission the research?
- *Secure sales by improving staff training.* Which staff? How much training? In what areas? In-house or external training?
- *Make more contacts with customers.* By post, phone or face-to-face? How often? For what purpose?

So to recap:

*Look at the options*

- take each objective one at a time
- brainstorm a choice of approaches you could take to achieve it
- make each suggestion as specific as you can

# Week One
## THURSDAY

*I NEED YOU TO BE MORE SPECIFIC. SHOULD THE EXHIBITION STAND BE ROYAL BLUE OR NAVY BLUE?*

## Consider the practicalities

Now that you have a list of objectives, each with a choice of ways to achieve it, you need to start finding out which approach is best in each case.

The way to do this is to examine the implications of each option from a practical point of view. In each case you need to calculate:

- *The potential revenue* from achieving the objective using this method.
- *The cost* of using this method.
- *The time implications* – how long will it take to achieve it and when could you start – in other words what would the schedule be?
- The implications for *staffing* – could it be done by the existing staff, or would you need to bring in experienced people or contract out? (This obviously has an impact on your costs as well.)

Week One
## THURSDAY

> - Will you need to run any *training* in order to put this approach into operation? How long will it take? Do you have suitable staff who could be trained up effectively?
> - Are there any *transport* implications? Would you have to commit to more deliveries? Or start shipping overseas? Or increase your fleet size?

You should have enough information to be able to do these calculations quite easily. Then you'll be ready to weigh options against each other. If any of your calculations show that a particular option isn't going to be cost effective, either revise it or abandon it.

## Select the best route

You should find that by the time you've identified all the feasible options, and then considered the practical implications of each one, it isn't difficult to choose the best way to meet your objectives.

## Week One
# THURSDAY

Occasionally, you'll find that there really isn't much to choose between two or more of the options. If this is the case, don't waste time over the decision of which option to take. If either will do the job equally well, pick either. It probably doesn't matter.

There is one thing, however, that you must consider: combining options. This often results in the best of all worlds. Take our example of reducing delivery times to under four working hours. If you remember, we identified three basic options for doing this:

> - Contract out all your deliveries to someone else.
> - Change your working system so orders are processed faster, drivers check in more frequently, and so on.
> - Employ more drivers.

These options are not mutually exclusive. Once you've weighed up the practicalities, consider mixing some of the options. For example:

> - Change your working system but *also* contract out some deliveries at peak times.
> - Change your system *and* employ a part-time driver from 2 p.m. to 4 p.m. each afternoon.

When it comes to objectives that relate to increasing awareness of your company, or your products or services, you'll find that there are often several approaches that will work. They can frequently be mixed, and often they will support each other if you mix them to give you a better result than they ever could alone.

## THURSDAY

For example, you can combine direct mailshots with telephone selling to excellent effect – the combined approach will give better results than either could on its own. Or you can support an appearance at an exhibition with advertising in the trade press. Or you can run several awareness campaigns quite independently of each other, such as a feature article in the local paper, a trade exhibition and a telemarketing campaign. This last approach would be particularly suitable if you need to increase awareness in several distinct markets.

*Budgeting*
Once you have decided which options to choose, it should be fairly straightforward to calculate the cost of meeting each objective. You've already costed each option, after all.

All you have to do is add up the individual costs of meeting all the objectives, and you have your overall marketing budget. You already know how much revenue you expect it to generate, and that it will more than pay for itself.

It will sometimes happen, nevertheless, that you simply can't afford to invest this much at once, until you've started to see some return. In this case you will need to go back and revise the options.

If you can't reduce the costs, put some of the lower-priority objectives on hold until the increased revenue from the first few is available to pay for them.

In this case, budget in this revenue, and also show in your budget that you will be reinvesting this revenue once you have it – later in the year – to put your other strategies into practice.

# Week One
## THURSDAY

At the end of all this, you should have a clear list of objectives, with your action plan for meeting each one. This will not only outline how you will meet the objective, but will also give a schedule for doing so.

## Summary

That's really all there is to it. You simply take each objective, look at where you are now, and then work out how to get from one to the other.

First, work out what your options are. Then take into account the practicalities:

- cost
- time
- staffing
- training
- transport

Then choose the best route based on this information.

Consider the possibility of combining two or more options. Then draw up a budget and, if necessary, revise your strategy to fit your overall budget. Once you have selected and listed these action points, you have drawn up your marketing strategy.

You've now done all the serious hard work you need to in order to draw up your marketing plan. All that's left is to put the whole lot together on paper.

# FRIDAY

Week One

# Putting the plan together

Congratulations. You've done all the thinking work. Now you simply have to put your plan down on paper in the right order. This is a fairly straightforward process which will get you from the huge pile of material and notes on your desk, to a few smartly presented pages which are easy to understand.

*Putting the plan together*

- assemble your data and review the plan as a whole
- establish the content
- plan the design and layout
- write it up clearly and simply

The aim is to end up with a document that you can work from efficiently, and which you would be proud to show your bank manager or any other outsider to whom you need to show it.

Week One

# FRIDAY

## Assemble your data and review the plan as a whole

The first thing you need to do is to collect together all the finalised information for your marketing plan. Not the books and documents you used to research it, not the lists of notes; just the answers, so to speak:

- answers to the questions we asked on Monday
- competitor comparison table
- SWOT analysis
- objectives
- sales forecast
- marketing strategy

Keep the rest of your notes and research data – survey results or whatever – in a safe place. You never know when you may want to refer back to them, so don't throw them away.

Now have a look through the material you've still got on your desk. It's a good idea to do this after you've had a break from the detailed work of planning the strategy – the next morning is a good time for it. The aim is to give yourself an overview of the whole thing.

You may find when you do this that a couple of things don't quite fit together, or there's something important in the early research that has somehow failed to make its way into the objectives or strategy. Or there might be an important question you couldn't answer at the time that you now feel you can. So this is your chance to review the plan as a whole, rather than looking at it in bits, as you have done up to now.

## FRIDAY

## Establish the content

The next step is to work out what is going to go into the final plan. Don't get upset at leaving out things that you spent ages working on. For one thing, you needed to do the work in order to arrive at a really effective plan. And for another thing, you'll keep the material for reference and – as you'll see in the next chapter – there'll be plenty of opportunities to refer back.

Also, you may find that the bank manager or the shareholders or someone may want more background detail on certain aspects of the plan. That's when you'll be able to produce from the filing cabinet all these extra documents that never made it to the final document.

So what is going to find its way into the final plan? Well some things are compulsory and some are optional. There is a list of things – which we'll look at in a moment – that really have to be there; everyone expects it. But that doesn't mean that everything else is banned.

You want to keep the document as brief as you can – between about ten and 25 pages – but if there's other information which in your case you feel is particularly important, then you can include it.

As for the compulsory information, the following things should always find their way into the finished plan:

> *Core contents of the marketing plan*
>
> Where your business is now:
>
> - key facts about your products or services
> - key facts about the customers
> - key facts about the competition (including the comparison table)
> - SWOT analysis
>
> Where your business is going:
>
> - your objectives
> - your sales forecast
>
> How your business is going to get there:
>
> - your marketing strategy

You'll notice that you only need to include the key facts about your products or services, your customers and your competitors. Only you will know precisely what these are.

The point is that once you've answered some of your early questions, you'll find that some of the answers repeat each

# FRIDAY

other, and some of the information turns out – once you have it – to be less relevant than it might have been. So you won't necessarily need to reproduce the full list of answers that you researched.

You should be able to judge this for yourself and, if in doubt, keep the information in there. You can always put it in an appendix at the back so it's out of the way for anyone who doesn't need to read it.

As well as the core contents of the marketing plan, there are one or two other practical inclusions you need to make, to render it easier to read and to use.

> *Other contents of the marketing plan*
>
> - Cover page – stating company name, address, phone number and the date the plan was prepared; also give your own name and phone number.
> - Contents page.
> - Summary (we'll look at this in more detail in a moment).
> - Appendices – if you think it would help to include some of your extra information in an appendix.

The first three of these – cover page, contents and summary – should go at the beginning, in that order. The summary is extremely important. It may not matter much to you – you know what's in the document anyway – but if you have to show your marketing plan to the bank manager, potential investors and so on, they may well decide whether or not to read the whole plan purely on the basis of the summary.

## FRIDAY

So you need to know what goes into the summary. Everything in the document, really, but in brief. Just give the results of key points from each section:

- Where you are now – include a brief description of the products, type of customers and key competitors. Give the most crucial one or two strengths and opportunities. Since the summary is usually for people who you are hoping will invest, lend or whatever, it's best not to call attention to your weaknesses at this point. They need to be included in the plan – it wouldn't be credible without them, and a smart investor will spot them anyway – but they don't need to go into the summary.
- Where you are going – summarise your key objectives and give the bottom line of the sales forecast; don't bother with the monthly or weekly breakdown.
- How you are going to get there – again, summarise your strategy, and don't give the detailed specification of each action point, just the first stage you went through. So you can say that you will 'increase your customer base by 30% through advertising and exhibitions' without giving details of which exhibitions you plan to attend, and so on.

As far as the length is concerned, the point of the summary is to give a brief précis, so you need to keep it short. Aim to keep it to one sheet of paper, but if the whole document is long, you may have to run over onto a second sheet.

Although the summary goes at the beginning, you will no doubt have realised for yourself that the sensible thing is to write it last. If you do this, you'll find it far quicker and easier.

Incidentally, you'll probably find it a very helpful mental exercise as well. It tends to focus the mind on the absolutely central issues in a way that can give you a much clearer vision of where you're leading your business.

## Plan the design and layout

We've already seen that the finished document should be between about ten and 25 pages long – nearer ten for a small business. This may seem rather long, and the reason for this is simply that if you want to impress people with your plan, you need to present it professionally and clearly. And to do that takes up more space than presenting it badly. You could cram the plan into four or five pages, but it would look impenetrable and be hard to read.

So let's take a look at the most important rules of layout and presentation for creating a smart, professional document.

*Packaging*
The first thing to consider is the packaging. You don't want to present someone with a few stapled pieces of paper and tell them it's your marketing plan. But at the other extreme, you shouldn't have it leather bound with your company name engraved on the cover in gold leaf. Apart from anything else, this gives the impression that the contents are likewise engraved in stone. A marketing plan is a flexible document and it should give that impression.

By far the best approach is to use a good-quality laser or inkjet printer, and print out your plan on good-quality, plain white paper (not laid paper, which is the finely textured paper often used for letterheads – it doesn't take print so well).

Then have the whole thing bound with, for instance, a spiral binding and a clear plastic cover front and back. That will look smart and professional but not over the top.

*Space*
Your marketing plan will look much better, and be easier for you and anyone else to read and use, if you double space it and use reasonably wide margins. It will look more professional if you justify the text (in other words, line up the right-hand ends of the lines). This will also help to focus the eye on the text, which makes it look more important.

*Make it easy to follow*
Having included a contents list, you will naturally number the pages to help other people find their way around the marketing plan. You will also need to include clear

headings and sub-headings to make sure the reader can find the section they are looking for. This also has the benefit of breaking the text up a little more so that it looks readable and approachable.

*Keep it simple*
Limit yourself to two fonts (types of lettering) for the whole document. Use one for headings and one for text. Or stick to just one throughout if you like. You can use different sizes, bold, italics and so on, but only in moderation.

The aim is to produce a document that is clean, readable and easy to follow. You're supposed to be exercising your marketing skills, not your prowess as a designer. Fussy or fancy designs distract the reader from the content, which is the part that matters in a marketing plan.

Make sure any tables, such as the sales forecast, or competitor comparison table, are neat and simple. A page of text with tables or charts on it quickly looks confusing and messy if the graphics are at all fussy.

So don't play around with loads of different line thicknesses and typefaces. Just use bold type for column and row headings and keep the whole thing as simple as possible.

By the same token, don't start showing off with clever icons or bits of clipart. By all means put your logo on the title page, and perhaps even at the very end if there's a lot of the last page left blank, but leave it at that.

## Write it up clearly and simply

Now that you have a smart-looking, well-presented marketing plan that contains all the essential information, the only thing left is to make sure that whoever you show it to can read it.

There are a few guidelines worth following to make sure that your style is clear and easy to follow, and that people enjoy reading your plan. If the language is convoluted or over-complicated, it can be so hard to work out what the individual words and sentences mean that it becomes impossible to take in the overall meaning of the document.

> *Guidelines for writing clear English*
> 
> - Use ordinary, everyday language – don't try to be clever.
> - Use short words.
> - Use short sentences – average 20 words and don't exceed 40.
> - Use short paragraphs – they should never look deeper than they are wide.
> - Don't use jargon that your readers might not be familiar with.

## F R I D A Y

- Avoid legal terms and pompous words – such as 'herewith' and 'therein'.
- Use active rather than passive verbs – make the subject of the sentence do something rather than have it done to them: *The boss phoned me rather than I was phoned by the boss.*
- Use concrete rather than abstract nouns – abstract nouns often end with '-tion': write *car* rather than *transportation*.

## Summary

You've completed your marketing plan. Today we've worked through the four stages of putting the plan together. First of all we assembled the data and reviewed the plan as a whole – the first proper opportunity for an overview of the work you've done up to now. Then we looked at the three stages of transferring the work to the final document.

*Establish the contents*
First of all, establish what exactly is going into the report. There are the core contents, that set out where you are now, where you are going and how you are going to get there. And then there are the other ingredients – the cover page, contents, summary and, sometimes, appendices.

*Plan the design and layout*
Next we looked at the packaging and design of the marketing plan. We established that it should be presented in a way that looks smart and professional but not over the top. Then we looked at how to use space, page numbers and headings, and the importance of keeping the design really simple.

Week One

# F R I D A Y

*Write it up clearly and simply*
Finally we considered the importance of using simple, everyday language so that the document is easy to read and take in. We looked at the most important guidelines for writing clear English, such as keeping words, sentences and paragraphs short.

So now you have your completed marketing plan, and all that's left is to make sure you get the most out of it. After all, you want to make all the work that's gone into it worthwhile — and it will be.

# SATURDAY

Week One

# Using the marketing plan

We've spent the last few days putting together a marketing plan from scratch, and you should now have a smart document sitting neatly on your desk. So this is a good time to recap everything we did to get here.

> *Drawing up a successful marketing plan*
> - asking the right questions
> - researching the answers
> - setting the objectives and sales forecast
> - planning the marketing strategy
> - putting it all together

It hasn't been difficult, but it's taken a fair bit of work and it seems a shame to waste it. So the last thing we're going to do today – but by no means the least important – is to find out what you're supposed to do with the damn thing now you've got it.

Week One

# SATURDAY

## Asking the right questions

On Monday, we had a look at the first stage of the marketing plan: drawing up a list of questions. The important thing is to ask the right questions so you end up collecting all the information you're going to need later.

We established that there are four areas you need to ask questions about:

- your product or service
- your customers
- your competitors
- your business

To begin with, you have to specify exactly what it is that you're marketing. If you never focus on this, you'll never notice if it needs to change. We looked at some of the most important questions to ask:

*Questions about the product or service*

- What is the product or service?
- Where do the raw materials come from?
- What is the packaging like?
- How is the product transported?
- Where is it sold?
- In what form does it reach the customer?
- Does it need explaining?
- Is it easy to use?
- How easy is it to increase production if sales go up?

# SATURDAY

Next, we examined the sort of questions you need to ask about your customers and potential customers. Of course, if you're just starting out in business, all of your customers will be potential.

We discussed the importance of asking yourself uncomfortable questions, such as 'What do your customers dislike about your product?' Only by investigating these areas will you really learn what you need to know about how you can keep improving your business.

> *Questions about the customers*
> - Who are they?
> - What are their buying trends?
> - How much will they pay?
> - How do they know about the product or service?
> - Where do they buy it?
> - What do they like about your product or service?
> - What do they dislike about it?
> - What do they like about this type of product or service?
> - What do they dislike about this type of product or service?
> - Why do your existing customers choose your product or service rather than your competitors'?

The next area we asked questions about was the competition. You need to check out any other business that your potential customers might go to instead of buying from you. They may not be selling the same product – it could be a competing type of product. If you sell electric egg whisks, companies selling rotary whisks are competing with you.

# S A T U R D A Y

> *Questions about the competition*
> 
> - What product or service are your prospects using at the moment?
> - Who are your competitors?
> - Do they offer anything beyond a basic product or service, and if so, what?
> - What has each of your competitors got that you haven't?

We also drew up a table of comparison with your competitors. We listed you and your competitors across the top, and the various factors to compare down the side. This gives you an at-a-glance picture of where you are doing well or badly against the rest of the field.

Lastly, we asked questions about the business, which we did using SWOT analysis.

> *Lists to draw up using SWOT analysis*
> 
> - Strengths
> - Weaknesses
> - Opportunities
> - Threats

## Researching the answers

On Tuesday, we researched the answers to all these questions. We found there were three places you could go for information:

# SATURDAY

- Off-the-shelf information.
- Your customers and potential customers.
- Other people.

### Off-the-shelf information

- your own records
- libraries
- trade associations and regulatory bodies
- trade press
- government departments
- your local enterprise agency

### Your customers

- existing customers
- potential customers
- ex-customers

You can get information from customers by talking to them, phoning them or writing to them, and we looked at the pros and cons of all these approaches.

### Other people

- suppliers
- competitors
- non-competing businesses
- advisors

# Week One
## SATURDAY

# Setting the objectives and sales forecast

Once you've collected all your information together, you need to do something with it. You've already established, by answering the lists of questions, where your business is now. So it's time to work out where it's going.

*Identify your critical success factors*
Go through the answers which you now have, and identify which factors are absolutely vital to your success. These are the things without which your business cannot thrive.

First of all, go through your competitor comparison table and see where your performance is falling short of the average. Then see where everyone, including you, is scoring highly. These are the areas that are likely to be critical. Check these against other answers if you're sceptical and, once you're satisfied, note them down as critical factors.

The weaknesses and threats in your SWOT analysis are also worth checking through, to see if they bear out any other indicators of where you absolutely must improve your performance. They are not an answer in themselves, because not every weakness is crucial, or even avoidable.

*Establish your objectives*
Now you need to set yourself objectives based on the areas where you need to improve. Top of the list should be your critical success factors. You'll also want to look through your other information as well to work out what needs to be done.

# SATURDAY

Week One

In general, you're setting yourself objectives for the next year. However, in some cases you may be aiming to achieve a certain thing much faster than that, or to reach a particular objective over several years.

Each objective should be specific, so you know exactly what you're aiming at. Don't aim *'To speed up delivery'*; aim *'To deliver 95% of orders within four working hours, and the remainder within six hours'*.

We also looked at how to set priorities if you can't afford either the money, or the time, to pursue all your objectives straight away.

*Draw up your sales forecast*
This is a forecast of what you expect your sales to be, not a fantasy of what you'd like them to be. There are half a dozen factors, other than your sales figures for last year, that you should take into account to help you estimate your sales as accurately as possible.

> *Factors that will help you estimate sales*
>
> - the market
> - the products or services
> - the competition
> - the customers
> - contract payments
> - seasonal patterns

Week One

## SATURDAY

# Planning the marketing strategy

The final stage of preparation involves converting your objectives into action plans. In other words, having established where you are now, and where you are going, this is the time to establish how you are going to get from A to B. The three main stages to achieving this are:

- look at the options
- consider the practicalities
- select the best routes

*Look at your options*
You need to examine, for each objective, all the plausible options you can think of for achieving it. We looked at the kind of approaches you should consider within each of the five main areas of marketing that your objectives are likely to fit into:

- increasing awareness of your company and your products/services
- increasing existing customers' loyalty
- securing sales
- generating higher turnover
- increasing your knowledge of your market

*Look at your options*

- take each objective one at a time
- brainstorm a choice of aproaches you could take to achieve it
- make each suggestion as specific as you can

# SATURDAY

*Consider the practicalities*
The next stage in drawing up your marketing strategy is to look at the practical implications of each option. You need to consider several aspects.

> **Practical considerations**
> - potential revenue
> - cost
> - time implications
> - staffing
> - training
> - transport

*Select the best route*
It should be fairly clear which of the options you identified is going to be the most effective. If there's nothing to choose, it doesn't matter which you go for. Bear in mind the possibility of combining options; this can work very well. We considered one or two ways in which you could do this.

Finally, we looked at the budgeting for your marketing plan. Once you've added up the costs of all the options you plan to adopt, you have a budget. Sometimes you really can't afford to launch into all these marketing schemes straight away. So we finished by looking at what you do if this is the case. By the end of Thursday we had a list of objectives, with a costed and scheduled action plan for achieving each one.

# SATURDAY

## Putting it all together

On Friday, we pulled everything together into a finished document. We started by assembling all the data we were going to put into it, and then reviewing it all together, to make sure there was no repetition or inconsistency. Then we established the precise contents of the final document.

> *Establish the contents*
>
> - Cover page
> - Contents page
> - Summary
> - Where you are now:
>   key facts about your products or services
>   key facts about your customers
>   key facts about your competitors
>   SWOT analysis
> - Where you are going:
>   your objectives
>   your sales forecast
> - How you are going to get there:
>   your marketing strategy
> - Appendices (if you need them)

After that, we looked at the key points of layout and design, including packaging, spacing, page numbering and headings. We also established the importance of keeping the design clear and simple.

Finally, we looked at the guidelines for writing clear English, using short words, sentences and paragraphs.

# SATURDAY

## Using your marketing plan

And finally ... What are you going to do with this marketing plan? You're going to wring every last drop of value from it, that's what. And you will be able to derive plenty of benefits from it if you use it wisely.

You've already learnt a huge amount doing it, and come up with strategies you would never have arrived at without it. You also have a professional and thorough document you can show to anyone who needs to see it, from your bank manager to consultants, investors and incoming directors.

But you don't want to frame it and hang it on the wall, looking impressive, as a memento of all your hard work. You can get far more value from it as a working document that you refer to regularly.

*Implement the plan*
For a start, you will need to implement the strategies that you have set in the plan. You've written yourself an action plan with a schedule and a budget, so you can start putting it into practice.

*Update the plan*
You'll remember that we started with a list of questions which we researched the answers to. There were probably a few answers that you couldn't find at the time and had to make an educated guess at. Well, you can fill some of them in as you go along.

This is worth doing for two reasons. For one thing, you may have guessed wrong, and the right answers might affect your strategy so you need to know about them in order to keep it up to date.

## SATURDAY

The other reason is that if you keep your marketing plan regularly updated, you will never have to go through the work of putting it together from scratch again. If you let it sit at the back of a filing cabinet for five years, it will be virtually useless at the end of that time. If you need it then, you'll have to start again.

So make yourself an action point to fill in the guesstimate questions as soon as you can. Be on the lookout for the information you need.

You should also schedule an update session (with action points) every so often. Once a year is enough for a lot of companies. If your business or market is changing fast, once every six months might be better. You should make a point of checking every fact to see whether it needs updating. Your product range may have changed, or a new supplier may have arrived on the market. Most facts may not need altering, but if you don't consciously check, you'll miss something.

# SATURDAY

*Week One*

Take your competitor comparison chart as an example. Have any new competitors arrived on the scene? Has one of your competitors revamped and improved their approach to customer care? Are you still doing as well by comparison with the rest of the field? If not, are you doing better or worse?

*Review the plan*

You also need to review the plan – again, once a year is usually sufficient but you might want to make it more frequent. Do this shortly after you have updated it.

If you have achieved the objectives you set out last year, you are going to need a new set of objectives, and a new strategy to achieve them. Many businesses take a couple of days out for their directors or senior managers to get together and hammer out next year's plan. But you could set aside a long session every few months if that suits you better.

Your update will tell you about any changes in the market, your customers' attitudes, your product, the competition, your strengths and weaknesses, and so on. These will help you devise a new set of objectives, using the same approach as for the original plan.

*Use the plan proactively*

Keep using the plan to generate ideas. Look at the SWOT analysis and ask yourself if there's anything else you could be doing to build on your strengths, or make the most of opportunities.

Week One

## SATURDAY

When things go wrong, use the plan to tell you why. Suppose you start missing your sales targets. The odds are that you'll be able to work out why if you look through your marketing plan. And you'll be able to find a way to get back on target.

Suppose the reason you're missing your targets is because a new competitor has arrived on the scene. Don't give in – fight. Update your competitor comparison table and use it to help you brainstorm ways to maintain and build your share of the market.

So you see, a marketing plan isn't a tedious document you're obliged to prepare to keep the bank manager happy. It's one of the most useful business tools you'll ever lay your hands on, and the more you learn to use it, the more indispensible you will find it.

*Schott's Original Miscellany · Calendar*

## — ASIMOV'S ZEROTH LAW OF ROBOTICS —

'A robot may not injure humanity or, through inaction,
allow humanity to come to harm.'

*On this day in 1988 the national debt of the UK was £197,295 million, or £3,465 per person.*

# 31
*March*

© Ben Schott · www.miscellanies.info

# Viral Marketing

**RICHARD PERRY AND ANDREW WHITAKER**

**WEEK TWO**

# Dedication

*For Amanda and Clare*

Thanks to all those people who have supported us in bringing this book to life. Special reference to the guys at DS. Emotion, Gyro, Hodder & Stoughton and the Chartered Management Institute.

# Acknowledgements

The author and the publisher would like to thank the following for permission to reproduce material in this book.

Circus Restaurant and paybox US invitation reproduced with the permission of Paybox UK Ltd, Staines, Middlesex.

'What is your No 1 reason for going online?' research data printed with the permission of Forrester Research, Amsterdam, Netherlands.

Time2flirt SMS text message reproduced with the permission of Time2flirt, London.

Every effort has been made to trace and acknowledge ownership of copyright material but if any have been inadvertently overlooked, the publisher will be pleased to make the necessary alterations at the first opportunity.

# CONTENTS

# Week Two

| | | |
|---|---|---|
| **Introduction** | | 102 |
| **Sunday** | Get the basics right | 103 |
| **Monday** | Vital viral ingredients | 121 |
| **Tuesday** | Guiding content principles | 133 |
| **Wednesday** | Viral hosts, vehicles and characteristics | 142 |
| **Thursday** | Keep it simple | 157 |
| **Friday** | Start on the right foot | 167 |
| **Saturday** | Get going | 183 |

Week Two
# ■ I N T R O D U C T I O N ■

Like everything, the dynamic marketing world never stops changing – evolving constantly with developments that turn yesterday's 'new and improved' into today's 'end of line clearance'. The best products and services manage to evolve with their environment, retaining a constant appeal to their target audience – the best marketers remember those traditional principles and apply them to new opportunities.

For the marketer, this changing world has created a consumer far more informed than ever before. Higher levels of media awareness and even an increase in cynicism towards traditional marketing and selling techniques have certainly created a far more mature, challenging and competitive marketing environment. The sharpest marketers realise that when something new comes along, those that embrace these fresh disciplines and communication routes will have one more tool they can use in their eternal quest for mind and market share.

For the 21$^{st}$ century marketer, one such new discipline is Viral Marketing – a technique which captivates the audience and the marketer alike with its ability to deliver a truly fresh approach to marketing communications.

The opportunity with viral marketing is unique – to use your audience to spread your marketing message, while simultaneously adding their endorsement to it. What is more, they do this instantaneously, to many contacts, with the click of a button.

Over the course of this week you will discover how to plan, implement and measure a successful viral marketing campaign and, therefore, how to embrace one of the most exciting marketing communication developments this generation has seen.

Week Two

# SUNDAY

# Get the basics right

## By the end of today you will know:

- the background to viral marketing and what it is exactly
- why viral marketing can be so successful
- how viral marketing works and its benefits
- the pitfalls to watch out for

We will start the week by looking at some of the basics behind viral marketing, from what it is and how it works, to why it has become such a powerful communication medium. From here you will be able to appreciate and understand why this relatively new technique is receiving so much attention.

To begin, let us define viral marketing. We do not want to get hung up on lengthy and complex definitions, but it does make for a good starting point. For our purposes viral marketing will be defined as:

> The voluntary spread of an electronic message from one consumer to one or many others, creating exponential and self-perpetuating growth in its exposure.

Over the next 7 days our focus will be to consider viral marketing as the activity of forwarding *electronic messages* from one consumer/user to a number of other people. These electronic messages can take a number of different forms. The most common by far is e-mail.

Week Two

# SUNDAY

## Viral marketing: an overview

The principles on which viral marketing are based are not new, we have been spreading viruses for years. Think about this:

When was the last time you recommended a good film that you had already seen to a friend?

Or

Have you ever given a friend the telephone number of a good restaurant for an important dinner date?

> *Things you may have recommended:*
> - a holiday destination
> - a clothing shop
> - a restaurant, bar, café
> - an airline
> - a medical specialist
> - a vehicle make or model
> - a garage
> - a business supplier
> - a book, film or music album

These informal suggestions form part of a referral process known as 'Word of Mouth' (WOM) – passing on information to a friend or associate based on your own experience.

A few years ago, before the internet and e-mail came along, viral marketing was being called WOM and in fact, apart from the distribution method, there is not a lot of difference between the two. There are many examples of the latest

## SUNDAY

trend or fashion being spread, not by multi-million pound television advertising campaigns, but rather by individuals simply talking about it, seeing it or hearing about it and creating a ground swell of interest. Think of the phrases, *'I was reading . . .'*, *'I've just heard . . .'* or *'Have you seen . . . ?'* This is where it starts! Cast your mind back to crazes such as the Rubik's Cube, Cabbage Patch Kids and more recently Micro Scooters, Absinthe and Pokemon – all of these products owe much of their success to WOM marketing. WOM marketing can, when successful, be a marketer's dream ticket; consumers drive brand awareness and product demand themselves.

In many ways the easiest way to understand viral marketing is to consider it as 'super-charged Word of Mouth over the Internet'. I receive a piece of communication from a friend, associate or company, I like what I see so I tell others by forwarding the electronic communication. It all happens at the click of a button, which explains another name for viral marketing; 'Word of Mouse'.

Week Two

# SUNDAY

## Background to viral marketing?

Viral marketing, as we know, has actually only been around for a few years and only a few savvy marketers have fully taken advantage of its potential. It has become the marketer's latest buzzword, mainly because of some well publisised success stories, such as Hotmail, Levi's Flat Eric and Virgin cinema tickets, to name just a few.

The term viral marketing was first coined by Steve Jurveston of venture capital (VC) firm, Draper Fisher Jurveston. Jurveston and his partners were the venture capitalists behind Hotmail, and it was their idea to add the now infamous tag line '*Get your free, private email at Hotmail*' on to the end of each message. With this, the automatic digital referral process was recognised.

Jurveston initially referred to this process as viral marketing in a 1997 issue of Netscape's newsletter describing the phenomenal success of Hotmail. The term has grown in popularity ever since – Iconocast even gave viral marketing the award for *Internet Buzzword of the Year* in December 1998!

Viral marketing offers marketers an additional weapon in their armoury. On shoestring budgets, successful viral marketing campaigns can increase sales, improve market penetration or market share and enhance brand awareness.

Many of these marketing objectives could be achieved through one traditional marketing communications media such as advertising, direct marketing or PR or through a combination of them. However, viral marketing offers a unique opportunity to supplement (or even replace) these traditional activities with a campaign that offers results at a uniquely low cost, targeting an audience with near-limitless reach.

> *The wrong sort of virus*
>
> This book is about the positive outcomes that can be achieved through viral marketing initiatives, however connotations of the word viral or virus can create all sorts of unpleasant images. Today, the word is also synonymous with computer viruses – bugs that travel around global computer networks in a matter of minutes, often causing havoc and losing millions of pounds in computer downtime. Code Red, Melissa and the Love Bug are just some of the more well-known examples we hope you have not had the misfortune to experience.
>
> Naturally our use of the word viral is about embracing new technologies and using customer advocacy to drive awareness, interest and demand – something all together more positive.

## E-mail and viral marketing

The close link between viral marketing and e-mail is obvious and it is important that we realise why, in order to capitalise on potential viral success.

E-mail is the third most popular way for people to communicate, following face to face interaction and the telephone. This popularity stems from a number of advantages the medium can offer:

Week Two

# SUNDAY

> - Instantaneous written word, both in creation and reply.
> - One-to-one, or one-to-many communication without the need for physical proximity.
> - Informality – e-mail has its own language and is becoming ever more relaxed, for example smilies :-) and saddies :-(.

The uniqueness of e-mail is the cornerstone of viral marketing success.

## Is viral marketing the same as e-mail marketing?

There can be some confusion that viral marketing campaigns are in essence, e-mail campaigns under a different name. This is not true – the host medium provides a key similarity, but that is where the commonality ends. An e-mail campaign can have a viral element if it contains sufficient motivation to forward it on.

E-mail as a communication channel is perfect for the fast dissemination of information, which is a key factor in how viral marketing achieves the results it does. Within e-mail marketing there are many instances where this is not accounted for and opportunities to encourage a viral effect are missed. Below are two examples of e-mail campaigns that have been received in inboxes.

The first example includes a viral element by suggesting that we should recommend a friend and providing a

# SUNDAY

Week Two

mechanism to enable this, the second includes no such mechanic and does not enable the viral process.

*Example one: Circus Restaurant and paybox UK invitation*

---

Dear Richard,

**Circus Restaurant and paybox would like to invite you to an exclusive dining experience!**

Sign up to paybox and you will be entitled to enjoy a £40 three course evening meal with a complimentary glass of champagne for only £20 by paying with your mobile phone! Any evening from Monday, 19th of November until Friday, 7th of December 2001.

1. Sign up to paybox here
   Please allow two weeks for your application to be processed.

2. Reserve a table
   Telephone Circus Restaurant on (020) 7534 4000 quoting the "special paybox menu".

If you want to invite a friend, partner or colleague, **just forward this invitation**.

Please print out this email and bring it with you as confirmation of the offer.

THE TIMES, October 2001

*"perhaps the most innovative and flexible is the recently launched Paybox, backed by Deutsche Bank. The process is almost as fast as handing over cash"*

Any questions? Please do not hesitate to contact me.

We wish you a pleasant evening.

Yours sincerely

Elizabeth Cooper

---

paybox uk Ltd :-)))

Consumer hotline 0800 58 729269
http://www.paybox.co.uk
Knyvett House The Causeway, Staines TW18 3BA

# SUNDAY

The example above features a 'send to a friend' option to encourage referrals, whereas our second example, a standard e-mail, or 'e-shot' as they are often known, has no such referral method.

*Example two: MAD.co.uk newsletter*

---

Dear Richard

For top editorial content in your industry, go to mad.co.uk every day for current and reliable news. With content taken from 12 leading industry titles plus a breaking news service throughout the day, mad.co.uk has all the news you need to stay ahead.

mad.co.uk has been first with many stories this month including the inside line on the future of Excite UK and job losses at Cordiant, Circle.com and IPC. Other stories broken by mad.co.uk since the start of August include The Body Shop's campaign against Esso, new account appointments by Jaguar and strategic marketing changes at BT Cellnet, to name but a few. We have also provided up to the minute commentary on the battle between Havas and WPP for control of Tempus.

———————Sponsors Message———————
Think differently about your world, think imaginatively about the challenge you now face, think hard before you choose an agency partner . . . Think!

Redefine your thinking.
http://users.mad.co.uk/advert/default.asp?ad=38&id=21479 –

———————————————————————————————

To subscribe at any level today go to
http://users.mad.co.uk/advert/default.asp?ad=39&id=21479 –

All the team
mad.co.uk

If you do not wish to receive further emails from mad.co.uk please click here

http://users.mad.co.uk/users/nomoremails.asp?usr=21479

---

Of course, there is a lot more to viral marketing than this, and day by day we shall uncover the key ingredients you should consider.

# SUNDAY

## Key benefits

One of the fundamental elements of successful viral marketing is that messages are forwarded on to friends, family and associates who usually know the sender. The fact that a virus allows marketers to tap into people's existing networks, allowing them to take advantage of the trusting relationships that already exist, does much to explain the power of viral marketing. Who would you take advice from – a nondescript ad, website or brochure, or a personal message sent from a contact in your network of friends, family or associates? Consider when you check your e-mail and you see a mail from a friend. You will always open it, relishing the personal contact just as you would a letter or phone call.

When a recipient chooses to forward any message they have received, they advocate or endorse its content, by associating their name with the message content. In this way, everyone who uses Hotmail becomes a brand advocate every time they send an e-mail, in essence Hotmail's own customers are doing the selling. Trusting relationships and personal affinity are vital to viral marketing – tap into these and watch your virus grow and grow.

These trusting relationships can occur in different strengths and tiers; e-mail creates and sustains secondary friendship levels and you may find yourself communicating with people who, in day-to-day life, you may not have the time or opportunity to keep in touch with. For the viral marketer, these second level contacts greatly increase the size and opportunity for an individual to forward a message.

## SUNDAY

We can summarise some key benefits of viral marketing:

- The massive adoption of the internet has created an online population of millions, all of whom can be reached with the click of a button.
- The speed in which the information travels cannot be matched by any other communication means. Its exponential effect is unique. Within seconds a message can reach countless people, spread all over the world.
- The self-perpetuating nature of viral marketing means that the cost per direct contact is minimised. Take the example of Hotmail who, with a budget of only $500,000, attracted over 10 million users in a single year, putting an acquisition cost per user below 5 cents each!

# SUNDAY

- Viral marketing has a proven correlation between exposure and improved brand recall levels, website usage and customer loyalty unlike traditional techniques like advertising and public relations. This is mainly due to the referral process coming through established trusting relationships.
- Viral marketing gives instant credibility to a company or product and is by far the most user-friendly type of marketing. This is driven by the brand advocacy created by sending on the message.
- Viral marketing can be measurable, offering the marketer the opportunity to track and analyse how a campaign has performed.

## Why do we refer?

We all subscribe to referral principles every day – it is human nature to pass on information of value and that has a shared interest. There is a 'feel good factor' in passing on a useful piece of information. For many years WOM has been a favoured marketing mechanic for generating loyal and profitable customer relationships; positive WOM delivers considerable benefits.

Viral marketing is most commonly undertaken for the benefit of the individual 'infected' – the benefit may be educational or entertaining, and whether it is intangible or tangible, the sender believes the recipient will receive gratification from being exposed to the virus.

Week Two

# SUNDAY

## Natural vs. encouraged

Viral marketing is increasingly a planned marketing activity. However, this is not always the case – even the best marketers do not always recognise what the consumer wants or what they may pick up on. Do you think the team behind Hotmail really expected the phenomenal success they enjoyed? The answer is no – they may have hoped for a strong uptake, but could not have foreseen such a record-shattering outcome.

There are essentially two types of viral marketing. The first covers campaigns that are meticulously planned and agonised over by organisations and creative agencies, such as the recent Spielberg *AI* viral campaign. This example is arguably the most complex viral campaign yet and is rumoured to have cost over $1 million, the most expensive. Revolving around a host of websites identified in the film's trailer, the campaign requires a high level of user involvement and perfectly fits the description of 'encouraged'. Such campaigns are designed specifically with the user's interests and profile in mind.

Secondly there are those that are picked up more naturally, and without such a high degree of planning. Examples could include such things as messages passed between women alerting one another to the dangers of the date rape drug which was widely publicised in America after some women suffered such terrible ordeals. The shared interest (or in this case shared concern) meant that with little planning, the message travelled widely through a viral referral process.

Importantly, this example reinforces research that a bad customer experience will be communicated eight times,

Week Two

# SUNDAY

compared to a good experience comunicated just once! The natural example epitomises this and is a warning of how a viral campaign can work against you, just as easily as it can work for you.

## The viral dimension – how does it work?

So what is the difference between viral marketing and say, advertising or even direct marketing?

When you place an advert in a magazine, its exposure is constant – you will know roughly how many people will see it from circulation figures and readership surveys. The exposure can vary on a number of factors – position, format, and colour – but broadly speaking, the level of exposure is planned to attain a certain level as an integral part of the media schedule. The same applies to a direct mail campaign – if you mail 20,000 contacts you can assume, fairly accurately, that around 20,000 contacts will be exposed to your message.

With viral marketing that level of exposure planning is removed. Initial distribution can be carefully considered (we will examine this further on Friday), and marketers can hope the campaign will take off. However, there is little that can be done to proactively define how many people, in total, will be exposed to the message. Viral marketing is not a science, but more of an art. If you are after accurate forecasting, then use another communication technique. The best you can do to help guarantee success is to follow the ideas and principles we detail here.

When successful, through the self-perpetuation of the viral marketing initiative, exposure of the message can reach levels unparalleled elsewhere in the marketing world. The exposure patterns of most viral marketing executions show strong elements of exponential growth. The early phases may be slow, but as a critical mass is reached, the exposure of the message increases spectacularly. This exponential trend gives viral marketing a unique ability to disseminate a message incredibly fast.

*Exponential growth*

> **Tony Blair gets the viral message – fast!**
>
> The speed of dissemination of one of the viral marketing games created for the UK elections in 2001 was carefully monitored by the authors after its launch two weeks before the country took to the Polls. 'Crouching Tony Hidden Hague', a Street Fighter style game was launched to a target database of 2000 contacts. Within 24 hours 15,000 different people had played the game in five continents.
>
> What is more, the feedback loop was closed when a senior aide to Tony Blair called the game's creators within six hours to say he would be showing the PM the game that evening.

## The enabler – the growth and acceptance of e-mail

As we mentioned earlier, viral marketing has been enabled by the growth of the internet and the use of e-mail. Therefore, it is important to understand how the habits of e-mail use and penetration have implications for viral success.

# SUNDAY

Week Two

We all recognise how prolific the use of e-mail is, most certainly everyone reading this book will have an e-mail account; in fact it is more likely that we will have at least two, one for work use and one for more personal matters.

*Number of people online*

| World total | 513.41 million |
|---|---|
| Africa | 4.15 million |
| Asia/Pacific | 149.99 million |
| Europe | 154.63 million |
| Middle East | 4.65 million |
| Canada & USA | 180.68 million |
| Latin America | 25.33 million |

Source: Nua Internet Surveys, August 2001

The number of electronic mail boxes around the globe is estimated at a staggering 891 million, with more of them now outside the US than within. In 2000, the number of mail boxes saw a growth figure of 67 per cent from 533 million in use at the end of 1999. What is more, the International Data Corporation (IDC) predicts the number of mail boxes to be around 1.2 billion by 2005.

With so many mail boxes around the world, it is no wonder that the number of e-mails sent on an average day reached 10 billion worldwide by the end of 2001. And there is no end in sight for this growth – by 2005, IDC predicts that over 36 billion e-mails will be sent every day. Our own research, conducted specifically for this book, revealed that 53 per cent of respondents send between 6–20 e-mails per day, while 28 per cent send between 21–50 e-mails per day.

# S U N D A Y

E-mail usage may be considerable but it is also enjoyable. Pew Research, in a recent study, discovered that 70 per cent of e-mail users look forward to checking their e-mail, with 40 per cent saying it is one of the first things they do in the morning, and a further 40 per cent indicating that it is one of the last things they do at night.

*'What is your No. 1 reason for going online?'*

| Research company | No. 1 reason for going on online | % of response |
|---|---|---|
| Jupiter Communications | e-mail | 92% |
| Forrester Research | e-mail | 89% |

## Three key observations

- As e-mail volume increases, there will be more e-mail noise and the user may begin to feel overwhelmed, therefore viral marketing success is by no means guaranteed.
- People like e-mail; a viral marketer can take advantage of this but should be wary about spoiling someone's enjoyment!
- Understand your customers and how they act and use this intelligence to execute your campaigns.

## The pitfalls of viral marketing

When you release your virus, you instantly lose control. Only the bravest marketers should attempt it. It is not for the weak hearted – half-baked or weak ideas simply will not work. Be brave and bold.

# SUNDAY

Week Two

It is also wise to remember that success is far from guaranteed because referral is such a personal decision. Campaigns that fulfil every success criteria have bombed, whereas campaigns that ignore all the recommendations have seen remarkable success. Viral marketing cannot be controlled and so it is important to think about how you can determine if your campaign has been successful.

Viral marketing is not appropriate for all products and all companies, and many consider it to be limited to larger brands with a focus on youth and fashion. Viral marketing for corporate organisations and those in the business to business sector is more difficult, but there are successes. The trick is not to come across as patronising, desperate or overtly 'salesy'.

## Keep it legal

Individuals, not organisations, drive successful viral campaigns. As an individual you do not need your friend's permission to send him or her an e-mail. However, as a professional marketer working on behalf of an organisation, you do need to fulfil a number of legal requirements in the initial dissemination of the message to your target audience.

## It is not the Holy Grail . . .

Viral marketing has been deemed by some as the answer to a marketer's prayers – a quick, cheap way to broadcast a message, drive awareness and generate hot leads. Yet, while viral marketing is a powerful marketing tool, it is by no

# Week Two
## SUNDAY

means the panacea that some have made out. The advantages of a viral initiative will become clear over the following pages – as will the pitfalls – and the underlying theme of carefully planned research and targeting will come to the fore.

## Summary

Throughout the day, you should have gained a broad understanding of the basic principles and driving forces behind viral marketing. Hopefully you will have begun to see how viral marketing campaigns could be integrated into your own marketing activity. Tomorrow we shall look at how planning is essential for a successful viral marketing initiative.

Week Two

# MONDAY

# Vital viral ingredients

## Today you will begin to understand the following:

- How planning is as important as execution when creating a successful viral marketing campaign.
- The importance of understanding your audience.
- Why simplicity is such a critical success factor.

A viral marketing campaign needs to be approached in the same way as any other marketing initiative. Considerations like objective setting, targeting and message definition are as important as ever. The basics remain the same, it is only the medium which is new. Today we set out to identify the fundamental planning considerations that need to be included.

## Set your objectives

Objective setting encourages you to focus on the results you wish to achieve and helps to ensure a planned and systematic approach to a campaign. Traditionally, marketers have been told that objectives they set should be SMART:

**S**pecific
**M**easurable
**A**chievable
**R**ealistic
**T**imely

This rule still applies when conducting viral activity. Setting objectives at the outset of the campaign allows a marketer to

## Week Two
# MONDAY

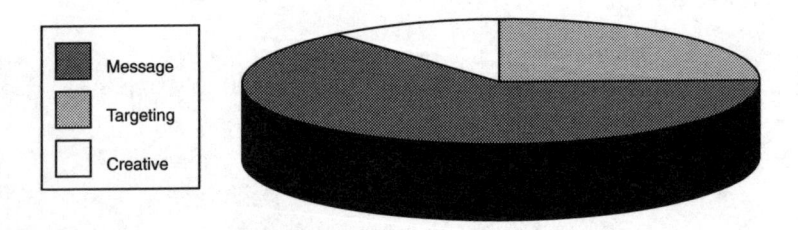

ensure that the campaign has been well considered. Once objectives have been established do not file them away – use them to guide the campaign development and if they change, adapt your approach accordingly.

Objectives such as, generating awareness, improving recall levels, building the brand and reaching as many people as possible, tend to be more qualitative in nature and subsequently can be difficult to measure. Try to make these more specific, for example:

- Acquire 1000 new user e-mail addresses.
- Generate 5000 new unique visitors to the site.

Or even:

- Generate a 10 per cent increase in sales, through cross-selling opportunities.

Week Two

# MONDAY

The objectives of a viral campaign do not have to be limited to hits on a website, registrations or new users. The objectives may aim to create a buzz around the brand in order to enhance or change perceptions or create a brand association. The John West Salmon and Budweiser's 'Wassup' campaigns are good examples of this – both are humorous MPEG (Moving Picture Experts Group) movie clips where the entertainment value creates a positive feeling around the brand, thereby stimulating a referral.

## Identify your target

By definition, once the virus is released it cannot be controlled and can reach anyone, so you may question the validity of targeting in the first place. However, correct targeting at the beginning is fundamental to success – you need to ensure that the contacts who receive your message, especially those you initially target, have a sufficient interest level in your content. Once the virus begins to be spread by your audience, targeting should occur naturally; those sending it to friends and associates will generally have a good understanding of the characteristics, interests and personality of the recipient. The importance of a *shared interest* is highlighted here as a fundamental element of successful viral programmes.

The stronger the element of shared interest, the stronger your chances of success. A great example of this is Friends Reunited.

www.friendsreunited.co.uk is a website that brings together old school friends all across the UK. The site has captured the imagination of the public to such an extent that its success has

Week Two

# MONDAY

become newsworthy in its own right. The coverage generated in the press and radio fuelled the referral process that was already occurring naturally, to a point where some users of the site began placing paid advertisements in local papers to encourage old school friends to register. This almost unique example shows how the power of a good idea and a strong shared interest turns simple referral marketing almost full circle, generating its own PR and promotion.

At the beginning of 2002, Friends Reunited had over 4 million members. For a more in-depth review of Friends Reunited, take a look at the site itself at www.friendsreunited.co.uk.

## Understand your target audience

Research is always relevant – try to understand the motivations and profile of your audience. Ask them questions and test your ideas on them, more importantly listen to their feedback. Sometimes the best form of research can be your own gut feeling; the greatest marketers have entrepreneurial characteristics. Balance your own thoughts and beliefs with those of others – either learnt formally through facilitated research, or informally by listening to your colleagues' opinions.

For example, if you are developing a game, get a few people to play it – see how long they play it for, ask them to comment on its playability, and look out for problems with it.

If you are working on an offer to use as an incentive to respond, check that those within your target find it enticing and are interested enough to bother to respond to it. Consider

**Week Two**

# MONDAY

whether you are going to use a prize draw as an incentive, or whether everyone who replies will receive something.

If you are developing a 'funny' (i.e. a joke or movie) make sure that it is not just you and your colleagues that find it amusing. People's senses of humour can vary considerably and what may be entertaining to one person may well be offensive to another. You need to strike the right balance, without diluting your idea.

This research process is not a one-off activity; it should be encouraged when the virus is alive and this way you will gain a huge amount of real-time intelligence on your target audience. We will cover some practical approaches to tracking on Saturday. If you are using an agency to run your viral campaign, make sure that they have tested their idea and do not forget to ask them if they have executed similar campaigns before and, if so, how they worked.

Week Two

# MONDAY

## Audience-centric planning

It is vital to plan your campaign around your audience. It is no good coming up with a campaign that you think is a winner, if the people you want to communicate to simply cannot partake in it.

> **DVD launch is a little too PC!**
>
> When a leading Hollywood studio launched one of its recent blockbusters on DVD, some very clever technology was built into the disk. If consumers put the DVD into a DVD-ROM drive in their computer, they could access a special website with exclusive trailers for the film's sequel. That is as long as the consumer had a PC. If they had a Macintosh, that was too bad. Mac users couldn't access the special content until a glitch in the programming had been corrected.
>
> The use of technology as part of an innovative, multi-channel strategy was excellent, but the lack of planning and testing caused an embarrassment, highlighting the importance of thorough testing.

## What does audience-centric planning mean?

In short, audience-centric planning is putting the audience experience at the heart of what you do. When planning any activity that touches your audience, it is important to consider how they will react. In larger advertising campaigns it is often possible to research exactly which campaigns will be more effective, and in the direct marketing world it is common practice to test different executions.

# MONDAY

Week Two

In the digital world where it is not as simple to test different executions with the audience, many viral marketers opt for the easy route and plan their viral executions around a lowest common denominator in terms of content, message, level of involvement required or technical usage environment. Yet, while this is one solution to ensure that the campaign is audience-centric, it is not the best way because many powerful, engaging vehicles will be discarded in the hunt for the safe bet. With this in mind, taking the lowest common denominator route is in itself limiting the potency of the campaign.

Through gaining even just a basic understanding of your target audience it is possible to develop some sensible parameters that reflect the level of technical sophistication of your audience.

## Take an example – personal e-mail at work

We all do it at work! Send and receive the odd personal e-mail . . . Have a few sneaky minutes checking that Hotmail account . . . So, while it may be an obvious assumption that a business-to-business campaign is likely to land in a working environment, it is also wise to remember that consumers work too.

In fact, according to research undertaken specifically for this book, 79 per cent of e-mails are opened at work. So unless the intention of the campaign is to annoy the user (and yes, some campaigns do aim to do this!), it is worth considering how an informal viral campaign will be received by your audience if they are at work. Sudden loud sounds, for example, could embarrass the user in a quiet office, prompting him or her to click 'quit' followed by 'delete'. That said, as with all audience-centric planning, the skill comes in finding the perfect balance.

Week Two

# MONDAY

## What message are you trying to convey?

At the heart of viral marketing is a good idea. From this starting point, the assumption is that the people you send it to will think that it is so good they will pass it on, and so on and so on.

To guide your good idea, try to ensure that you have identified a single-minded proposition or clear single message to convey. Too many times marketers try to communicate multiple messages at one time – focusing on a single message will help to ensure brand recall and avoid any message confusion in the target market (i.e. Hotmail – 'Get your free, private e-mail at http://www.hotmail.com'. Short, simple and single minded).

In the following example the powerful message, once again, is short, simple and single minded.

> **THAMES WATER** have set up a website associated with Water Aid and will donate a total of £150,000 pounds (which will provide safe drinking water for life to 6,000 people in Africa and Asia) if they have 2,000,000 visitors to the site in the next 12 weeks. It only takes a few seconds to visit the site and click on the 'Click Here' message at: http://www.givewater.org/

## Check out the competition

Before you release your virus, try to find out if the competition has conducted any similar activity – get yourself on their e-mail listings, see what offers and promotions they are running and how these stack up against yours. Are they targeting the same people as you and are they using the same medium? All this will give you the intelligence to create a campaign that stands out from your competitors.

The continual battle in generating awareness is gaining mindshare, and although viral marketing is great for doing this, you need to remember that more and more people are pursuing this activity. What is more, our survey into e-mail use for this book showed that 55 per cent of respondents received between 6–20 e-mails per day, and a further 26 per cent received between 21–50 e-mails per day. These figures illustrate that e-mail inboxes are becoming as noisy as any glossy magazine filled with ads.

## How does the activity integrate with your overall marketing strategy?

Your viral marketing activity must be integrated within your overall marketing strategy and other marketing communications. Campaigns created in isolation will not benefit from wider activity that you may be conducting and vice-versa. We recommend that you do not approach a viral campaign as a quick fix to a problem.

Integration refers to more than simply following corporate guidelines or using the same strap-line. A viral campaign reinforced with other activity will have a greater overall effect. Furthermore, you want to lean over and touch people with your campaign, create a buzz in their workplace and encourage them to discuss it down the pub. When you can achieve this level of online and offline integration, your chances of success are greatly improved.

# MONDAY
Week Two

*An example of integration: Metz targets students*

A recent campaign into the student community by Metz, the alcopop drink, demonstrated the power of ingenious marketing integration. The campaign leveraged the Metz 'Judderman' character and the unnerving music of the TV ads. The site, at www.spinechillin.com, featured Judderman taking the visitor through his mysterious forest, leading them to a spinning fridge where the visitor entered a competition. This action required the visitor's e-mail address and that of a friend, who subsequently received an e-mail alert. The campaign further integrates with a student's favourite haunt – the student union bar – by using a promotional poster and sticker campaign.

## The role of creativity

The use of creativity within any piece of marketing communication can have a significant influence on the overall success of your initiative. Creativity can be defined in a number of ways – from the way you seed or release the virus, to the call to action, to the medium, and obviously to the content itself.

Creativity can determine the success level of your campaign. However, whether your campaign is carried out in-house or by an agency, there is a temptation to make it as unique and creative as possible, sometimes forgetting the message, objective and more importantly the user along the way. Be as creative as you can afford to be, but always remember who you are talking to and what you want them to take from the communication.

> *The AA encourage the Battle of the Sexes*
>
> Motoring organisation the AA extended their recent TV and poster advertising campaign – based on domestic arguments – through the creation of the 'Argumate', a humorous interactive game where the user can test their skills in avoiding arguments and confrontations. The results were collated to determine whether men or women are better at avoiding arguments, building on a battle of the sexes angle which was central to the viral idea. Users could e-mail the game to friends and family, encouraging the viral effect. Visit: www.argu-mate.com.

This example extends the creative platform and creates a fun and interactive dimension to the offline activity. It also demonstrates a good starting point for developing viral executions that integrate creatively with the overall message.

## Summary

Today we have looked at some of the key elements you need to consider when developing your viral campaign. Many of these are fundamental to an effective execution and, as with the majority of successful initiatives, the greater the effort spent on planning, the greater the chance of your virus spreading.

Week Two

# TUESDAY

# Guiding content principles

## By the end of the day you will have learnt:

- Why content is so critical to a good viral initiative.
- The difference between driving sales and building brands in viral campaigns.
- How to maximise your chances of engaging with your audience and getting them to drive your viral campaign forward.

Today we shall look at the different ways to structure the content and how to make sure that it engages its recipient and ensures its spread. We will also look at some well-known examples to find out how their content underpinned the success they enjoyed.

## Great content makes for great viral campaigns

Think of any e-mail you have received recently. Just any message from those in your inbox. The chances are that you are thinking of a message for two reasons – firstly because of who it came from, and secondly because of the content it contained. It may have been a nice message from your partner, or a really good joke from a friend, or one of those movie clips where a skateboarder attempts some impossible trick and it all goes horribly wrong.

You are remembering this e-mail because it has somehow moved or engaged you momentarily. If someone sent you a

## TUESDAY

message with boring or irrelevant content, there would be no reaction. E-mail itself is an empty vehicle – it is the content that makes it a powerful communication tool.

The same basic rules apply to viral marketing initiatives. The most fundamental success criteria for any viral campaign is the content and the personal referral – the make or break factors in getting the campaign to lift off. If you think back to any of the memorable viral campaigns of late – whether it was MTV's 'Stereo MPs' for the election, or Budweiser's 'Wassup' MPEGs, the principle holds true. It is the content that makes the difference between 'forward' and 'delete'!

## So why does content reign supreme?

In any marketing activity, it goes without saying that the message to be communicated needs to be planned and researched in order to maximise effectiveness, as we discussed yesterday. In any advertising or direct marketing campaign, the content is one of the key success factors of the initiative and, as such, is mapped out with the greatest care. If the communication fails to engage the recipient, it is simply ignored. The same is true of viral marketing – each and every recipient needs to be engaged by what they receive.

Think about the content when it reaches its tenth round of recipients – people who may not have heard of your company, be familiar with your product or even understand your proposition. Does the content still engage them enough to want to send it on to their friends and colleagues?

# TUESDAY

Week Two

## Striking a balance between subtle and overt sales messages

The basis behind marketing is increasing demand or raising awareness for your product. Deciding on whether your message will be overtly sales driven or more brand building is a key decision for any viral marketer. If the objective of your campaign is to generate short-term sales and you lead with a sales message, there is a danger that if your offer is not good enough, your virus will die quickly. However, leading with more subtle sales messages contained within an overall branding proposition will help improve long-term sales as well as build your brand. So how do you decide what is right for you?

*Overt sales*

If you have a very strong offer and call to action, you can focus on these in your viral activity, without fear that the virus will not spread. As a consumer, if you are sent a great

Week Two

# TUESDAY

offer, you will want to let your friends know about it, just as you would tell them about a great sale on the high street. In the example below, from *The Sunday Times Wine Club*, the offer appears so good that it was forwarded to a select number of contacts – friends who share an interest in wine

---

### YOURS FREE – A 12-bottle case of wine normally £70.20!

Dear Mr Whitaker,

From any angle, this is THE best quality wine deal in the UK – 12 bottles of award-winning wine . . . absolutely FREE!

They're serious quality, every one of them . . . like Australian Chardonnay from the World's Best Chardonnay trophy winner, vintage-of-the-decade Bordeaux, a smoothly oak-aged Rioja style and our most scintillating Sauvignon . . .

Simply order The Club's August Highlights mixed case at just £69.99 (plus £4.99 p&p) and receive a Deluxe Dozen of special occasion reds and whites (normally £70.20) – FREE!

Better still, every bottle is backed by The Club's famous guarantee of enjoyment. Don't like them (for whatever reason!), we'll refund you in full, no questions asked.

So give us a try. You've nothing to lose and twelve superb wines to gain. To take full advantage of this once-only offer, and to see the wines, simply go to www.sundaytimeswineclub.co.uk/XA21or call The Club's Express Orderline on **0870 444 7200** (quoting **XA21**).

Best wishes,

Adrian Bentham

Wine Director

The Sunday Times Wine Club

If you would prefer not to receive any further offers from The Sunday Times Wine Club, do please let us know by simply replying to this e-mail, putting the word "unsubscribe" as the subject.

# TUESDAY

For the viral marketer, the risk with overtly sales-led activity is that without an exceptional offer and call to action, there is no reason for the recipient to spread the virus. Furthermore, an overt sales message can encourage the sender to be more selective – creating a smaller community of more qualified recipients at the expense and risk of limiting the exposure of your message. The quality and not quantity argument speaks for itself here.

Take another example. When a leading cinema chain offered free tickets, the virus spread exceptionally quickly, because the offer was so powerful. However as the offer was limited to 20,000 free tickets and the uptake was so strong, the virus died quickly. Gauging the success of this campaign depends on the cinema chain's objectives – if it was to get 20,000 people to their site and claim a free cinema visit, then yes, it was very successful. If the objective was to build the brand, then the tens of thousands of people who received the virus as it died down and could not get a free ticket would be less favourably inclined to that particular brand.

## So what about viral campaigns that build the brand rather than drive sales?

Viral marketing offers an exceptional opportunity to build the brand. Many brands have invested in viral marketing with a focus on the brand; the trick is to ensure that the content is so creative and engaging that it merits passing on to a friend, despite the lack of an explicit offer. Due to the aspirational nature of the 'cool' content, the person forwarding the message becomes part of the 'in crowd'. In essence, the opportunity to be able to impress others through an action is driven by basic human motivations – people like to be liked!

Week Two

# TUESDAY

Brand-building campaigns can positively affect your sales figures, but it is likely to be more long term as customers and prospects build an affinity with the brand, have higher levels of recall or recognition and ultimately become predisposed to the product or company.

A good example of this is the recent MTV video clip, created as a viral campaign for Christmas 2001. This spoof piece of home video showed a young boy opening his presents on Christmas day to find that his gift happened to be a genuine, fully functioning Star Wars light sabre. The boy swings the weapon around his head and accidentally decapitates Grandma. Aimed at a specific audience who would see the entertaining side to this movie, the virus reached thousands from a small launch group within just a few days.

This example illustrates that not all campaigns require a specific action, i.e. visiting a website. Some, such as the MTV example, reinforce brand values and create a buzz around the content.

## Avoiding apathy

How many times have you received a piece of direct mail containing the latest, greatest offer that frankly you just do not need? And how many times have you thought *'so what?'* before throwing it in the bin? For a direct mail campaign, this kind of reaction can be tolerated – this reaction is even expected from 98 per cent of the recipients, so long as the other 2 per cent think *'that's just what I've been waiting for'* and respond to the campaign. Unfortunately, with viral initiatives this success criteria is not the same.

# TUESDAY

If a viral campaign is to have sustainable growth, out of every 100 people to receive the virus, we need another 100 referrals – anything less would mean the virus slowly starts to die. If only two people feel sufficiently moved to click the 'forward' button, they will each need to send the mail to 50 people, which is pretty unlikely. If they only sent it to ten people each (i.e. 20 referrals in total) the virus would be in rapid decline. It is important to stimulate a reaction in as many recipients as possible to maximise the number of referrals.

What reaction should your viral campaign prompt from a user? There is no answer to this because the communication objectives of any initiative will be specific, if not unique, to that campaign. Take a charity viral e-mail, for example – here the desired result may well be sympathy and concern or simply awareness of the problem, compared to a Budweiser campaign intended to make people laugh, drive aspirational awareness and reinforce subconscious perceptions that 'Bud' is cool.

While the reactions can be very different, all viral campaigns have a common enemy – *apathy*. Prompting a response – any response – is essential for the campaign to grow. Failing to elicit any response means that the campaign will die because the content fails to move the recipient. That lack of engagement means that the virus will go no further.

## Passing the *'What's in it for me?'* test to avoid apathy

It is imperative that the user engages with the content and gets something out of it. This may be tangible (i.e. money off a product) or intangible (i.e. an emotional reaction). If the

Week Two

# TUESDAY

content fails to elicit either of these reactions, you will end up with a dead virus. In order to get a positive reaction, your content has to pass what we call the *'What's in it for me?'* test.

Before you go to the effort and expense of developing your viral campaign, there is a simple way to see if you will pass this test. Put yourself in the shoes of the recipient and ask yourself the questions identified below – if you can answer some or all of them positively, your campaign stands a chance of passing the test. If not, you may need to think about the proposed content again.

- Is there a benefit or an offer? Is it compelling enough to make me stop what I'm doing and shout about it to my friends?
- Does it make me look cool/good/educated? In other words, does it position me how I want to be seen?
- Is there a reason for me to pass it on? What is it?

# TUESDAY

- What would I tell a friend the benefit is? Is it clear to me?
- What will I remember from the campaign? Is there something long lasting?
- How would I convince a sceptic that this is something good?
- What questions or objections would I get from that sceptic, and would I have an answer?
- Could the people I send it to misunderstand something? Is there anything that could make me look bad?

Simply ask your target audience what they would do if they received your virus. Explain how the campaign will work and the response you want from the recipient and ask if this is a reasonable expectation.

Remember that you are relying on your audience to forward the message. They will only forward something if it reflects positively on them, so your content needs to be sympathetic to their preferences. You are in the hands of your audience and you need to keep them at the forefront of your thinking.

## Summary

Today we have covered the principles that should guide the direction of your content and how to maximise your chances of creating excellent content. Much of today is theory – tomorrow we shall start to put this into practice.

Week Two

# WEDNESDAY

# Viral hosts, vehicles and characteristics

## Today, we will cover:

- The different ways your message can reach your audience.
- How different content can be applied for maximum advantage.
- The three main content characteristics your campaign can adopt.

Today we are going to cover the type of virus you will be trying to spread. We can break this down into three areas. Firstly, the host, which is where the virus resides. Secondly, the vehicle by which the message is carried, for example an MPEG movie. And thirdly, the characteristics that are present within this message, for example is it purely for entertainment purposes, or is there an educational element as well?

## The host

There are a limited number of hosts for a virus. The two main options are e-mail and a website. This book predominantly relates to these two, but there are a couple more that are worth noting, mainly mobile phone text messages and hand-held devices such as Personal Digital Assistants (PDAs). We will touch on the latter two briefly, later in this section.

# WEDNESDAY

*Week Two*

## *E-mail*

As people are now very familiar with e-mail, it lends itself well to spreading a virus. When e-mail is the host, the virus is contained within the body of the e-mail, or as an attachment to the message. Although there may be a website or other call to action referenced, the virus can be spread and understood simply by forwarding the e-mail to another person.

The great advantage is that the spread is made easier by simplifying the actions required to become infected, i.e. you do not need to visit a website. The main disadvantage is that there are limitations with the type of content you can spread – such as the size of a file attachment and any special applications that are required to view the content.

## *HTML or text?*

One of the key questions when using e-mail is whether to use a plain text or an HTML (HyperText Markup Language) (an e-mail designed using HTML may contain graphics, rather than a pure text-based e-mail). The basic answer is that both can usually be created within an e-mail (known as a multi-part e-mail) and your e-mail application will detect what it can read. As a rule of thumb, approximately 80 per cent of e-mail users can read HTML e-mails and IMT Strategies reports that as of September 2001, 57 per cent of marketing e-mail received by online users was in HTML format. The type of e-mail you send depends upon your content and your audience.

## *Websites*

Due to their massive adoption, websites make a perfect host for your virus. When a website is the host, the recipient will need to visit the website to be infected and experience the virus.

Week Two
# WEDNESDAY

Many of the issues regarding inclusion of content within the body of an e-mail are avoided if the content is on a website, mainly because the user's environment can be more controlled. For example, games, interactive competitions and large file-size content can sit easily on a website, but spreading these within an e-mail is more difficult. Tracking the virus is also easier when the host is a website – we will cover this more on Saturday. There are again disadvantages that need to be weighed up, a key consideration is that it requires the user to visit the website, adding a further obstacle to the infection process. You will also be placing a large amount of strain on your Web server. Finally, not everyone who has access to e-mail necessarily has access to the Web such as users of interactive TV and restricted Web browsers.

*An example of a simple Web-hosted campaign from the NSPCC*

```
SUBJECT HEADER: Re: Chariddy . . .

Donate to the NSPCC for free. It'll take
two seconds . . . Just click on this
link, and then the green button to have
Microsoft give the NSPCC 8p on your
behalf. Pass this on to your friends.

http://www.nspcc.org.uk/donate-4-free
```

In this example the recipient is required to visit the website to complete the infection. Without this action the virus is incomplete.

# WEDNESDAY

Week Two

## Other hosts

We mentioned that other hosts are available and although far less common than e-mail and websites, text messaging and PDAs are becoming more widely used.

### *Mobile phones*

Short Message Service (SMS) or text messaging can also play host to a viral campaign. This is currently being utilised by a limited number of companies. As with any new technique, success levels vary and much depends upon the content of the message. Initial indications suggest that SMS as a viral vehicle is more likely to be successful in the youth or younger professional market places.

*Example: Time2flirt mobile phone campaign*

> time2flirt d8 4 diary!
> 12 Dec, Embargo,
> 533b Kings Road SW10.
> Get yr mobile ready
> 4 some flirting fun
> :-) frwrd this
> 2 any1 u know

The above example to promote a London club night used simple text to convey the message. SMS is more limited than e-mail and websites hosts. Text-based messages are the most popular, however ring tones and phone logos are other examples of viral elements that can be transmitted to mobile phones.

*Personal Digital Assistants (PDAs)*
PDAs can also be used to host a virus. These small hand-held devices are becoming ever more widespread and many applications (usually free downloads) are spread using this method.

If the content is rich enough and it is free, then a viral effect can be created. The virus is usually a 'natural' spread and tends not to be actively encouraged by the content originator.

## Which one is best for you?

It is impossible to specify the single best host because the choice must depend on the campaign and its objectives. What we can say is, stick to what you know and if it is a good idea it will spread. You will probably get more success from e-mail and websites than using other hosts.

## The vehicles

The viral vehicles are wide and varied. Below some of the vehicles are listed that you may have received. The vehicle is not particularly important within itself; you can use any of them to convey your message and build the viral effect.

Week Two

# WEDNESDAY

### *Examples of viral vehicles*

jokes
stories
tests, e.g. personality tests
trivia questions
warnings and spoofs
still images
sound files
movies
competitions
incentives and offers
games

We have investigated some of the limiting factors that will affect the use of the vehicle and you will find out more about these on Thursday.

Week Two

# WEDNESDAY

## *Quick reference guide to attachments*

You may be sending out content attached to an e-mail. If so, here is a simple guide to the types of file you could be sending, the file format, and the plug-in a user will need in order to view the content you are sending.

| Content type | File format | Plug-in/Software |
| --- | --- | --- |
| Movie file | MPEG (.mpg)<br>QuickTime (.mov)<br>AVI (.avi) | Windows Media Player<br>QuickTime Player |
| Static image | JPEG (.jpg)<br>GIF (.gif)<br>TIFF (.tif)<br>BITMAP (.bmp) | Graphic package or Web browser |
| Sound file | WAV (.wav)<br>MP3 (.mp3) | Sound card and player |
| Program | Executable (.exe)<br>Projector | No software – just need PC for .exe or Mac for projector |
| Moving Web graphics | Flash movie (.swf) | Flash Player |
| Uneditable document | PDF (.pdf) | Adobe Reader |
| Text document | .doc<br>.txt<br>.rtf | Microsoft Word or Text editor |
| Spreadsheet | .xls | Microsoft Excel |
| Web page | .htm | Browser |
| Compressed file | .zip | WinZip<br>Stuff-it Expander |
| PowerPoint | Slide show (.pps)<br>Presentation (.ppt) | Microsoft PowerPoint |

*Which type of vehicle is best for you?*

As recognised all along, much depends upon the type of campaign you are promoting and, indeed, the budget that you have available. If you are working on a low budget campaign, the chances are that you cannot afford to go and shoot a movie clip – however, you might be able to produce a research document that your audience will find valuable. When you have set your objectives and got to grips with your audience, the choice of vehicle will become more obvious.

For your reference, here is a table based on research for this book. It shows how likely recipients are to forward on a particular vehicle. This is only a rough indication – the reality will be more determined by the potency of the specific content.

(Please note that in our survey we asked respondents to rate the likelihood of forwarding a message on a scale of 1 to 5, with 1 being unlikely and 5 being very likely to forward.)

| Unlikely 1 – 5 likely | 1 | 2 | 3 | 4 | 5 |
|---|---|---|---|---|---|
| A joke or funnny story | 9% | 19% | 23% | 25% | 24% |
| An incentivised competition | 16% | 31% | 21% | 17% | 15% |
| An education message | 21% | 33% | 28% | 12% | 6% |
| An amusing movie/image/sound file | 19% | 21% | 23% | 28% | 9% |
| A work-related document | 12% | 14% | 15% | 34% | 25% |
| A game | 27% | 23% | 22% | 20% | 8% |

## The characteristics

OK, so we know about the types of host and viral vehicle, now it is time to look a little more deeply at the fundamental characteristics of what makes viral content so contagious. All successful campaigns – in fact all communication – aims to stimulate an emotional response. But viral marketing has a twist – as viral marketers we need to create an emotional response which will in turn motivate the recipient to continue the spread of the message.

We have identified three main categories Entertaining, Educational and Rewarding – viral campaigns will fall into one of these. However, they are by no means mutually exclusive – in fact if your campaign can feature two or all of the characteristics, your chances of success will increase.

## Entertaining

The most popular and, arguably, the most successful type of viral activity has an entertaining value. If you think about the type of content that you have personally spread, the chances are that entertainment is pretty high on the list.

We usually associate this with amusing content – whether it

## WEDNESDAY

Week Two

is a straight joke or amusing movie clip. Some of the well-known viral examples can be classified as entertaining, for example Levi's' Flat Eric and Budweiser's 'Wassup' initiatives. Here the sender has a feeling of 'coolness' by being associated with the content of the message.

### *So how do you apply entertaining content to your own campaign?*

If you are going to follow this option, your primary objective should have a brand-building focus and not a sales-led one. Therefore, you need to ensure that your message is not overtly sales focused, but more subtle in nature.

For example, when Flat Eric was initially released by its PR and advertising agencies there was no reference whatsoever to Levi's. It was only when the viral campaign officially launched to coincide with the ad campaign that the Levi's brand was promoted. Before the official launch, this piece of unbranded viral marketing had seen prolific growth, purely because its content was so innovative, cool and entertaining. It was only when the advertising campaign broke that any brand association was made, thereby exploiting the mass awareness already generated.

The core objective in Levi's campaign was to raise awareness of the new product and regenerate the flagging Levi brand. By association, if this was successful there would be an increased demand and subsequent revenue generation, which ultimately there was.

Such examples illustrate how the user can discover the brand for themselves, and it gains acceptance and familiarity, rather than having a brand or sales message forced on to them which can alienate and encourage non-acceptance.

Week Two
# WEDNESDAY

It may go without saying, but you need to make sure that your content is actually entertaining – Levi's used one of the best advertising agencies in the business and they got their result – outstanding, award-winning, creative. You do not necessarily need to have a huge budget, however, you do need to have a good idea.

## Educational

Most commonly, educational content is spread to a more select group of recipients, purely because it does not have such a broad appeal as entertaining content. Shared interests, which define how far a virus will spread at each referral, are likely to be more specific in this scenario. Think of a free piece of research you find on the internet – you are unlikely to send this out to the entire company, but you may well send it on to your project team or boss, if it relates to the work you are currently undertaking.

Week Two
# WEDNESDAY

Alternatively, imagine that you are on the Web, checking out your stock portfolio and notice some top tips on some potential purchases; you remember some friends who might find these useful and send the information to them. You have just taken part in your own educational viral campaign, created and executed by yourself. The chances are your usage of this site will increase, as will your loyalty as a result of your action.

That said, educational content could also have a very broad appeal – take the example of a charity viral campaign, which serves to alert the population of a problem such as water shortage in developing countries. Such an issue has a wide shared interest and, therefore, a larger potential audience.

### *So how do you apply educational content to your own campaign?*
Content with educational characteristics is particularly flexible because it can be applied to campaigns with either brand-centric or sales-centric objectives. The nature of the educational message will, as ever, depend upon your target audience and what they find interesting or relevant.

Educational content is a good choice for improving positive associations, while raising awareness and building the brand. It can work particularly well in business-to-business campaigns, where valuable information can be used to propel the virus. Often this information is already within the knowledge pool of the organisation and simply requires a campaign to be wrapped around it.

# WEDNESDAY

## Rewarding

The third characteristic of contagious viral marketing is rewarding, or perhaps more accurately, a direct, tangible reward. This usually manifests itself in the form of incentives, time-limited offers, promotions or competitions. They are the most blatant types of response-driven viral marketing and most appropriate when short-term demand generation is the primary objective.

Reward-focused viral marketing campaigns will contain a direct and personal benefit to the recipient. Any company can create a rewarding campaign, whereas some may find it more difficult to create an educational or entertaining execution. In business-to-consumer marketing, the reward is usually aligned to the individual, or in a business-to-business context, the reward may focus on the company or both the company and individual. For example, if you order a specific type of product, there could be money off (a benefit for the company) together with a free gift (for the individual).

# WEDNESDAY

Central to the success of a reward-based viral content is the need to ensure that the reward is appealing to the target audience. The *Sunday Times Wine Club* example identified yesterday is a great example of a simple direct response e-mail that has gone viral. Why? Because the offer was strong for this shared interest group. The plain text e-mail execution was simple and the offer was a winner.

### Online retailer forces the issue . . .

In June 2000, an online wine retailer sailed very close to the wind with a viral initiative to boost their UK customer base.

The viral vehicle was a competition to win a group holiday for the entrant and four friends, whose e-mail addresses had to be specified. These friends all then received an e-mail from the company explaining that they had been nominated for the competition by their friend, but that the group's entries would be invalid if they did not confirm their entry for the competition, thereby registering for the site.

Understandably many of the 'friends' were alienated by the dot-com company, as they felt the company had been put under pressure to register, so as to avoid letting their friends down. Clearly these people would not be favourably inclined to that particular brand after that, even if they did enjoy the odd tipple!

Week Two
# WEDNESDAY

***So how does rewarding content fit into your own campaign?***
Reward-based content can offer a simple route to viral success. If the offer is compelling enough, it will engage the user and spread amongst the shared interest group.

With this type of content it is essential to identify what response you want from the reward you are offering. In some cases this is very simple, such as a 'Buy-one-get-one-free' offer. In other cases the response could be to click on a website, enter a competition, request information, trial a new product or make an appointment. Once you know what you want your recipients to do, the all-important call to action can be developed. As always, keep it simple and clear and you will enjoy a greater level of success.

As this type of content is so focused on generating a response, it is most commonly applied in campaigns intended to drive revenue rather than build the brand. Although, as we mentioned yesterday, both of these objectives have an indirect effect on one another. In this sense, a good offer that spreads around the internet like wildfire will not only drive revenue and uptake, but will also build brand awareness.

## Summary

Today we have looked at how to give your viral idea the right host and vehicle, while also considering the most appropriate characteristics to help ensure viral success. Tomorrow we shall look at some of the pitfalls to avoid when creating your virus.

Week Two

# THURSDAY

# Keep it simple

## By this evening you will understand:

- The factors that can limit the success of your viral campaign.
- How technology can get the better of you if you are not careful.
- Key factors to consider regarding where your content should reside – i.e. on a website or in the e-mail itself.

It goes without saying that in any marketing activity, there are numerous ways for a campaign to go wrong, which can greatly limit the success the campaign would otherwise enjoy. All of these limiters can be applied to viral marketing campaigns as much as to traditional media, however the viral campaign has an added dimension – technology. With content viewed and passed on through connected electronic devices, the technical platform provides yet another area where mistakes can be made, and the success of the campaign can be restricted. As marketers are familiar with the limiting factors offline, the focus of today will be to shed light on these new technology-based success limiters.

## Do not let technology get the better of you

As previously identified, the most common way to limit the success of a campaign is by alienating or omitting potential users, and technology is very good at doing just this. However, many of the key technical limiters (identified below) can be removed through careful planning. The factors are split into two lists, representing the two basic 'host' environments discussed yesterday, namely e-mail and websites.

## Limiting factors for content within an e-mail

*Speed:* 79 per cent of people who can, will pick up their e-mail at work. For these people, who usually have the luxury of a fast network connection, speed is not often a major concern (although waiting even a short time can be frustrating). Nevertheless, most people connecting to e-mail away from a work environment do so on a 56k modem (in other words a modem that – in theory – transfers 56 kilobytes of data per second. In reality however the data transfer rate is likely to be just one-third of this). And so, one of the main success limiters for e-mail-based viral campaigns is speed. With a large attachment included, the e-mail may take a long time to download, frustrating the user even before they have seen its content.

# THURSDAY

Week Two

> The table below displays the research conducted specifically for this book about how long people are prepared to wait for files to open.
>
> | Time allowed before quitting | Percentage of respondents |
> | --- | --- |
> | Less than 30 seconds | 21% |
> | 30 seconds to 1 minute | 48% |
> | 1 to 2 minutes | 19% |
> | 2 to 3 minutes | 11% |
> | More than 3 minutes | 1% |
>
> As you can see, if the time to open the file is more than 1 minute, then you will have lost nearly three quarters of your audience.

If your audience is likely to have a large proportion of home users with slower connection speeds, the effect of file size becomes very important. A typical attachment of 100k would take a few seconds to come through, however a movie file of a couple of megabytes could take nearer 2 minutes. With users paying for a telephone call to their service provider, this can understandably be very annoying. On top of this, files in excess of 2 megabytes may crash the connection altogether! When this happens, the chances are that the user will not try to pick up the message again, stopping the virus in its tracks.

With this in mind, the first rule for attachments is a simple one – the smaller the better. Failing this, think about optimisation – this technique can help reduce file sizes in the majority of cases.

Large file attachments can also cause significant issues if you are launching your virus internally i.e. if a number of people are sending the e-mail at the same time it may crash your own web server.

Week Two

# THURSDAY

*Firewalls:* more and more confidential information is passed via e-mail and the potential for security breaches is very high. As a measure to safeguard a company's material against dangerous computer viruses (such as Melissa or the Love Bug) or against hackers, many larger companies implement a firewall which acts as a security fence, screening who and what can pass into the company's IT environment. What is more, as e-mail – and internet usage is now so prevalent in today's working environment, many companies are using their firewalls to help stop abuse of the IT infrastructure. In an increasing number of companies, viewing certain types of content, such as pornography or pure entertainment, is not permitted. The firewall can examine content and it may be applied as a filter to ban such unsuitable content.

While implementing a firewall is undoubtedly a very sensible move for the organisation, it does have an implication on the viral marketer looking to spread a campaign through an e-mail attachment. Often certain file types will not be allowed through the firewall, either because their content will be deemed unsuitable or due to the possibility of transmitting a dangerous computer virus. The most commonly refused files are video files (such as MPEG or AVI) and executable files (self-running files) such as the .exe files for a PC or Mac program files. If your content is in this format, spreading it by an e-mail attachment may not be the most effective method.

*Plug-ins:* from your audience-centric planning you should know the level of sophistication of your audience. Remember this when you come to choose the host and vehicle for your campaign; it is easy to create a campaign that takes advantage of technology that your audience does

Week Two
# THURSDAY

not have. Using functionality like Macromedia Flash can make your content more dynamic and engaging, but if the audience does not have the Flash player plug-in (an additional piece of software that can be downloaded from the internet) they will not be able to see the content at all. Even the specific version of the plug-in can cause problems. There are no hard and fast rules to follow. You need to choose a sensible compromise that will suit your audience without compromising your campaign.

*Platform:* do you work on a PC or a Mac? Or even a UNIX machine? It is an important question to ensure your campaign is open to the widest target audience. The platforms are increasingly inter-operable (in other words, they talk to each other much better!). However, there are still some inconsistencies which may mean that the content you have included in your e-mail attachment will not work on a particular machine. The most common by far is an .exe file. Although these are great for PC users because they require no other software to run, for Macintosh users they are simply a waste of time – they cannot be used. The reverse is also true – a Mac program file (which does the same job as the .exe file) will be useless to a PC user. Other examples exist, but the underlying rule is a simple one: test it. Try to run your campaign on as many machines as possible, from Macs to PCs and UNIX machines, and from the oldest to the newest. This is the best way to identify any problems before your users tell you about them!

*E-mail application:* as with any software application, there are many variants and versions of e-mail application. However, unlike, for example, a word processing application, with e-mail there are now two very distinct

## THURSDAY

methods to access messages.

1. Through a typical desktop application such as Microsoft Outlook, Quick Mail or Lotus Notes
2. Through a Web-hosted interface such as Hotmail

The main difference is that by definition, the Web-hosted e-mail systems show content as a Web page, so sending out an HTML mail will not cause any problems because HTML is the language used for the creation of web pages. The vast majority of desktop applications will also be able to display an HTML e-mail. In some of the older desktop applications, however, HTML can cause a problem, resulting in the message content turning into line after line of meaningless code.

The prevalence of these old desktop applications is reducing all the time and, as HTML e-mails are now so common, users of these applications will usually know the problem when they see it – and will often be resigned to the fact that their application is rather out of date. That said, it is something that can limit the effectiveness of your campaign and, as such, deserves a mention in this section. With this in mind, the rule is simply to be aware of the problem. If you feel there is a likelihood that your audience may have some old software, plan the campaign accordingly, eradicating the use of HTML in the e-mail message. Alternatively, incorporate a multi-part e-mail that will detect whether the e-mail application can support HTML, if it can not, it will show a text only version.

# Limiting factors for content hosted on a website

*Speed:* this is still an issue for viral campaigns where content is hosted on a website. Users are increasingly used to Web pages which load quickly, so long loading times will have the same effect as slow downloads on e-mail campaigns. Keeping file sizes to a minimum will give a faster file transfer time and using techniques such as streaming for movie clips (which allows the movie to begin playing the early parts while the latter stages are still downloading) will help get your content in front of a user more quickly. Also remember to include a loading progress bar for big or slow files – a user will be more likely to wait if they can see how much time is needed for the content to appear.

*Browser version:* just as e-mail applications vary, so do browsers (the interface through which a user views a Web page). Similar to e-mail applications, the same basic rules apply. If you are hosting content on a website, check it works on as many browsers as possible, from the latest and greatest to older, less advanced versions. Functionality changes with each new release, so make certain that your content can be viewed effectively on a browser version typical within your target audience, not just on the very latest version. If you are working with a marketing or new media agency, ask them to advise you on this, and check with them that they will design the Web pages to work effectively on the two main choices: Microsoft's Internet Explorer and Netscape's Navigator.

*Plug-ins:* as with content attached to an e-mail, web-hosted content may require a plug-in. The same rationale applies –

make sure your campaign is accessible to your target audience by understanding their technology environment. There is no point in creating a campaign using the features from the latest Flash 5 version, if the majority of your audience only have the more common Flash 4 on their machines; these people will be unable to see the content. Achieving that all-important compromise is vital.

*Corporate policy:* previously mentioned in the section above on firewalls, many companies have strict policies on internet usage. With 79 per cent of e-mails accessed from a work environment, it is important to consider the effect this can have. For the viral marketer it is an uneasy position – on the one hand trying to respect these policies, yet on the other hand trying to create a campaign which is extremely engaging and by its nature will distract the user from what he or she should be doing. Again, this is an example of where the viral marketer must find a balance.

*Functionality:* one common limiting factor that is easy to address is the usability of Web-hosted content. The obvious rule to heed is to keep it simple. No matter how Web-savvy the audience, the easier you can make it, the better. Keep the number of clicks (how many links a user has to follow to reach the desired content) to a minimum – any more than three clicks and there will be a drop off in users.

It is also wise to develop the functionality of the site around the guidelines specified by the World Wide Web Consortium. These guidelines, while not legal requirements, do set out a framework for good practice for the functionality of a website, ensuring the site works effectively for as many people as possible, in particular those with special needs. You can check out these guidelines by visiting www.w3.org.

A final limiting factor for Web-hosted content is the vital issue of *scalability*. If a campaign does take off and the site receives a high number of visitors, the last thing a viral marketer wants is the site to crash due to heavy traffic levels. Scalability, as a technical element of a viral marketing initiative, is examined in more detail on the marketinginspiration.com website.

## Making Web-hosted content run smoothly, with a little help from your friends

When it comes to technology, marketing professionals often are not the best people to understand and implement robust IT architectures that will deliver the perfect platform for a Web-based viral marketing campaign. So, call in the experts – for those with the luxury of an in-house IT resource, involve representatives in your campaign. If you work with an agency, pass the technical bit over to them. For those lone rangers tackling the campaign alone, speak to your Internet Service Provider about your objectives. Once aware of these, your technical support will help to ensure that the technical platform achieves them.

## Summary

Today we have looked at the factors that can limit the success of your viral marketing initiative and the actions that you can take to minimise their effect. It has been quite a

Week Two

## THURSDAY

technical day, but hopefully you have gained a new understanding of a key difference between viral marketing and traditional word of mouth – the technology involved in distribution. As well as this, do not forget the basics, like targeting, the proposition and naturally the strength of the idea in the first place – these will all have an impact regardless of any technology issues. Tomorrow we will look at the ways that you can launch your virus.

**FRIDAY** — Week Two

# Start on the right foot

## Today, you will learn:

- How to successfully launch your campaign using direct and indirect launch pads.
- How to sustain your viral campaign over time.
- There are different types of recipient of a viral message and how this can affect success levels.

After learning how technology can limit the success of a viral campaign yesterday, we will spend today examining the options available to launch and sustain a viral marketing initiative. We shall look at the importance of timing, before finishing with an overview of how people react to a viral campaign, and the difference that this can make to their propensity to pass on your message to their network of friends and associates.

## Getting your virus out there

There are a variety of ways that a virus can be launched into a target community, together with a number of ways to ensure that the life of the virus is sustained.

Many critics of viral marketing cite the fact that the medium involves a lack of targeting control and that this is its biggest weakness. However as already mentioned, the campaign will only pass between individuals where there is a shared interest in the content; this acts as a natural filter to keep the virus broadly within its target audience. Therefore, arguably, using personal relationships and networks as your targeting method is more effective than a purchased data list, where targeting assumptions are based on mass profiling information. With this in mind, viral marketers can counter this criticism with the knowledge that this self-selection acts as a natural targeting mechanism.

Self-selection does of course mean that you can expect a degree of fall out from the initial launch – do not worry about this, a certain amount of natural filtering is inevitable even if you have followed the principles discussed earlier in the week.

## The viral process

The following diagram below shows what happens when someone receives a piece of viral marketing. Ideally that person will receive the communication, take a look at it, be engaged in some way and decide to forward the message on. However, at any stage the virus can be dismissed: a user could fail to (or be unable to) open the communication; take a look but not be interested or engaged; find the content engaging, but simply decide not to forward the message on. All of these reactions mean that the virus has died for that person.

This illustration highlights just how important the content of your campaign is – if the content is poor or the characteristic(s) inappropriate, a larger percentage of the recipients will not be engaged and will dismiss the campaign rather than send it on.

*Content engagement process*

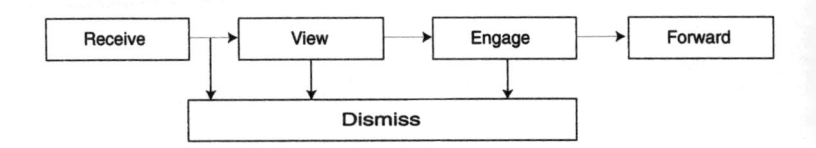

Receive → View → Engage → Forward
↓ ↓ ↓
Dismiss

## Viral marketing launch pads

The following chart details the main options for launching your campaign. Remember that the launch of your virus can be staged, allowing the spread of the campaign to be orchestrated over a period of time throughout a wide community – this may have the advantage of avoiding a quick peak and subsequent quick death of the virus.

The launch can use one some or all of the methods identified. The choice depends very much on the target audience, as well as on time and budget. The simple fact underpinning this is that the more launch pads that can be built into the campaign, the better.

It is wise to remember that the launch process is critical to success and, in fact, is the only stage within a live viral campaign that can be controlled. Once you set the campaign free, it lives or dies at the hands of the recipient.

Once launched, a good virus will spread itself. So how do you get the campaign to the inboxes of people who will pass it on?

Week Two
# FRIDAY

**Direct launch pads:** Friends, family and associates | Purchased database | Opinion leaders | The supreme opinion leader | Existing customer database

**Indirect launch pads:** User groups | Chatrooms | Message boards | Other platforms | Your own website | Affiliate programs

↓ ↓ ↓ ↓

**First referral**

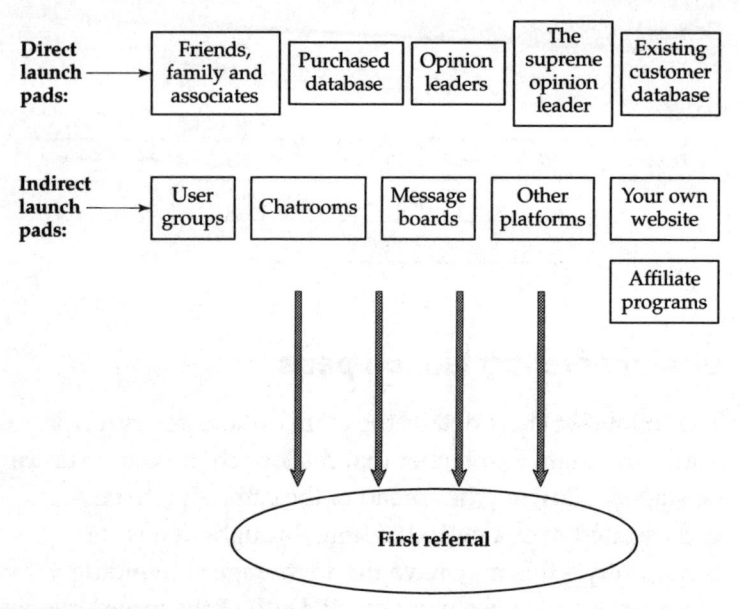

## Direct launch pads

These offer a direct communication channel to the recipient – in nearly all instances this occurs through the use of e-mail. This method is used predominantly to launch the viral campaign, rather than to offer an ongoing method to sustain the referral process. In this sense direct launch pads offer a short 'blast' of high volume referral in place of the steady stream created by the indirect launch pads.

### Friends, family and associates

One of the simplest and best ways to launch a viral marketing initiative is to use your existing network of friends, family and associates. As we have identified, viral marketing relies on the relationship and trust between the sender and recipient, so using your own network allows the first step of the process to be taken within an environment

## FRIDAY

where that trust is strongest. Numbers may be small from this launch pad, but by asking people in your organisation, your friends, family and associates to launch the virus, a strong initial push can be created.

Naturally, targeting is still important within this audience – sending your retired parents a campaign about 18–30 holidays is unlikely to impress them! It is important to select those contacts that still fall within your target audience.

### *Purchased databases*
Lists of e-mail addresses can be readily purchased, with all manner of databases available. When working with a purchased list, it is important to stay within legal and ethical requirements. Make sure that the list you buy is permission based (in other words the contacts on the lists have given their permission to be included on the database). Also ensure that the list is opt-in (referring to the contact having actively requested to be sent information from third parties, rather than simply *not having specified* that they do not want to receive any third party communication, know as an opt-out list).

Week Two

# FRIDAY

The cost of these lists varies, depending on the level of targeting sophistication. For example, a list of doctors working in the North East, specialising in orthopaedics will be more expensive than a list of men aged 18–26. Cost also depends on the usage of the list; it can be purchased for a one-off use, multiple use or unlimited use, during a pre-defined period. If you choose the latter, remember to request updates on the data to ensure that it remains as up to date as possible.

## *Opinion leaders*

This type of contact helps you by helping themself. Opinion leaders receive an associated benefit from using their personal reputation to promote your message. Their motivation for spreading a virus stems from the perception that they will:

Roughly between 20 per cent to 40 per cent of any target

- achieve higher levels of self-respect
- end up with higher esteem in the eyes of others
- feel good because they have helped someone else

audience will have some kind of natural opinion leading effect. However, it is possible to identify and seed very powerful opinion leaders in your initial distribution list. These people are identified using personal knowledge and lateral thinking, however PR agencies may also offer a way to identify the opinion leaders for your market. For those without the luxury of a PR agency, a good place to start is to think about those individuals who hold most sway in your sector or whose opinions are most valued.

Week Two

# F R I D A Y

### *The supreme opinion leader*
Given their position of authority and respect, journalists are uniquely powerful opinion leaders. It could be worth spending more effort targeting journalists because they have all the characteristics of a powerful opinion leader. In addition, they give you the opportunity to spread your viral idea through their publications to a very wide audience.

Locating journalists is a relatively easy job; they will always be credited in newspapers, websites and articles, as well as listed in media directories.

### *Existing customer database*
It would be foolish to omit your existing customers from your initial distribution because these people already have a relationship with your organisation, provided they have given their permission to be contacted. Follow the normal targeting principles of selecting who is interested in your proposition.

Week Two
# FRIDAY

Bear in mind, particularly if your customer database is especially large, that you will usually receive a more positive response if you identify people who have the characteristics listed below:

- Positive talkers – advocates who have probably already recommended you or your organisation.
- Those who have had a positive experience with you.
- Those who have volunteered information rather than been asked for it.
- Those who have told you that they like what you do.

### *Hewlett Packard talk to their customers*

HP launched a successful business-to-business campaign through targeting existing customers with tailored news articles. Segmented by date of purchase and product, users received information on upgrades, maintenance and performance improvements, with a simple 'Recommend A Friend' option to encourage the viral effect.

The objective was to drive traffic to their website, and HP achieved a click-through rate in excess of 10 per cent from contacts from their own database. However, even these results were eclipsed by the click-through of up to 40 per cent for those recipients who had been referred by a friend or colleague, demonstrating the uplift created by a personal referral.

> **Five top tips for writing the perfect initial message**
> - Keep it short.
> - Avoid overt sales messages.
> - Let the audience discover the campaign for themselves.
> - Give a moving call to action.
> - Avoid corporate tone – keep it friendly and informal. Even make it look like a referral itself!

## Indirect launch pads

Indirect launch pads offer an effective way to launch and sustain a viral marketing campaign. They work through the promotion of the campaign on shared interest 'third party' media, where communication is broadcast from one to many.

### *User groups/communities*

User groups are online communities, based around chat platforms where individuals with a shared interest can interact with each other. As such, they offer an ideal seedbed for your viral campaign. Identify the user groups that contain the largest concentration of your audience and join in! (A simple Web search should go a long way to finding the user groups most relevant to your proposition.) Once you have joined the community, you can start to reference your campaign in discussions and forums, driving people towards the content. Remember, however, to get your timing right and try not to be too overt or salesy. User groups exist for the benefit of the users and for them to share their opinions. They are not a marketing tool, so be careful not to alienate or annoy the community members.

Week Two

# FRIDAY

For a great introduction to the world of the user group, visit www.geocities.com, which claimed 1.4 million members and 400,000 home pages in 2001, or www.tripod.com, with 1 million users and 1.6 million member-created pages. Others include Talk City, WBS, the Mining Company and the Globe.

*Chatrooms*
Outside the more formal user group environment, other popular chatrooms exist where it is easy for you to promote your viral content. Chatrooms appear on all sorts of websites. By thinking laterally about the habits of your user, you should be able to identify which chatrooms will offer the greatest exposure. Select only those chatrooms where users have a strong shared interest in your proposition, and – when the time is right (i.e. when the chatroom is busy) – make people aware of your campaign.

*Message boards*
Much like the informal chatroom, message boards offer a simple, albeit highly visible, opportunity to promote your content. Whereas chatrooms are active, real time environments, message boards are more passive forums for interaction. Popular message boards offer a longer lasting method to increase awareness of your campaign.

*Other marketing platforms*
Remember that all communication platforms can form part of an indirect launch pad and serve to encourage the spread of the virus through creating awareness and driving individuals to the content. Once exposed, these people may become part of the process, referring the virus themselves. There is no limit to which platforms can be used, from

# FRIDAY

*Week Two*

### Buddy Lee for President

Lee Apparel successfully launched a viral marketing campaign to raise awareness of their dungaree products through message boards and chatrooms. The campaign featured the Buddy Lee doll – an icon from the 1960s – pushed as a presidential candidate. After a number of fake 'fan' sites were created, the marketing team used chatrooms to push 'Buddy For President' to create the impression that support was growing underground.

This clever launch technique underpinned a highly successful campaign, which saw 250,000 entries to a Buddy Lee competition and helped to fuel a sales increase of 125 per cent.

collateral and marketing material through to vehicle liveries. Remember your e-mail signature because it is so easy to change and can be very effective. Hotmail's famous example set the standard and Blue Mountain continue to use the technique, alerting every recipient of their e-greetings cards to their service through a strong e-mail sign off. Remember to integrate the customer touch points – it is important to consider viral marketing as an integral part of an overall marketing plan.

### *Your own Website*

It may be obvious, but do not forget your own site when it comes to launching your virus. Promote your content on the site, advertise it on your Home Page and make sure that when visitors come through to the viral content, the referral method is obvious. The most effective method is to include a 'recommend a friend' or 'e-mail this to a friend' button, which will encourage your visitors to participate in the viral effect.

*Affiliate programs*
Encourage your partners to include the virus on their website. This can be part of either a formal commercial agreement or a simple reciprocal arrangement. A button or text link will drive traffic through to your site, pulling users into the viral process.

### *Do not miss out on data collection*

If you include a 'recommend a friend' button within your campaign, be sure to make the most of it. Do not limit the visitor to just one referral – give them the option to mail multiple contacts with your content, thereby increasing the spread. Also remember to take their details, so you can tell the recipient who referred the content to them if you are going to forward the content on their behalf.

Remember that data collection is important, but data protection regulations are more important. You cannot use the e-mail addresses of the people who have been referred content because they have not opted-in to your database. However, the sharpest marketers will have offered the visitor referring the content to their friends the ability to opt-in to future communication, thereby making his own data valid.

Week Two

# F R I D A Y

## Timing

Once the campaign is live, it is impossible to control the timing (there is no way to regulate when a recipient will hit the forward button once a message is in their inbox). However, the timing of the initial distribution is easy to control for the direct launch pads. Moreover, the timing of this message can have a dramatic impact on the success of your campaign in making that all-important first referral.

Timing depends very much on the audience you are talking to. There are, however, certain broad rules to follow:

- Avoid Monday (especially Monday morning) as people are gearing up for the week.
- Lunch-times are good – particularly if your target includes desk-bound professionals.
- Avoid weekends for all campaigns – people have better things to do at this time than check their mail.
- Friday afternoon is good because the working week reaches its most relaxed period.
- Avoid overnight distribution because spam (unsolicited e-mail) is usually sent out when servers are quiet. You do not want your campaign to be competing for attention against a load of junk e-mail.

There is no substitute for experience, so try, try and try again. Watch the response carefully and see which times are gaining the highest response, then focus on this time for your future campaigns.

## What happens when the campaign is launched?

People's propensity to forward a piece of content differs for each and every viral campaign. It depends on a number of environmental factors ranging from their mood and how busy they are, through to their position in society and affinity with your brand or proposition. That said, through our research we have identified four basic types of individual reaction to a viral campaign, outlined below.

- *Killer:* this person does not pass the message on, killing the virus there and then.
- *Selector:* this person will choose a small number of 'select' people to forward the message to – usually less than five.
- *Supporter:* a good person to know – this person will send the message on to between five and ten people.
- *Volumiser:* the ultimate recipient – this person will send the virus to more than 11 people.

Details from our research identified how these categories break down in terms of e-mail reaction:

| Type of e-mail reaction | Percentage of respondents |
| --- | --- |
| Killer | 2% |
| Selector | 76% |
| Supporter | 16% |
| Volumiser | 6% |

We all know volumisers – the person who seems to always send out the jokes or movie clips to a huge mailing list. While it may seem that these people are the ideal people to hit with a viral campaign, remember that volumisers can also have a negative effect on your campaign. We have mentioned the self-targeting nature of viral campaigns where recipients choose to pass the message on to contacts with a shared interest, thereby keeping the campaign broadly within the target market. We have also stressed the difference between targeted e-mail and spam; it is good to remember that even within a personal network, volumisers can be guilty of 'spamming' their friends and colleagues. People may receive your content from a volumiser, despite a lack of any shared interest in the content. This will create a 'killer' reaction when that recipient realises that they have been sent something in which they have no interest and therefore have no inclination to send on.

## The death of your virus

Ultimately your virus will fizzle out and die. A time will come when the vast majority of interested people will have been infected and have forwarded it accordingly, or the campaign has failed to stimulate a strong referral process, limiting its exposure. Through natural fatigue, any virus will have to die sooner or later. The only thing a viral marketer can do is to use the launch pads we have discussed to maximise the life span of the campaign.

## Summary

Today we have covered the different ways to launch and sustain a viral marketing campaign, and the importance of planning the timing of the initial distribution to maximise the chances of gaining the first referral. Tomorrow we shall look at how to track the performance of your campaign, and

## Week Two
# FRIDAY

how to turn this tracking information into tangible analysis. Finally, we will recap what has been learnt this week, creating a list of ten critical success factors.

## SATURDAY

*Week Two*

# Get going

## By the end of today and the end of the week we will have:

- Recommended how you can measure your campaign.
- Given advice on how to track and report on your campaign.
- Summarised what we believe are the *critical success factors* for viral marketing campaigns.

Over the last week you have covered a lot of content and been given much food for thought. Hopefully, along the way, you have been able to identify how a viral marketing campaign could work for you. Today we will look at the final element – the tracking and measurement of your virus to prove that your campaign has been a success. Following this we will take a brief review of the week, identifying ten critical success factors for viral marketing.

## Measuring the immeasurable

In today's competitive business world, marketing needs to be measurable. Gone are the days when the advertising executive could famously state, '*I know half of my advertising budget is wasted, I just do not know which half*'. There is tremendous pressure to analyse all expenditure in order to ensure that it has been used in the most effective and efficient way possible.

# SATURDAY

Marketing in general and viral marketing in particular, are often perceived to be rather intangible – a murky world of costly campaigns without any real way to monitor Return on Investment (ROI). However, the reality is very different. Strong tracking and analysis has allowed marketers to demonstrate just what a fundamental return their campaigns can produce.

## Campaign tracking

Tracking a viral campaign will vary according to the host environment – whether the campaign is hosted on a website or sent as an e-mail attachment. It is very simple to track visitor numbers to a website, whereas monitoring the spread of an e-mail is far more difficult – but not impossible!

For both options, the first step is to track the response of the initial launch. If you have used any direct launch pads this is quite simple – track the click-through to your initial e-mail. There are a number of companies who offer e-mail tracking such as E-circle, Expedite or Responsys, or your agency may use some bespoke software, however, you should be able to check the performance of the initial direct launch.

Once the user-to-user referral process begins, the tracking methods are different for the two host options. For campaigns based on e-mail, tracking is usually lost at this point, but there is one way to gain a small insight into how far the virus has spread. By including in the e-mail itself, a transparent graphic file which is hosted on a website, you will be able to measure how often the e-mail is opened and by how many unique users. This works each time the e-mail is opened by a user who is connected to the internet – a request is sent by the computer to the website for the Web-hosted graphic file (please note this does not apply to all platforms, for example cable access e-mail does not support this). Once the request is received, the image is sent back down to the user. All this can happen without the user even knowing their computer had requested a Web-hosted graphic, providing the viral marketer with all the information they need to run analysis on the tracking information collected.

While both legal and perfectly ethical, it must be stated that this method of tracking is not totally accurate. Users viewing the content offline will not be counted in the overall figures because no request for the Web-hosted graphic can be made. That said, this process does give the viral marketer a rough measure of the overall usage of the campaign.

Rather more detail can be gained from Web-hosted content, simply through using any of the many Web usage

## Week Two
## SATURDAY

monitoring software packages. These packages, such as Web Trends, will look at the log files which record usage of a site and create useful, concise reports showing a whole raft of information which is useful in its own right. Typically the report will show:

- Number of unique users (i.e. not the same users coming back for a repeat visit).
- Number of new versus returning users.
- Where groups of users came from – both geographically and digitally (where they were referred from).
- How long users typically used the site for.
- At what point users left the site.
- What the most active time periods were (by day and time period).

Even better than these static reports are 'live' reporting tools, which offer real-time reports on exactly who is on your site. These packages, such as Live Stats from Media House Software can often be downloaded; sometimes they are even free of charge for a trial period and they can give amazing insight into how the campaign is performing. As well as providing the basic reports detailed above, live reports allow you to feel the excitement of the campaign; you can see 'real' people coming on to the site to view your content.

For any reporting tool to work, you will need to have access to the log files from the Web server – these should be available, but remember to ask for them up front. If they are not saved they cannot be recreated and you will lose valuable information. If you are working with an IT colleague or agency, make sure they know that you need to run reports on the site usage.

## Turning statistics into information – the analysis and ROI measures

With the statistics you have gleaned from the campaign tracking, you will already have the raw information to show how successful the campaign has been. Although this offers some insight into the performance of the campaign, calculating a real return on the investment is a great way to put flesh on these bones. The simplest and most effective way to calculate a return is to consider the investment and results in terms of equivalent marketing spend. Take a look at the example below.

Let us say that your campaign website had 50,000 hits and cost £10,000. Firstly your cost per hit is 20p. Next think how many page impressions on banner advertising you would have needed to generate the same 50,000 hits. Presuming an optimistic 2 per cent click-through means you would have needed 2,500,000 banner impressions. At a rough cost of £100 per thousand, you would have paid £250,000 for those same 50,000 hits. So this rough comparison of effectiveness gives a ratio of 1:25 – in other words your spend on viral marketing has been 25 times more effective than online advertising media spend.

Whilst this comparison method is by no means 100 per cent accurate, it does give an insight into the overall effectiveness of the campaign, which is the best basis for deciding on how the marketing budget should be split.

A more tangible measurement is data capture. The data you collect can be used to give valuable insights into who your customers are, what they do, their likes and dislikes. It also boosts the size of the company's database, ready to improve the effectiveness of future marketing initiatives.

> ### *What data to collect?*
>
> The data you collect has two elements: Who and What.
>
> The **Who** element is simple, standard information detailing who that person is: name, sex, address, postcode, e-mail address, telephone and mobile number. This information allows you to recognise the individual.
>
> The **What** element adds insight into what that person is like. Here it is important to get the information you need. This could be simple information like age or marital status, or in a business-to-business context, job title or area of responsibility. If, for example, your target market is golfers, remember to ask if that person has a handicap or is a member of a club. This information will help you to build up a profile of the individual. Once segmented, it is easier to tailor communications to a segment's specific requirements.

## Ten critical success factors

Over the last week you have looked at all the key features of a successful viral marketing campaign. We shall now review the key points made during the week, producing ten critical success factors of a viral marketing campaign.

# SATURDAY

*Week Two*

### *Understand your audience*
The success of a viral marketing initiative is less to do with those who orchestrate it, and everything to do with the target audience. Identifying and understanding them is essential. Audience-centric planning will help guarantee that the end user is kept at the forefront of your mind. Understanding the audience will drive the entire campaign, from the initial idea, message, chosen characteristic and vehicle, to the timing and creative execution.

### *It starts with a good, simple idea*
This primarily refers to the content of your message, although simplicity is key throughout the execution. You need to ensure that the message is as potent further down the line as it is for the first recipient. Make sure that everyone can understand it consistently.

### *Exploit human behaviour*
Consider what consumers like and apply this to your target audience. Would the campaign idea pass the *'What's in it for me?'* test.

Remember your initial objectives and reflect these throughout – are you generating sales with an offer or are you building awareness with a brand message? Make sure you select the most appropriate vehicles and characteristics to do the job.

And finally, remember what annoys people – reconsider the research results mentioned on Wednesday in order to understand people's propensity to become infected with the virus.

# SATURDAY

## *Keep it open*
The more complex the execution, the greater the chance that it will not work. Understand your audience and create a campaign that fits their profile. Do not fall into the trap of choosing the lowest common denominator because this will compromise the creative execution. Rather, aim for a balance between technical innovation and access. Remember that the easier and smoother it is for your audience to experience your content, the more likely they are to send it on.

## *Make sure it scales*
If your viral campaign features Web-hosted content, make sure that your technical platform is up to the job. A successful campaign will place an increased burden on your IT architecture and, if this fails, the campaign will fail too. Talk to your technical people and your service provider or hosting partner to make sure that the systems in place can handle the volume of traffic that you are hoping for.

## *There is more than one way to catch a virus*
When launching or sustaining your viral campaign, you have more than one option. Consider the balance and mix between direct and indirect launch pads, for example, e-mailing your closest friends and family or customer database, while penetrating user groups and exploiting your own website.

## *Integrate the touch points*
It is unlikely that your viral campaign will work in isolation; integrating both your marketing strategy and other marketing activities is crucial. Give people the same customer experience in your virus as they would expect elsewhere – both in terms of the message you are trying to convey and the creative execution.

Week Two
## SATURDAY

### *Keep both eyes on the results*
You can track your campaign by using some specific technologies arguably, however, final analysis is actually more important. Use the techniques mentioned earlier today to turn statistics into ROI information. Learn from your successes and your failures, and do not forget that some results will be instant, some will be delayed.

### *Get the right team involved*
Like all marketing initiatives you need the right people on board – engage with your Web team and technical people, talk to your product specialists and choose your marketing or new media agency wisely. Visit www.marketinginspiration.com for some helpful guidance and an agency resource centre.

### *Be committed, single-minded and have some fun*
Your commitment to viral marketing is an essential factor. Too often marketers avoid viral campaigns because of a mythical fear factor or because of a misguided view that viral marketing cannot work for them. The key is to give it a go – commit to a simple test campaign and see it through – you may be amazed by the results.

A first attempt at viral marketing does not have to be the most sophisticated campaign ever produced. You do not need six figure budgets. All you need is a good idea and the knowledge you have learnt over the last 7 days.

## Final thoughts

Viral marketing has been praised and criticised more than any other medium in recent times. Nevertheless, the

# SATURDAY

potential returns speak for themselves and the medium is here to stay. So, when planning your next marketing campaign, keep the following points in mind.

> - Which marketing medium makes every participant a brand advocate?
> - Which is the most user-friendly type of marketing?
> - Which marketing vehicle is delivered with immediate credibility?
> - Which marketing tool quantifiably improves the efficiency of marketing spend and ROI?

The answer is clear to us – viral marketing is an essential part of the 21$^{st}$ century communication mix.

# Building a Brand

**PETE LAVER**

# WEEK THREE

# CONTENTS

# Week Three

| **Introduction** | | 195 |
|---|---|---|
| **Sunday** | From products to brands | 197 |
| **Monday** | What have we got? | 212 |
| **Tuesday** | Completing the audit | 229 |
| **Wednesday** | Positioning | 243 |
| **Thursday** | Bringing the brand to life | 252 |
| **Friday** | When the brand speaks | 265 |
| **Saturday** | Managing the plan | 279 |

### Dedication

To J W H Life
For his unstinting support.

# INTRODUCTION

Week Three

Success in business derives from getting, keeping and using competitive advantage. Branding is the most powerful way to do this. The world's biggest brands belong to the world's most profitable companies.

Brand marketing is centuries old and began when businesses that had established a reputation in the market added a brand mark to their products to distinguish them from competitors' products.

Today, brands can be companies, products or services. For simplicity, this book refers to corporate brands. If you are working with a product or service brand, the generic principles are the same the main differences arise in the marketing mix.

Brands offer compelling benefits over and above conventional marketing:

- Brands support premium pricing on high volumes, creating improved sales and profit margins.

## Week Three
# INTRODUCTION

- Brands are one of the few investments that do not wear out. In fact, the older they get, the stronger they get. The high prices paid for brands reflect the long-term return in shareholder value. Brands capture investment, reducing risk.
- Strong brands compete on price and quality and they compete in the third dimension of intangible brand equity. This encourages innovative marketing and results in strong, differentiated markets.
- Brands own a place in the minds of their customers (the only advertising space worth paying for) and have an astonishing resistance to change. Lowenbrau and Stella Artois beers both date from the middle ages and have outlasted civilisations.
- Brands support and defend innovation. Lycra was quickly copied as a product, but customers want Lycra. The brand defends itself and, in addition, can be legally protected.
- Brands segment the market and create options for growth through extension and brand families. Developing a brand is much less risky than starting again.
- Brands are surprisingly resilient in the face of mismanagement!

Much lip-service is paid to brands, but few of us treat them with the respect they require if they are to deliver their full potential. Building a successful brand is what this book is about. Achieving this task in a competitive environment is a challenge, yet it is achievable. Over the next seven days you will be guided through the processes of building a brand from first principles and growing its equity in the short and long term.

It's great fun, so let's get started.

# SUNDAY

Week Three

# From products to brands

- What brands are and how to use them.
- The benefits of branding and the brand building process.

## The brand building process

Four crucial questions must be answered powerfully and effectively to achieve a winning brand strategy. Can you answer them for your business?

1 What is your business for – what is its essence?
2 How do you define and segment your customers?
3 What differences exist between your business and those of your competitors and how do you capitalise upon these differences?
4 Which channels to market are most beneficial to you and do they form the focus of your business activity?

The questions seem simple and yet most of us find it extremely difficult to provide clear, precise answers. The answers are essential, however, because they form the foundation of a successful brand plan. Keep your initial answers and see how they have changed by the end of today.

There are five outputs of the brand planning process:

1 4C analysis (company, customers, competitors, channels)
2 Positioning
3 Growth vectors
4 Growth drivers
5 Action

## SUNDAY

*4C analysis*

4C analysis (the name is taken from the first letter of each key field – company, customers, competitors, channels) guides you, step by step, through your strategic analysis and creates the opportunity to achieve your all-important competitive advantage.

- *The company*: the company or brand audit will develop the anatomy of the brand and its equities. What the business stands for, its unique essence, will emerge from this and lead to an understanding of what the brand should be telling its audience.
- *The customers*: traditional segmentation methods target customers and prospective customers without any discrimination between the two (mention this to anyone involved in sales and be prepared to duck!). In contrast, 4C analysis guides you to a complete customer map, taking these vital components into account. The analysis will identify the most suitable customers to target for the brand. At this point you will know what to say and with whom you will initiate the discussion. The output from this piece of work will define your customers precisely in terms of what they need. You will also have a measurement of customer loyalty; the driving force behind profitability.
- *The competitors*: we choose our competitors as surely as we choose our customers. You will need to make an industry model based on the needs you serve and competitors who meet similar needs. The output of your work in this field will be a clear view of the specific differences between your business and those of key competitors expressed as a competitor map. Exploiting these differences reveals your competitive advantage.

## SUNDAY

- *The channels*: there are many means by which the brand's products and services can reach its customers. These include retail and wholesale outlets, the internet and direct mail. But brands are known by the company they keep. To be in the wrong company sends out the wrong signals. This part of the process involves mapping available and potential channels to market in terms of current and future potential.

*Positioning*

Effective positioning focuses your brand in the eyes of consumers, precisely where you want it in relation to your competitors. In other words, it highlights your point of difference and creates competitive advantage. Using the data collected from 4C analysis, you refine your brand map to select the most relevant message to communicate. Your customer analysis provides the data to select your primary audience. Your competitor analysis enables you to select the most appropriate competitor against which you are capable of establishing a significant point of difference. Finally, channel analysis leads to the selection of the most appropriate trade marketing channels.

| Company | Customer   | What to say       | To whom             |
|---------|------------|-------------------|---------------------|
| Channel | Competitor | Where to sell it  | Point of difference |

Figure 1. Distilling data from 4C analysis to create a positioning statement

Week Three

# SUNDAY

The situational report, derived from 4C analysis, defining the essence and components of the brand. This will inform all the creative work on the brand from now on and ensure consistency over the long term.

*Growth vectors*

There are only a limited number of directions (vectors) that any business can follow in order to achieve growth. Essentially, you can sell more, put up the price or find a combination of the two. You need to evaluate each potential option in turn, relative to the current position, and select the best route forward.

*Growth drivers*

Tactical alignment of the brand plan lines up behind a clear positioning, like shoppers forming an orderly queue. For example, an exclusive, expensive market position implies high specification products at premium prices sold through exclusive outlets and advertised in top quality magazines. The traditional 4Ps approach to building a marketing mix can be very restrictive. This refers to product, place, price, promotion – key drivers of success could be reduced queues, better packaging, stronger relationships with important customers and so on. Instead, you can look at each element of the marketing mix and rank them in order of importance to your customers. In so doing, you will flesh out the drivers of success for your brand and align them to match your strategic initiatives. Finally, you can create a 'tracker' to check and measure performance. Overall, the process is seamless and effective and the tracker adds the feedback loop so that you can learn and benefit from successes (and set-backs).

*Action*

Finally, the plan can be put to work. The positioning, strategies and aligned mix can be worked into a project plan to drive the brand forward. Using sales and market data and the brand tracker provides feedback mechanisms to help you keep the business in control.

However complicated your business may be, this proven process ensures that the answers are clear, direct and simple for each question. Great ideas can only come from clearly setting out the issues and pinpointing clear achievable outcomes.

## Understanding your brand

The first stage of 4C analysis sets out to understand and map the identity of your brand. Before starting, take a moment to understand the definition of what a brand is, before moving on to brand identity and image.

*What precisely is a brand?*
At the most basic level a brand is described as a name, a symbol or a sign that denotes ownership. Today, some of these symbols and signs are worth billions of dollars in recognition of the profits that will probably accrue to their owners.

> **Definition**
> A brand can be defined as a reputation in the market which has an identity (the source of the brand) which has been translated into an image (customer perception) that confers competitive value in additional sales or premium prices or both.

# Week Three
## SUNDAY

A brand is capable of being much more than a trademark. A brand lives inside its customers' minds and forms a shared set of beliefs within that group. A shared belief or paradigm is astonishingly tenacious and provides competitive advantages of enormous value. The best brands take on some of the aspects of a human personality. They become an invisible friend: 'My mate Marmite', for example.

## The brand identity and image

Identity comes from inside the business, not from the customers. A clear understanding of the identity of your brand will ensure its consistency. Later on you will repeat this exercise, this time asking your customers in order to identify your brand image. The differences between identity and image comprise the strategic gap. Your aim is to retain the identity by adjusting the image and never the other way around.

> The image of a brand is what the audiences of the brand (customers, suppliers, potential customers, etc.) believe now. This may be true or not true and it may be good or bad. The identity of a brand is what it really is and aspires to be. Being unduly influenced by image is a mistake for a person or a brand. The finest people and the best brands have a set of values and beliefs that are not for sale and not liable to change easily. For a brand or organisation, this bedrock of principle is the anchor that holds its identity together and helps it to resist what is sometimes called strategic drift. Image is a vital concern but the direction of change and its management should almost always be towards changing the image of the brand, not its identity.

# SUNDAY

Week Three

> A downed pilot was being interrogated by his captors. 'What is your mission?' they barked. With pride he immediately responded, 'Our mission is to provide unfailing commitment to aerial bombardment technology with total focus on accuracy, quality and maximum damage at minimum cost.'
>
> Mission statements are a corporate ego massage – forget them. A corporate or brand identity statement will describe the purpose of the business (its essence) and how it should be perceived and behave. Add a sensible list of company policies and the job is done.

Your brand can be understood by building a brand identity map (Figure 2) starting from its inner core (essence) and moving outwards towards its attributes (properties and appearance) and behaviour.

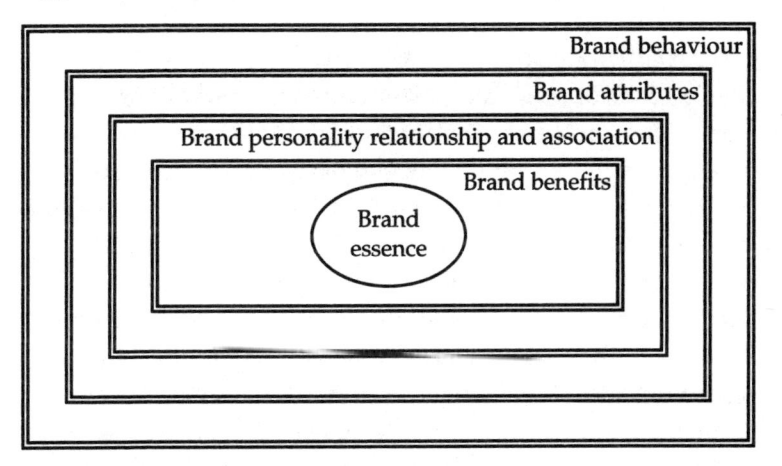

Figure 2. The brand identity map

## SUNDAY

Identity maps are atomic in structure. At the nucleus are the core values and purpose, which attract the other attributes into orbit around them. The core is resistant to change, while the attributes toward the edges need to change incrementally with the times. The map should contain only attributes (sometimes called equities) which can be understood and used strategically. Finally, the map should present the holistic face of the brand. It should be recognisable as an entity that can be understood and worked with. There is nothing wrong with a little imaginative moonshine in the identity map, provided you can sustain it. Many brand reputations are built around a good story even though it does not withstand much scrutiny. River Island is an example of a romantic brand that invites the consumer to share the fantasy. Clothing for extreme conditions would probably be a step too far for them, however, and best left to Berghaus.

Let's look at each element of a brand identity map.

*The brand essence or core*

The essence or core values of strong brands stand for something and communicate powerfully to people who share or aspire to similar values. The brand is a signature rather than a product or service. Aristotle said, 'If an axe had a soul its soul would be cutting.' Similarly, the invisible presence of a brand resides inside its products. The soul of the brand is its essence. People who wish to be cool may identify with and buy Virgin or FCUK. The brand's essence communicates directly to its audience by hooking into similar values. For instance, a damaged Rolex is not so valuable as a perfect example, but it is still worth much more than a fake. A damaged Rolex retains its soul; a fake never had one.

Week Three

# SUNDAY

Answer the following questions to determine the values of your brand:

- What does your business do?
- What does it value?
- What would you like to hear people say about it?
- Does your business have a standpoint – something it believes in above everything else?
- Does it have a heritage?
- What story does it have to tell?

*Brand needs*
Human needs are functional, social and psychological. Our most important needs are functional, such as food and shelter, but once these needs are met social and psychological needs take priority. Social needs reflect the strong desires of most of us to belong and be accepted by others. Psychological needs are inner-directed and egotistical, for example, wanting to be at peace with ourselves or to achieve our potential. The

# Week Three
## SUNDAY

extraordinary power of branding is its ability to associate with these desires and to build relationships with customers.

For instance, if you were marketing a professional football club, the needs that create the desire to attend the matches might be identified as follows:

| Need category | Need |
| --- | --- |
| Functional needs | Food, drink, comfort, warmth, security – crowd control, entry and exit arrangements |
| Social needs | Tribalism, hospitality, community, competitive association with success, access to the stars |
| Psychological needs | Hero worship, touching the dream, excitement, entertainment, joy |

Each set of needs requires a marketing solution, but some elements will be more important than others. Traditional fans will be more interested in the tribal and community elements, while less committed fans will be driven more by excitement and entertainment. Corporate clients will put hospitality at the top of their agenda, but the children will go for hero worship. Football may be the product, but motivation is the selling point.

- What needs does your brand serve?
- Are these needs predominately functional, social or psychological?
- Make a list of these needs.

# SUNDAY

Week Three

*Brand benefits*

Human needs are met by brand benefits and not product features. One important need within most of us is to define and improve our self-concept. Our self-concept is multifaceted. For example, it includes what we think about ourselves and also what we think others think about us. Many of us will make choices based upon our self-concept in terms of how we wish to be perceived or in terms of how we think others perceive us.

Reflect a moment on these two stories.

### Story 1
The wind whipped over the bonnet of the Porsche causing him to pull up the collar of his Armani jacket. Sweeping to a halt outside the Dorchester he caught the aroma of Chanel No. 5 as he opened her door. Pausing to offer her a Pall Mall and lighting one himself, he led the way inside where he ordered a bottle of Heinseck. He reflected wryly that the champagne was worth it just to see her voluptuous figure in her new Versace dress.

### Story 2
The wind whipped over the bonnet of the Astra Coupé causing him to pull up the collar of his Marks & Spencer leather jacket. Sweeping to a halt outside the Crown he enjoyed the aromatic mixture of Charlie and leather as he opened her door. Pausing to offer her a Camel and lighting one himself, he led the way inside where he ordered Fosters Lager. He reflected wryly that the drinks were worth it just to see her lovely figure in her new Gap dress.

# SUNDAY

What were your perceptions of the characters in both versions of the story?

The only change between the two stories is the brands used, but our perception of the characters changes radically. Brands address social needs by saying something about their users. They also address psychological needs by delivering the feel good factor. A designer label on the inside of a jacket helps the owner to value him or herself that much more.

- **What benefits does your brand deliver to meet each need that you have identified?**

*Brand relationship*
'Anyone who has a relationship with a bar of soap or a can of soup is either deluded or leading a sad life!' I believe that this viewpoint is entirely understandable, but incorrect.

Marshall McLuhan (who was Director of the Center for Culture and Technology, University of Toronto) points out that many products are, in effect, extensions of human beings. A trowel is an extension of the hand. The human hand, although clever, can dig a hole more effectively with a trowel. The addition of a spade creates an even larger hole and mechanical earthmovers can create tremendous holes. Each product extends the hand to do a different task of increasing size and complexity. Similarly, a car extends the foot and a computer enhances the functions of the brain. Some products are intensely personal, such as body lotions, and others very public, such as aeroplanes. However, they all extend human potential by extension of our natural capabilities. It is not surprising that we regard many brands with affection, considering the enormous gains in performance or pleasure that they offer.

# SUNDAY

*Brand personality*

Unconsciously, we humanise brands with human descriptions. This habit (anthropomorphism) is a vital aspect of branding.

When a lifstyle brand announces, 'I hate school', it identifies closely with a young market who feel the same themselves. Kodak is perceived as mature and responsible while Coca Cola is young. Chanel is a sophisticated woman and Levi is a rebel.

What is the personality of your brand? To discover this ask yourself some interesting questions, for example:

- If your brand was a person who would it be?
- If your brand held a party would you go?
- If your brand had a hobby, what would it choose?

Make a note of your instinctive responses.

*Brand association*

When we think of a strong brand, like Virgin, our mind conjures up not only the name or trademark but also a host of other associations. These may not always be at the front of our consciousness, but we can recall them when asked. We might, for example, associate the brand with usage occasion (e.g. cereal for breakfast, champagne for celebrations) and the types of people who use it.

People asked to imagine famous people climbing aboard a Virgin aircraft visualised pop stars, footballers and supermodels. A similar exercise with BA produced the names of politicians and similar worthies. Unlike these two examples, brand associations are not always favourable. In either case, this is essential information for your analysis.

Week Three

# SUNDAY

> • Think of a brand you know well and list the thoughts and associations that come to mind. Do the same with your own brand and make a note of the results.

*Brand attributes*
Brand attributes consist of the audio and visual signatures that signal the presence of the brand.

The Nike 'swoosh' and the Direct Line jingle and phone are examples. Some brands are associated with colours, such as Body Shop's dark green. The BMW propeller badge and twin-radiators act as signatures that ratify and endorse the brand. They signal authenticity, consistency and quality.

> • What are the audio and visual signatures of your brand?

*Brand behaviour*
Consistency is the key to effective branding. Lowenbrau was introduced in AD 1386 and is still here today. Rowntrees Fruit Pastilles were introduced in 1888. Brands offer a promise of quality and act as a beacon of consistency in a world of change. Marks & Spencer, Mars and Clerical & Medical Insurance are amongst the old, heritage brands that remain market leaders 100 years or more after their introduction.

Brands need to be consistent and to offer something that is perceived by their customers as superior to their rivals. They offer zero protection to shoddy products and services. Research shows that the big brands are more trusted than the church or the government. Abuse this trust and your brand dies.

# SUNDAY

> - How does your brand behave in relation to the values you identified earlier. Keep the results for later use.

## Summary

- You have looked at the astounding benefits of branding and started to think about how to exploit some of these for yourself.
- You have learned the overall structure of the brand planning process and made a start on creating your own brand identity.
- The future started today.

Week Three

# MONDAY

# What have we got?

- auditing the company and its customers
- auditing the brand and uncovering its value

## Profiling the brand

*4C analysis quick review*

4C analysis audits your brand and provides organised data that feeds directly into a brand proposition. On completion of each of the four stages of the analysis, you can prepare a straightforward chart specifying the conclusions reached. This consists of a brand identity map, a customer map, a competitor map and a channel plan. You have already begun the process by identifying some of the important elements of your brand's identity.

## Building your own brand identity map

Using the map structure outlined on Sunday, you can begin to illustrate your brand identity as a recognisable entity. The brand identity map is a useful container to capture the information collected earlier. It pulls the data together into a holistic framework. On completion, the face of your brand will be revealed.

The starting point is to work through the thoughts and ideas you have collected and to summarise the main points down to a phrase or even a single word. Decide which category each item fits, with reference to the brand identity map then enter it on to the map. The result may be very cluttered or very bare, depending on how you have got on

# Week Three
## MONDAY

so far. It is possible that you have discovered some important ideas that do not fit anywhere (the diversity of businesses is vast), in which case it may be necessary to create a new category on your map. The process is much more of an art than a science.

The example shown below presents a view of the BMW brand in the UK and goes a fair way towards explaining its success. The map for BMW suggests a unique standpoint of mechanical perfection that, coupled with its slightly younger image, has made the Ultimate Driving Machine one of the most successful brand identity programmes ever undertaken. At the core is cold precision. People rarely appear in its advertising. Its core values of thoughtful technology, performance and exclusivity are delivered through its tone of voice. Its German origin is important.

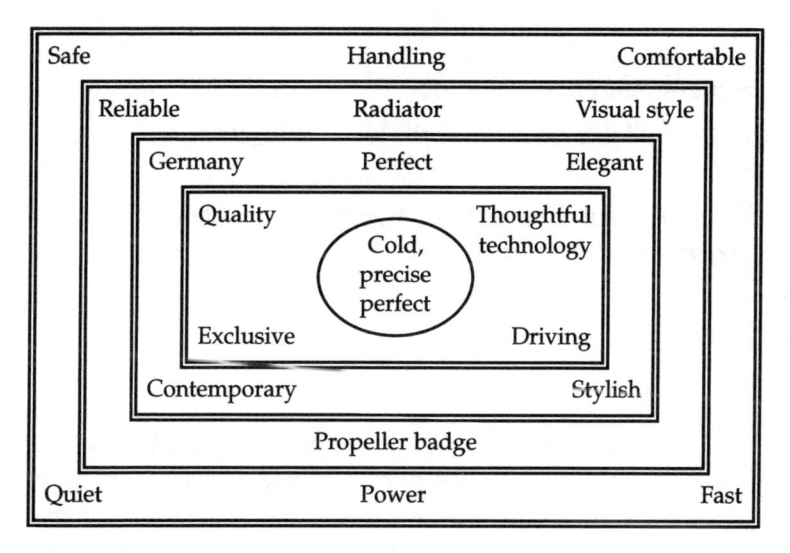

| Safe | | Handling | | Comfortable |
|---|---|---|---|---|
| | Reliable | Radiator | Visual style | |
| | | Germany | Perfect | Elegant | |
| | | | Quality | Thoughtful technology | |
| | | | Cold, precise perfect | | |
| | | | Exclusive | Driving | |
| | | Contemporary | | Stylish | |
| | | | Propeller badge | | |
| Quiet | | Power | | Fast |

Figure 3. Brand identity map for BMW

The BMW example (a personal interpretation) displays innovation and imagination, while remaining far-sighted and deliverable. A strong identity will not excuse poor products, but it will distinguish good ones.

It is often pointed out that the distinctions between categories can sometimes be hard to define. The important point is that the model has a definite structure from the fixed core in the centre, to the more readily changeable attributes towards the outside. The categories are a crucial guide to help you to construct your map.

Using the data collected from your brand on Sunday, complete your own brand identity map. You are seeking clues about what makes your brand distinctive and different from competitors' brands. It may seem that the answers will be obvious, but this is rarely the case. The guiding principle is to create a harmonious pattern with the selected equities complementing each other. The result should be a recognisable entity. Its attributes and personality should be present on the map and should be supportable.

## Benefits of the brand identity mapping process

The first benefit of the mapping process lies primarily in its ability to provide a holistic overview. The face of the brand will be looking out at you.

The second benefit lies in the descriptors you identify. Every one of them is a brand equity as valuable as any other major asset and much more valuable than most. Symbols and signs such as the Coca Cola Corporation bottle and IBM's logo are literally priceless. The fact that WHSmith and Boots the Chemist are trusted is almost certainly more valuable to those companies than any owned, physical asset. The most relevant equities in your business for today's marketplace will be used to develop your corporate strategy.

## The brand identity statement

The final stage is to create the brand identity statement. This document will lay out the brand identity, adding several elements that were not covered in the visual map. This is the anatomy of the brand, enabling everyone who works with it to understand its value and purpose. It provides a template to ensure that the brand's consistency, core values and purpose are maintained and protected. It will be used to set strategy and to advise staff and creative agencies about how to treat the brand. It should be protected because it is the brand blueprint and will outlast its creator. The table below sets out the areas to be covered, although you may wish to write it out in plain text.

| The Brand Identity Statement | |
|---|---|
| **Name** | **Content** |
| 1 The business purpose | What the brand is for. |
| 2 Core values | The essential nature of the brand. |
| 3 Benefit statement | The functional, social and psychological benefits of the brand. |
| 4 Personality | Young, old, male, female, sophisticated and clever or rugged and action-oriented. Reliable, trusted, independent. |

# MONDAY

| | |
|---|---|
| **5** Auditory and visual identity | The brand attributes including symbols, signs, colours, jingles, straplines, smells, taste, shape, form. |
| **6** The knowledge base | What the brand can do – its skills and therefore its operational zone, including brand extensions. |
| **7** Development | Developments, including future brand extensions. |
| **8** Tone of voice | Who it is and how it speaks. Friendly, man to man, woman to woman, boy to girl. Its relationship with its audience. |
| **9** Portfolio position | If there are other brands involved, how are they related, e.g. Nescafé and Gold Blend. How do their activities complement one another without getting in each other's way? |
| **10** Image | The significant differences between this identity and the actual image of the brand with its customers. This difference is your gap analysis. You now know what you need to do to bring the image in line. |
| **11** Behaviour | Unique ways in which the brand operates. |
| **12** Other | Any other significant points. |
| **13** Category and key competitors | What categories it operates in and who its main competitors are at present. |
| **14** Numerical data | Sales and profitability. Budgets and forecasts. Market share. |
| **15** Ratios | Return on net assets, asset utilisation, return on sales. |

Week Three

# MONDAY

## The brand book

Many brands develop the identity statement into a largish document, including the visual identity (logos, fonts, colour schemes, document layouts, etc). Be careful not to put your creative people in a strait-jacket. The addition of a mood board showing colour schemes, the preferred font and any brand icons (characters, logos, straplines) may well be sufficient to ensure consistency. One cigarette brand uses a mock cigarette pack with cards inside to outline the main design points.

Using the brand map, complete a brand identity statement (shown in the table above). There are a number of additional points that do not fit neatly into the map, which have been explained. Perhaps the most important is tone of voice. It is essential that the brand speaks consistently to its audience, which means understanding its relationship towards them. For example, it could be a man with a Manchester accent who talks man to man with an element of humour. The brand knowledge base explains what the brand audience think the brand can do and therefore creates a boundary in terms of the type of products or services the brand can sell.

- Can you describe the identity from the statement in a way that any ordinary person can appreciate?
- Does every word mean something valuable?
- Just as a complete personal identity card would contain a picture of the holder, so the map is the brand portrait. When you look at it do you see an entity you can understand and work with?
- Are there image gaps to be addressed? How will you address these?

Week Three

# MONDAY

## Profiling the brand audience

*The customer franchise*

All customers are not equal. Some are worth much more than others and prospects (potential customers) are not even customers yet. All too often marketing fails to make a clear distinction between customers and prospects. The brand identity is linked to its loyal customer base. The customers who buy from it comprise its real brand equity. A store chain that attracts 1 million customers a week has a 1 million customer head start on one that is about to open.

## Customer analysis

Modern consumers and business customers are streetwise. Intensive advertising and promotions have taught us to look for deals. Many businesses are learning the hard way that unselective recruitment of prospects is poor business. They take the deal and walk away. In this climate a customer strategy is vital. The solution is a good quality database that has the potential to reduce the complexity of big customer bases to a new version of the village shop. In a good village shop, big customers and regulars are given priority and shortages passed on to occasional customers and passing nomads. Loyalty is rewarded and promiscuous custom is welcomed, but never at the expense of more important customers. The shopkeeper's priorities are first to hold what he has (low churn rate) and second to sell more to his regular customers (share of wallet). He or she will know the value of regular customers (lifetime residual value).

In a typical customer analysis, 20 per cent of customers account for 60 per cent of sales and 50 per cent account for

Week Three

# MONDAY

10 per cent of sales. Few businesses can afford to ignore the 20 per cent, but many do. In fact, many businesses ignore them all and focus their effort on converting prospects, i.e. winning new business.

Repeat purchase rates vary enormously across business sectors and therefore loyalty will not be a major factor for some businesses. For most, where loyalty is an important consideration, the top 20 percent require special attention. Careful profiling will draw a picture of what these people (or businesses) are like and will enable you to search for more like them. It is important to hold on to the bread and butter customers too. Many are probably unprofitable, but they will be contributing to costs. Consequently, getting rid of them is usually a bad idea – just avoid giving them too much attention.

> **Golden rule**
> The most important customers are the ones you already have. They provide your income and your brand lives in their minds. By providing existing customers with great service you enable them to tell others about you. Word of mouth builds brands.

Review your database management:

- What systems do you have in place for recording and analysing transactions?
- Do your systems provide customer data of sufficient quality?
- If no, what can you do to change this?
- How well do you know your customers?

# Segmentation

It has been said that the current era will be the age of one-to-one marketing. It is certainly true that the one-to-one approach is increasing in importance, yet a sensible view takes account of larger groupings. When one message serves its purpose for an entire group, it is pointless and expensive to contact them individually.

The huge disparity between what businesses claim they can do with direct one to one marketing and the pitiful results usually achieved is amazing.

Segmentation should aim to discover and describe the needs of customers by identifying the different packages of motivators that exist within them. Only then can products be prepared to meet these requirements effectively. Segmentation is, therefore, fundamental to business strategy. It provides the information that leads directly into product and channel selection and effective communications.

The low-cost option is to treat everyone the same, but in today's overcrowded markets it is unlikely to be a viable approach for many. If there is a range of needs, you need a different approach for each.

*Benefits of segmentation*

- Segmentation continues a process that starts with what the business has been created to do and matches this to a precise evaluation of what customers need.
- It evaluates how these needs create the market.
- It describes the differences in these wants, creating segments that we know and enjoy working with.

- It starts a process capable of recognising and rewarding loyalty.
- It measures and prioritises these segments, putting them at the heart of the business, so that product, channel and communication strategy can be built around them.
- It develops a process for organic growth based on understanding and keeping and recruiting loyal customers.
- It leads to the prioritisation and selection of segments and to positioning the brand.

## Stage 1: identifying the market

Take some time to consider what the future might look like for your business. What will have changed five years from now? Ten years from now? What changes in social attitudes, communication methods and product usage will occur? Much business planning is carried out from the perspective of frozen time. Imagine you are driving a car into the future. What will you see?

## Stage 2: segmenting the market

*Identifying need sets – the six questions*
How, what, when, where, who, why? These six words form the basis of the majority of the questions it is possible to ask in the English language. Therefore, if you can define each answer arising from them in sufficient detail, they will detail the boundaries of any plan. For a segmentation study, the most important question is 'why?' This is because the answer arises directly from the fundamental values that

drive desire and create the want in the first instance. The buying process is an emotional proposition – you desire something and so you buy it.

*The anatomy of desire*

Our desires are filtered through our individual set of values. Values are deep-seated beliefs that, effectively, programme the brain. In other words, values determine how we think. If we think that one race is inherently superior to another, this may be part of our value system but we are unlikely to boast about it or confide it to a market researcher. Some values may be so deep-seated that we remain unaware of them and are unable to confide them to anyone, including ourselves. In addition, our self-image contains a perception of the person we aspire to be as well as the person we are. It is this aspirational individual who can easily surface in research. This individual generally believes in the right things. For example, he might not make purchases based on vanity, greed or sexual desire. The real individual may not be quite so well behaved.

*Needs*

Sometimes we want things because we need them, sometimes merely because someone else has something and we feel we deserve the same. In a complex social system, few products will sell on the basis of one clearly defined need. Usually a mixture will be involved and differences between the needs of customer segments will trace back to the manner in which these complex need sets are prioritised. For one buyer, the major need will be to minimise the cost while, for another, the major need will be to make a purchase perceived to be appropriate to his or her peer group. For a third buyer, the major need may be centred on an internally verified need, such as a connoisseur's belief in her ability to

Week Three

# MONDAY

make a superior choice. Brands link into these needs by association and exploit the habituation process, i.e. we have not got time to make a choice so we go with what we already know. In every case the process is about what the product can do for the buyer, not about what it owns.

*Why do they buy?*
Describe where their desires come from:

- The desire to be healthy, well fed and watered and sexually attractive.
- The need to be safe and protect and secure what we have.
- The desire to be liked and accepted by others.
- The desire to be respected for who we are and what we have achieved.

*Who buys our products?*
Describes the customer.

*What do they buy*
Describes their product preferences.

*Where and when do they buy?*
Describes their shopping behaviour.

*How do they buy?*
Describes the process (by credit, for example).

The plan is complete when all six questions are answered satisfactorily.

Need set analysis needs to be cunning to tease out the underlying preferences. If funds are light or the business is

# Week Three
## MONDAY

not large enough to withstand a large research budget, the task may have to be done intuitively. In either case the proof of the pudding is in the eating. There is no need to be perfect. If you make a significantly better job of it than your competitors, the path is open for a dramatic gain. The trick is always to be one step ahead of the competition. Sensible competitor analysis will reveal how they slice up the market. Can you beat them?

*Completing the customer profile*
*Who are they?*
It is useful to have a set of descriptions or profiles which can check for preferences in terms of behaviour, motivation and outlet choice. But beware, knowing that someone has plenty of money does not imply they will always buy premium products. They may well have plenty of money because they are careful with it.

*Where can they be found?*
This includes geographic data, such as country, region and area and urban, suburban and rural locations.

*What are they like?*
This explores demographic data, such as age, income, gender and social class. The business-to-business scenario includes size of business, type of industry, public or private ownership and centralised or decentralized.

*What do they value?*
This covers psychographic information such as life stage (child, adolescent, young adult, married with two children, etc.) and lifestyle (how do they live).

*Key drivers*
Once you know who the buyers are and you have a good understanding of the motivation that drives their purchase behaviour, you can find out what they buy, where they go to get it, and lots more pertinent information.

## Stage 3: screening segments

Some segments will be more attractive propositions than others. The segments should be screened and prioritised. The most attractive segments, which offer a good brand fit need to be selected, or at least prioritised, to receive the main effort. Some brands will niche on to selected segment(s) and others will have a wider appeal.

*The customer profile map*
The starting position is to map out the market segments you have identified. Figure 5 has five segments running vertically down the chart with preferences and known behaviours listed horizontally. The map should clearly describe the customer groupings and, if accurate, give a clear customer focus. Some datamining approaches (using huge computers to interrogate multiple databases) can provide 30,000 segments. However many you can find, you will only be able to effectively manage a number between five and nine. This is a human rather than a technical limitation. If you have more segments than you need, examine the potential for incorporating one or more together.

# MONDAY

|  | New fans | Traditional fans | Corporates | Young | Women |
|---|---|---|---|---|---|
| Prime Excitement motivation | Excitement | Tribalism | Hospitality | Joy | |
| Description | ABC 1 | C1C2 | AB | ABC1C2 | ABC1C2 |
| | £21k–£30+k p.a. | To £29k p.a. | +£30k p.a. | – | – |
| Product preferences | Tickets | Tickets, shirts | Food | Football kit | Tickets |
| Purchase behaviour | Credit card | Cash | Credit card | – | ? |
| Loyalty | Moderate | High | Low | Moderate | High |
| Buying process | Internet | Season ticket | Drinks | Xmas and birthday | |
| | Telephone | Stadium | Store | High street | |
| Channel split | | | | | |
| Stadium | 48% | 33% | 1% | 5% | 13% |
| Merchandising | High | Low | Low | High | ? |
| Media proforonce | Internet | Local press | Direct | Magazines | ? |
| Growth | High | Stable | High | High | V. High |
| Contribution | 55% | 20% | 3% | 7 | 15 |
| Size | | | | | |

Figure 5. The customer profile map

The customer profile map in Figure 5 shows an indicative view of segmentation for a fictional football club. The female segment is growing but undefined. The other four segments offer clear, differentiated segments.

# MONDAY

Identify what information you have available to design your segmentation and what is missing. How can you fill the gaps? Create your own segmentation map.

## Stage 4: targeting segments

Determining the targeting policy depends upon the strategic approach. Do you view the business as a niche player focusing on one or two segments, or a generalist attempting to cover the whole market? If you decide to exit a segment, remember that it may create a vacuum that will be filled by someone else. Also, big segments tend to offer lower profits, but provide critical mass. For most businesses, the best answer is to target a strategic segment, i.e. one segment to receive the main effort together with one or more secondary targets. Some useful factors to consider when screening segments are outlined below.

> **Size** The size of the opportunity. What is the total segment worth? What is its value in numbers of units of sale and the value of those sales?
>
> **Profitability** How profitable is it?
>
> **Growth potential** How deeply is the segment penetrated right now and, therefore, what is its likely rate of growth over the planning period?
>
> **Competitive strength** How difficult a segment is it to compete in? Will we do battle with strong competitors?
>
> **Brand strength** Is our brand respected and trusted in this market? What support has it had in terms of advertising spend? How well is it protected legally?

Week Three

# MONDAY

> **Distribution** How good is the fit between the current distribution arrangements and this sector? Is there a good fit with our existing supply and value chain?
>
> **People** Do we have the right mixture of people to make the most of the opportunity?
>
> **Money** What are the entry or growth development costs? Can we afford them?
>
> **Timing** Is this the right time to be making a strong move in this market? Are the economic and social trends favourable? What other signs and portents should we take account of?

Think about your focus. Describe the whole market you aim to serve (all the segments together). Which segment will be the main target of your effort this year? What segments will form secondary targets to receive some, but less, attention?

## Summary

Your customer and prospect segmentation analysis is now in place and waiting to be aligned with the brand identity. You are now ready to move on to the industry analysis (competitors and channels).

Week Three

# T U E S D A Y

# Completing the audit

- industry analysis: analysing competitors and channels to market
- building a powerful platform for the brand plan

The market analysis is complete, with a strong brand identity in place and a rigorous customer evaluation and segmentation study completed. The next phase is an industry audit analysing competitors and marketing channels.

## Choosing competitors

When antibacterial soap in dispensers reached consumers, it was positioned as a separate solution to existing soap. Existing competitors were bypassed and its delighted owners can now sell both types of soap. Sunny Delight achieved success by switching industry (or category as it is sometimes called) and moving into the chiller cabinets to compete against juices. Nicorette became a great success by switching category from doctors to consumers. In each case, the category switch moved the brands away from existing competition or into a new category without competitors. You are going to identify a competitive advantage, yet the choice of who to compete against is not necessarily obvious.

## Industry analysis

Competitor analysis evaluates the competitors and potential competitors who could or might supply your customers. A new industry (group of sellers) can enter a market and spoil

# TUESDAY

the party. Or you can move out. Cans replaced bottles as containers for beer and aircraft stole a large part of the shipping business. A new industry had discovered a new way of meeting needs in the marketplace. The pace of change is fast and wise businesses are alert to the comparative strengths of their potential as well as to actual competitors.

> WHSmith is a communication store, which meets the desire to send and receive information. This desire is satisfied by newspapers, magazines and books (receiving information) and by pens, paper and writing materials (for sending information). This interpretation identifies other retailers dealing in these products, including supermarkets, as existing competitors. However, technology (e-mail, internet, interactive TV, etc.) also meets the need to send and receive information. New competitors are feeding the existing market with substitute products.

## Industry maps

Markets often divide into economy, middle and premium priced subsets, as depicted by the industry map in Figure 6.

The vertical price axis is a straightforward measurement of average prices and the horizontal axis takes a measurement of perceived quality (what the customers believe, not necessarily a demonstrable truth). The three star markers at the base of the map compete directly with one another, as do the five in the central slots. This leaves the top two premium brands to battle it out for the high price points.

Week Three

# TUESDAY

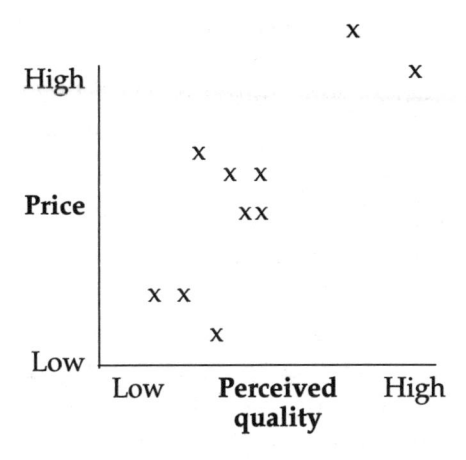

```
                        x
High  |                    x
      |
      |         x
      |           x x
Price |            xx
      |
      |
      |     x x
      |        x
Low   |_____
        Low   Perceived   High
               quality
```

Figure 6. An industry map correlating price and quality

The lowest of the stars represents a business with a clear quality and price advantage. It charges the lowest prices and is the best quality in its sector. The highest of the five central stars is overpriced and is likely to lose business. The business represented by the highest star appears overpriced compared to customers' perceptions and it stands to lose share.

Complete an industry map for your brand and interrogate it using the following questions as a starting point:

- Which brand holds the clearest price and quality advantage in your sector? What are the implications of this for your brand now and in the future?
- Which brand holds the weakest price and quality position? What opportunities does this open up for you?

Week Three

# TUESDAY

## Competitive advantage

Where, specifically, do your sources of competitive advantage lie? Take a couple of minutes to jot down your first thoughts.

Is your list painfully short, or worse still, empty? Sometimes the competitive advantages of a brand can be difficult to uncover, but for almost all brands they do exist. In fact, if they do not exist you are going out of business! Conversely, sometimes they are identified too readily and are later discovered to be insubstantial or untrue. 'Our people are our source of competitive edge' is a typical example. This statement may be true, but a wise manager would seek strong evidence before betting his or her career on it. If your list is long, revisit it and cross out any that now seem inadequate.

Teleology – the study of cause – provides a framework for a more thorough investigation. Four possible causes of competitive advantage arise:

1 *Organisational*: you are better organised than your competitors in some specific area or as an entity.
2 *Skill*: you have a skill advantage in one or more specific areas.
3 *Material*: you own, or have access to, superior physical and tangible resources. Your products and services are, in some way, superior.
4 *Soul*: an organisation that is aware of its purpose with clarity and precision rarely wastes time on non-essential tasks. Its is quite literally on a mission and the aura it grows around it is the stuff of legendary brands. This cause of competitive advantage is branding.

## TUESDAY

Competitive advantage lends itself to relational analysis ('better than, worse than'), rather than to precise measurement. It is likely, also, to be transient in the current fast-moving environment and so timing is invariably critical. A process is required that measures what advantages will occur and forecasts when to take advantage of them. This process begins with a comparative assessment of the key features of your product and service offer against your strategic competitors' offerings. The output of this comparative assessment can then be analysed in relation to the competitor analysis grid shown below.

| We are very strong<br>They are weak<br>**Attack** | We are very strong<br>They are very strong<br>**Accept or re-engineer** |
|---|---|
| They are very strong<br>We are weak<br>**Take corrective action** | We are weak<br>They are weak<br>**Opportunity** |

Figure 7.

*Competitor analysis grid*
Each of the four boxes of the competitor analysis grid represents a directional policy: attack; opportunity; accept; correct. The attack option is self-explanatory, but there is a further opportunity where a weakness is shared. The first organisation to take positive steps to correct this weak area will probably score significant gains when the benefits become apparent to its customers. Accept indicates competitive parity – a drive for gains here is likely to be expensive. Correct indicates a weakness to be addressed, but one which is unlikely to quickly turn into an advantage.

# Week Three
## TUESDAY

## Using a competitive advantage matrix

The next stage involves transferring the data you have amassed into a competitive advantage matrix (Figure 8). This will be your working document from which directional policy can be drawn.

| Elements | Attack | Correct | Opportunity | Accept |
|---|---|---|---|---|
| Organisational | | | | |
| Skill | | | | |
| Material | | | | |
| Brand | | | | |

Figure 8. The competitive advantage matrix

Against each of the first three causes of competitive advantage (organisational, skills and materials) list the key issues for your brand.

Compare the relative strength of each factor with a strategic competitor. Then, with reference to the competitor analysis grid record your responses within the appropriate boxes of the competitive advantage matrix. It should now be relatively simple to compile your competitive advantage matrix.

*Brand equity*

> The fourth cause relates to brand equity (value). In many categories, consumers are often unable to recognise their favourite brands in blind tests (with the packaging removed), i.e. cola drinks, baked beans, whisky, yellow fats, razor blades, analgesics (pain relief).

# TUESDAY
Week Three

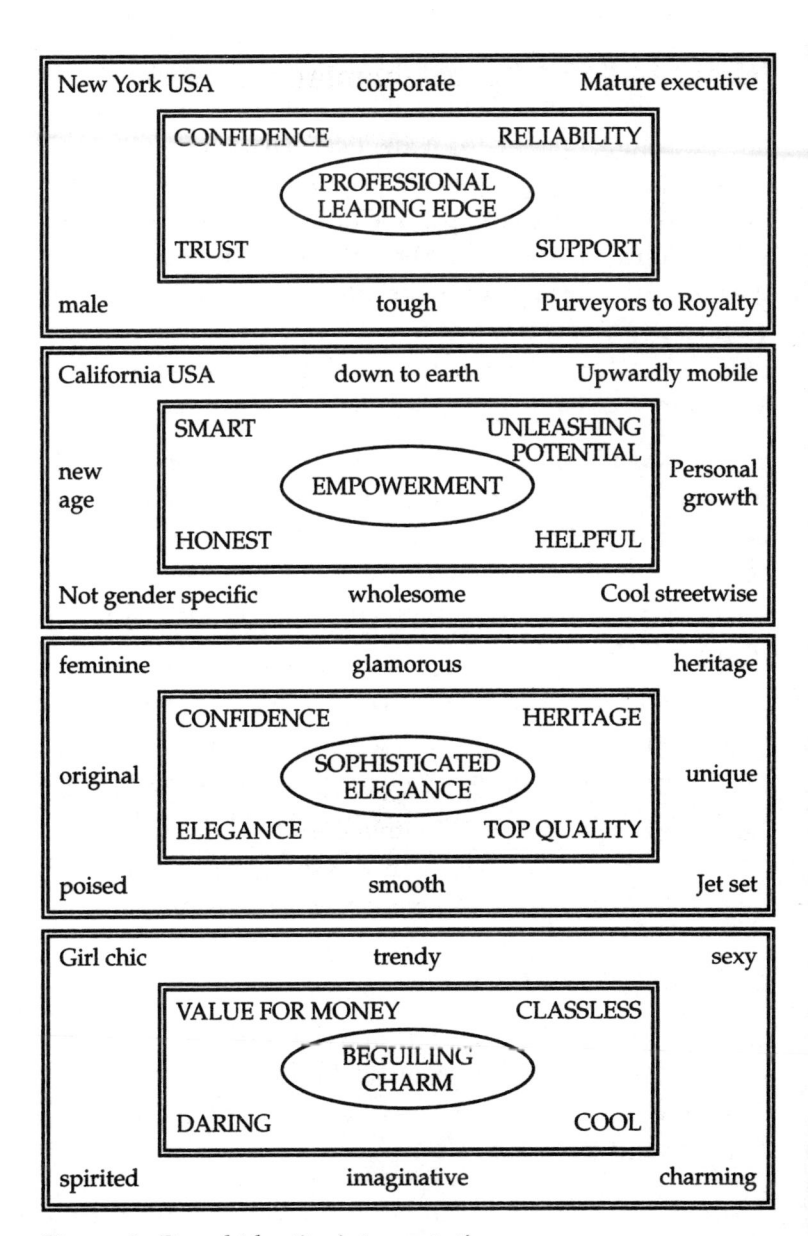

| New York USA | corporate | Mature executive |
|---|---|---|
| CONFIDENCE | | RELIABILITY |
| | PROFESSIONAL LEADING EDGE | |
| TRUST | | SUPPORT |
| male | tough | Purveyors to Royalty |

| California USA | down to earth | Upwardly mobile |
|---|---|---|
| | SMART | UNLEASHING POTENTIAL |
| new age | EMPOWERMENT | Personal growth |
| | HONEST | HELPFUL |
| Not gender specific | wholesome | Cool streetwise |

| feminine | glamorous | heritage |
|---|---|---|
| | CONFIDENCE | HERITAGE |
| original | SOPHISTICATED ELEGANCE | unique |
| | ELEGANCE | TOP QUALITY |
| poised | smooth | Jet set |

| Girl chic | trendy | sexy |
|---|---|---|
| | VALUE FOR MONEY | CLASSLESS |
| | BEGUILING CHARM | |
| | DARING | COOL |
| spirited | imaginative | charming |

Figure 9. Brand identity interpretation

# Week Three
## TUESDAY

In principle, the equity of your brand is easy to establish. Compare the results of a market test with the brand name and packaging present, to an identical market test with the name and packaging removed. The difference in sales value of the two tests, grossed up to the full value of all the brand sales volume, equals the equity of the brand, i.e. its value to the business over and above the sales they would still have without it. This value arises from the intangible 'marketing brand equity', which the brand is able to lever to gain sales and margin, or both.

A good way to compare and contrast brands is to make pairs of brand maps to show comparative differences and to extract their strengths and weaknesses. Compare the matched sets of maps shown in Figure 9 and notice how quite small changes in the chosen words create distinctly different identities.

To compare and contrast brand equity, complete brand identity maps for your competitors' brands. Carry out a precise evaluation of your brand position relative to theirs. Look for attacking options and shared weaknesses and transfer significant differences on to the competitive advantage matrix.

## Selecting the channel

Channel strategy is the last link in the 4C process. It examines the routes through which the company can make contact with its chosen markets (the groups of buyers of its products and services).

Week Three

# TUESDAY

# The value chain

The value chain is the total process that contributes towards the final performance of the brand. It leads downstream through the distribution outlets and communication activities and out into the consumer world. It also leads backwards, to the producers and suppliers sitting behind the brand. Value flows down the chain but profits flow backwards, paying the costs and profits of all concerned. The customers at the end of the chain finance the whole operation when they buy the end products and services. Therefore, wastage in the system, especially excess stock, is paid for by the customers. A competitor using a more effective value chain has a competitive advantage. In a competitive environment, the performance of the entire value chain is therefore a key measure of success.

*Downstream development*
Where the brand enters the consumer domain there are likely to be a number of options concerning the point of purchase location. For example, high street stores, convenience stores and out-of-town hypermarkets may find themselves competing with the internet and direct selling methods. It is important to look carefully at the options available and decide where your focus should be. Consumers are not always the direct customer. Some products form components of a larger product.

Week Three
# TUESDAY

## Channel analysis

There are four layers to consider in analysing channels:

1 Environmental analysis
2 Power structure analysis
3 Economic analysis
4 Identity analysis

## Environmental analysis

Socio-economic, political and technical changes may affect your various channels to market. The deregulation of the magazine market, for example, removed the monopoly of local newsagents and shifted sales towards the supermarkets.

Consider the socio-economic, political and technical changes that are likely to impact on your channels to market.

- Who are the likely winners/losers?
- What are the implications for your brand?

## Power structure analysis

Below the surface, the big issue is power management. If your system is a bus, who is driving it? The driving seat of the bus is the best place to be. If you cannot be the driver, you must at least be near the front. Being thrown off the bus is disastrous. Power is usually the result of concentration of force. If five retail chains buy from 20 suppliers, the power structure will favour the retailers. If two suppliers supply 100 retailers the power structure will favour the suppliers.

# TUESDAY

Power is often used coercively and it is important to know some strategies that can influence the balance of power in your channel options.

1 The best strategy is a strong brand with a differentiated market and a clear and sought after point of difference.
2 A balance of in-house and out-sourced suppliers can reduce reliance on both by giving you the option to move your business towards or away from either.
3 A strong research and development function should ensure that you are at the forefront of new developments and not threatened by innovative new products.
4 Erect barriers to keep out new players. For example, direct communication links with partners using unique software will make it harder for new players to enter the fray.
5 Build strong relationships with high value channel partners and consumer segments to strenghten your position.

Consider the power relationships of each of your channel options:

> • Will the balance of power enable you to achieve your profit and sales targets or will you be brought into line with larger, more powerful partners?

Number crunch each channel to ensure that you know the current worth of each in terms of volume and value, profitability and net contribution.

> • Are there any hidden costs?
> • What are the growth prospects of each channel?

# Week Three
## TUESDAY

*Identity analysis*

Your brand needs to be in channels that complement its values rather than detract from them. This might entail some hard choices. A key point is the intensity of the channel. A high value brand will need a low intensity channel, i.e. relatively few outlets with premium standards of presentation and service. An economy brand, on the other hand, will require a heavy concentration of outlets and will survive with lower standards of service.

Consider how your channel options relate to the identity of your brand:

- Is the intensity of each channel appropriate to the value of your brand?
- What service levels are required for your brand?
- Do you need to supply high levels of training or supporting material? If so, you will need a stronger level of integration and cooperation between the two parties.
- Which channels will require key account teams to service them and which, if any, can cope with a lesser level of support?
- What are the relative costs to serve?

Each channel will probably be skewed, relative to your customer analysis. In other words, customer segments will be strongly represented in some channels and absent from others.

- What information do you have that will help you to understand the customer structure of each channel?

# TUESDAY

Week Three

Finally draw a channel map similar to the one in Figure 10 (values are indicative only). Enter information on to the chart as shown.

| Channel | Grocer | Convenience | High street | Wholesale |
|---|---|---|---|---|
| Environment | Grow | Grow | Grow | Fade |
| Power | Weak | Fair | Strong | Strong |
| ECONOMICS | | | | |
| Size | 200 | 71 | 78 | 82 |
| Profit | 14 | 24 | 16 | 12 |
| Growth | High | Medium | Slow | Decline |
| Margin | 6 | 34 | 21 | 15 |
| Share | 3 | 4 | 2 | 4 |
| Loyalty | Weak | Strong | Strong | Fair |
| IDENTITY | | | | |
| Brand fit | Strong | Weak | Strong | Weak |
| INTENSITY (outlets) | 1000 | 250 | 301 | 72 |
| Service | Good | Poor | Weak | Weak |
| SEGMENT (share) | | | | |
| A | 24 | 25 | 27 | 24 |
| B | 12 | 35 | 27 | 26 |
| C | 33 | 35 | 29 | 3 |

Figure 10. Channel map

Week Three

# TUESDAY

## Channel evaluation

Your final task is to decide which of your channel options are to be the primary outlets for the brand, which should be secondary and, possibly, which channels are unsuitable and should be exited.

## Summary

You have carefully evaluated the channel options available, taking account of the big picture as well as the financial and brand identity issues. Power – the ability to push through with the brand objectives – has been an important consideration. Your 4C analysis is complete. The next stage is to pull the four separate pieces of work together into a coordinated and focused plan.

Week Three

## WEDNESDAY

# Positioning

- Preparing a situational report.
- Positioning your brand in the mind of its target audience.

## Preparing a situational report

Congratulations on completing your 4C analysis. What you have prepared is a brand audit comprising:

- A brand identity statement revealing the key elements of the brand's anatomy and personality.
- A customer map identifying your actual and potential customer base.
- An industry map examining your chosen competitors and identifying potential points of difference.
- A channel map examining your best placement for customer contact and sales.

Week Three

# WEDNESDAY

If you are involved with a major brand, it is likely that positioning and communications will be done in partnership with a creative agency. If so, this is the point to involve your account director. Agencies need to be involved to develop the strategy. Creative briefs developed by agencies are, in fact, positioning statements. Are you happy to pass the parcel onwards and devolve much of the responsibility to them? Working together would be preferred by most marketing directors. Rifts occur in most partnerships sooner or later, so decide on how you prefer to work (and who is working for whom).

## What will all this work look like when its finished?

Your challenge now is to transform the output of your analysis into a successful brand plan. This requires you to assemble all the relevant material you have collated and sift it carefully to shake out the less important data. What is left should provide you with a number of options that could potentially be taken forward. You will sift these options and identify the most appropriate for your purpose. At this point you will be able to see what your work is going to look like when it is finished. Once you know this, you will have translated your purpose into an outcome: you will have a strategy.

## Creating a brand plan

A brand plan contains three elements:

1 The brand identity statement
2 A positioning statement
3 Growth vectors and drivers

## WEDNESDAY
Week Three

*Brand identity statement*
This is the statement that you completed on Monday. Remember that this represents the anatomy of your brand and enables everyone who works with it to understand its value and purpose. This permanent and unchanging template ensures that your brand's core values, purpose and consistency are maintained and protected.

*Positioning statement*
A positioning statement identifies the elements of the brand to be positioned in the mind of the chosen customer segment (the output of brand and customer analysis). In addition, it uses a point of difference (from competitor analysis) and identifies the best channel to market (from the channel analysis). Unlike the brand identity, the positioning strategy will need to be changed or adjusted periodically as customer values and attitudes change.

*Growth vectors and growth drivers*
Growth vectors are the routes the brand will take, such as entering new markets or developing new products and services. Growth drivers are the elements of the marketing mix that are most effective in creating delighted customers and improving sales. For example, a vector would be the decision to create an extension to the brand and a driver might be the activities at the point of sale that are most capable of building sales and profits. Together, they inform decisions on business direction and the elements required to deliver results.

Week Three
# WEDNESDAY

## Strategic thinking

The strategic decision process is supported by systematic analysis but requires a degree of intuition (and courage) to arrive at a differentiated and persuasive proposition.

To build your brand plan you will need to pull together all the data you collected from the 4C analysis and summarise it in a situational report (SitRep). This report will feed into the positioning statement. The remaining work will be to identify the growth vectors and drivers for your brand.

## Creating a situational report

A SitRep is a working document. It contains a summary of your analysis that you can keep to hand and amend in the light of new information.

To pull together a SitRep for your brand you will need to answer the questions in Figure 11. Some people will be more than prepared to do this. Others, for a number of different reasons, may find that this more difficult. Don't worry, this is quite normal. If you are struggling, try using the techniques outlined on the following pages to liberate the required information.

Answer the questions set out in Figure 11.

# WEDNESDAY

Week Three

| 1 What is my preferred product and brand focus?<br><br>How will I leverage my competitive advantage?<br><br>Where will the profit come from?<br><br>Market growth %<br><br>Share gains %<br><br>Inflationary pricing %<br><br>Cost saving % | 2 Describe your general target market (all users and potential users)<br><br>Describe your strategic target (the segment of the market chosen for your main effort)<br><br>Describe your secondary targets (any other segments chosen for a special effort) | 3 Select a strategic competitor<br><br>(the one chosen for market share attack or strategic focus)<br><br>State what attacking and defensive measures you plan to take | 4 Select a strategic channel (the one you plan to make the focus of your activities)<br><br>Select a secondary target |
|---|---|---|---|
| **5 Competitive advantage**<br><br>What do you see as your main sources of competitive advantage? | **6 Assumptions**<br><br>What assumptions do you make about how the market is moving? What assumptions do you have about other factors (e.g. the economy) that are also likely to make an impact? | **7 More research needed**<br><br>What facts or assumptions do you need to find out more about? Where can you find additional information to help you to develop your marketing plan? | **8 Summary**<br><br>Summarise below the main findings from your 4C analysis. What is the overall picture for your market? |

Figure 11. Summarising the situational report

The following section notes some techniques to try if you are stuck.

*The note party*
Write down the equities of your brand using one note per equity. Do the same with the individual customer segments and then the various competitors and channels. The

# Week Three
## WEDNESDAY

purpose of this exercise is to experiment with a wide variety of combinations to identify the best options available to you. Assuming you organise the resulting notes into every possible combination and you have seven items in each box, you will be able to create 2,401 combinations. Many will be incongruent, but the promising ones will make an interesting story.

Summarise the answers into a story specifying your main points: How do you plan to grow? With what customer focus? Using what competitive advantage factor? Outputting through what channels? Work on what you have written until it is as compact as you can make it.

### *The dinner party technique*

The dinner party. Imagine you have invited six celebrities to dinner. Get each team member to nominate one celebrity who they admire. Then the team members are invited to become that celebrity and, in this role, suggest some new ideas. Whilst in character, people may feel more comfortable expressing new views.

If you suspect some people are afraid to contribute fully, hand out white squares of paper and a pencil to everyone. Ask them to write down their ideas, anonymously, on to the paper and then to screw up the paper and throw it into an empty waste paper bin. Retrieve the bin and write all the ideas on to the grid.

### *When the ideas slow down*

Study the analysis, discuss it with colleagues, have a bath, go for a walk, forget it and come back to it in a day or two. Reassuringly, marketing is a stochastic discipline, which means that there are no right answers (no company will ever

# WEDNESDAY

know if an alternative plan would have worked even better).

When you feel confident, return to summarising the SitRep.

*Finalising your SitRep.*
Your answers to the questions must be organised into a coherent format. You may choose to lay them out as a series of bullet points or write them out in report format. You now have the basis for the current positioning of your brand and its long-term development.

## Selecting positional strategy

A positioning statement takes the key points from the SitRep and arranges them to form the positional strategy of the brand. All other strategies will flow from this central position. The positional strategy should contain the following:

- *What do we want to say?* The primary reason for buying your products and services that you will present to your audience. The source of differentiation. It needs to be presented from the receiver's point of view, i.e. as a benefit not a feature. It is the promise of beauty and sophistication, not a health and beauty product.
- *To whom?* The selected audience you will speak to: your strategic segment and possibly some secondary targets too.
- *Why?* Your proof. The substantiation to the proposition, derived from your principal competitive advantage. It can be something big, for example, a

# Week Three
## WEDNESDAY

> major product advantage or something small if necessary. The skill is to create a scarce resource and make it attractive. The substantiation is often rational rather than emotional. The important point is that it must be different and attractive to the target audiences.
>
> - *Against whom?* This is the competitor you plan to gain share from. Sometimes this is not the case. If the market is growing it would seem to be a redundant element. It is almost always useful to select a strategic competitor. It prevents the strategy from being too introverted and, besides, even the best general would be confounded if he or she was unable to discover the opponent. Today, most business activity is highly competitive. If not, then it is either a public service or very profitable indeed. In the second case, it is likely become highly competitive in the near future!
> - *The brand essence* The core values of your brand give it credibility and must be accurately represented in the positioning statement. The brand's character, personality and tone of voice must be consistent with the message. In addition the brand's values and beliefs must be complemented and reinforced.

Write draft positioning statements for your brand following the format laid out above. Interrogate each one in turn by scoring it against the following questions on the basis of excellent (3 marks), reasonable (2 marks) and poor (1 mark). You may wish to add a weighting to each criteria.

# WEDNESDAY

1 Does it add value to the corporate plan?
2 Are our target markets valuable enough?
3 Is it consistent and coherent with our previous positioning?
4 Does it exploit competitor weakness?
5 How easy will it be to copy us?
6 Are there measures we can take to combat copying?
7 Can we afford it?
8 Have we measured it? Is it congruent with our forecast?
9 Is it distinctive, understandable, attractive and different?
10 Can we design contingencies?

Add up the scores to identify your best positioning statement.

## Summary

You have prepared a situational report that summarises the main conclusions and decisions arising from your audit. The findings of the SitRep have been translated into a positioning statement. In addition, the discarded positioning options have all been measured against criteria that can be argued and justified amongst your team and to your senior management. Your brand identity statement and positioning statement will guide and lead the remaining decisions that need to be made.

Week Three

# T H U R S D A Y

# Bringing the brand to life

- operational planning
- identify the most suitable growth vectors
- align the drivers of business success

## Selecting growth vectors

So far, you have audited the brand and compiled the main findings in the SitRep. Using this data, you have faced the difficult task of identifying the brand positioning and essence. The directional policy of the brand is established: you know where you are going. What you need now is a route map to steer by.

You still have two sets of big decisions to make. The first set involves how to grow your brand. Growth is invariably the aim of business. The primary measurement of growth is Return on Capital Employed (ROCE). ROCE is how much you earn represented as a percentage of how much money you have put into the brand to create those earnings. ROCE is a function of the two secondary ratios: Return on Sales Ratio (ROSR) and the Asset Utilisation Ratio (AUR). Simplified, the business can only grow if it creates more sales or a better margin on the sales it is making, or both of these together.

There is a strictly limited choice and, therefore, it is well worth considering each one carefully. For example, you could decide to focus on new products or on entering new markets. Your best options for growth can be referred to as your growth vectors.

**Week Three**

# THURSDAY

Having decided what route to take, the second set of decisions centres on changes you might want to make to the marketing mix. Broadly, the marketing mix divides into three key areas. The first is the goods and services you provide. Making these as well aligned as possible is your first task. The second area is logistics (the processes needed to get your goods and services to the right places at the right time and profitably). This requires tight management and successful partnerships. The third area is your communication with your target audience (and other public entities such as your owners, suppliers, etc.) about what you have to sell. Some changes in the mix will produce much better results than others. These can be called the growth drivers of the business. Your task is to find these and put them to work.

You have two tasks for today:

1 To identify the growth vectors for your brand
2 To establish the key growth drivers you need to work on to maximise the return on capital

## Growth vectors

Let's examine each possibility in turn.

## Improving profitability

There are two ways to improve profits: reduce the costs or put up the price.

*Cut costs*
Random cost-cutting invariably creates more, often hidden, costs. When looking for ways to improve profit margins the

## Week Three
# THURSDAY

focus should be on effectiveness, i.e. getting the job done properly and avoiding costly *firefighting* activities that go unnoticed in the formal accounts. Your channel analysis is useful here.

Look at your work on your supply chain. What changes can be made that will cut costs while maintaining efficiency?

- Can you reduce the number of suppliers?
- Can you tighten stock management?
- Can you strengthen the sales information system?
- Can you reduce paperwork by using the internet?

*Put up prices*

- *Value positioning*: putting up prices is the best way to make more money, provided the result is not a reduction in sales. Putting prices down is bad for branding and worse for profitability (unless it causes a very big increase in sales). Think about the problem as value rather than price. Could you offer:

1  Improved, perceived value at a higher price (a premium policy)?
2  More for the same price (can you add inexpensive extras or find someone else who will pay for them)?
3  Less value for a lower price (an economy policy)?

Revisit your segmentation and positioning:
- What possibilities exist for enhancing the range on offer to different segments?
- Would some segments benefit from improved value at somewhat higher prices?

- *Sensitivity analysis*: How sensitive are customers to price in your market? In some cases, an increase in price will result in a steep decline in sales, in others an increase can go unnoticed. It depends upon the customers. How familiar are they with current prices? To what extent are they prepared to shop around? There are often some segments which are not price sensitive even in a generally price sensitive market, for example younger, unmarried shoppers in supermarkets often have no idea what items cost.
- *Bundling*: it is not uncommon to find groups of products bundled together at a great overall price. Usually, there will be one or two that are substantially marked up in the overall price. Moreover, check the price points within a range – often some better sellers can be adjusted upwards and slower lines can be reduced in price.
- *Competitor reaction*: how will the competitors react to your actions? Work out what they will do and plan accordingly. If prices are to go up, wait until they put theirs up and follow behind. If prices are going down, be first and promote heavily.
- *Monitor Progress:* try to gauge the responses you get to price changes. Good customers tend to ask more of you, pushing up the cost-to-serve, while seemingly less valuable customers can be less demanding and therefore more profitable: know where your income stream is coming from.

Week Three

# THURSDAY

> Never treat a price as an isolated issue. Price is part of the overall value proposition. It is more about perception than reality. The cheapest product is rarely the best seller.

## Improving sales

To improve sales you must either benefit from an improved market or take business away from your competitors.

*Growing the market*

- *Increasing usage*: the first place to look to increase usage is amongst your existing customers. Warm leads are better prospects than cold ones. A positive action would be to target existing, high worth customers with new offers. A defensive action could involve introducing an early warning system to monitor high worth customers and respond rapidly to problems.
  Understanding what a good customer is like enables you to look for more like them, rather than attracting price and deal-driven customers who will take the bargain and walk away.
- *Extending range*: Brands can be extended to incorporate new products and segments. The core values of the brand must not be compromised and must have the same meaning and relevance in the new segment. Secondly, unless it fits the distribution channel a new range can be expensive. Most brand extensions fail, so be careful. A real howler could seriously damage your brand.

## THURSDAY

- *Market growth*: If there is room to grow the current market and add new users, then the best process is to revisit the existing marketing mix and find better ways of doing what you are already doing. In particular, look for distribution gaps where you are not currently available.
- *New markets*: can be new geographic regions that you were previously unable to cover or newly identified segments within your existing coverage. Genuine innovation sometimes creates new markets. No one wanted anti-bacterial soap or energy drinks until someone invented them.

*Growing market share*

- *Buying rivals*: a good strategy, if you can afford it, might be to buy your competitor and thus take them out of the market. This avoids the potentially disastrous outcome of provoking a price war where everyone stands to be a net loser.
- *Alliances*: the internet is an example of the changing nature of competition. Website owners form alliances and deals, linking themselves to selected partners in a collaborative partnership. This creates networks and excludes non-members.
- *Beating rivals*: developing this strategy means deliberately setting out to persuade existing users to switch from their current supplier to you. In mature markets this is sometimes the only option.

Week Three

# THURSDAY

*Golden rules*

> - New customers will be non-users, buying for the first time or customers attracted away from competitors. Be clear about which of these types you are looking for.
> - Wherever possible target influencers (e.g. family, friends, medical advisers etc.), the people to whom new customers will turn for advice. Include existing satisfied customers in this if you can (remember the power of endorsement).
> - Finally, make sure that your efforts to attract new custom do not favour prospects over loyal customers. Look for ways and means of communicating separately with existing and new customers to ensure that the separate messages do not cause conflict.

## Selecting growth drivers

What elements of the marketing mix have the most impact on your business? What is it that really works for your customers? Some of the possibilities include: prices, product range, product quality, availability, speed of service, quality of service, 24 hour access, packaging, absence of packaging, the smell of the product, accessibility, reliability, information.

The trick, of course, is to know what will make the *most* difference. Many people in marketing have no idea. Or worse, they have their own, uninformed, opinion.

List all the marketing mix factors that you think make the most impact on your business and then rank the list from most to

# THURSDAY
*Week Three*

least important. Add to the list your best estimate of how much you spend on each. If the result shows the largest expenditure at the top through to the least at the bottom, give yourself a pat on the back. For ease of reference, display the results to map your brand display curve, as shown in Figure 12.

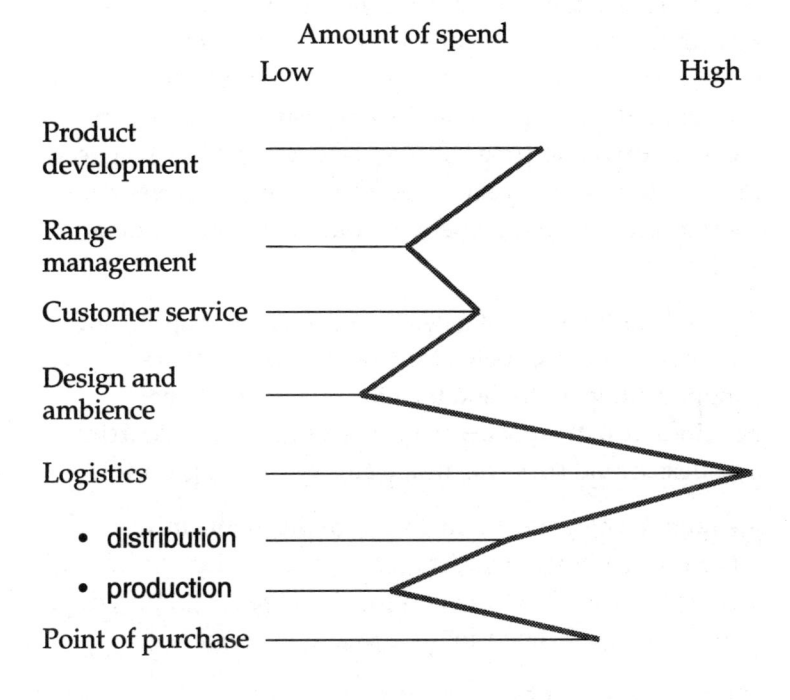

```
                        Amount of spend
              Low                             High

Product
development

Range
management

Customer service

Design and
ambience

Logistics

  • distribution

  • production

Point of purchase
```

Figure 12. The brand spend display curve

The curve is also a good measurement of differentiation. The design of your curve should show significant differences to the curve of your competitors.

Week Three

# THURSDAY

## Brand tracking

Now find out what your customers think about the key drivers you identified. Transfer the meaningful data collected into action by testing it to verify its efficacy. If the change results in an improvement, keep it going and roll it out. If the test does not produce the result you wanted, try something else. Try out variations until you get the performance improvements you want. Brand tracking builds a set of qualitative and quantitive measurements to gain feedback on brand progress. A good brand tracker will need to be customised to suit the specifics of your business but it should contain three elements: exploration, development, evaluation.

A brand explorer investigates issues, such as occasion and reason for purchase, new ideas, how your goods are shopped and paid for and the effects of promotional activities. It will probably make use of omnibus research, dipsticks (rapid surveys), usage surveys, focus groups.

A brand developer experiments with the media mix, advertising, point of purchase and outlet choice and product changes. Normally, it involves the use of focus groups, depth interviews, workshops and observation experiments.

A brand evaluator tracks results and recommends changes. It may evaluate extensions, campaigns, trade and brand performance (financial). It will probably make use of omnibus research, particularly market share, sales audits and dipsticks in addition to observation.

Use your brand tracker to understand and make adjustments to the brand spend curve you completed earlier.

# THURSDAY

*Week Three*

## Design value into the brand

No business has infinite resources. Therefore, you will never be able to solve every problem. It is necessary to make the best possible use of scarce resources. Design the marketing mix so that maximum resources are put into areas of high perceived value to the customers (and/or consumers). Switch costs away from areas that are less valued and into areas that are. Figure 13 illustrates this point.

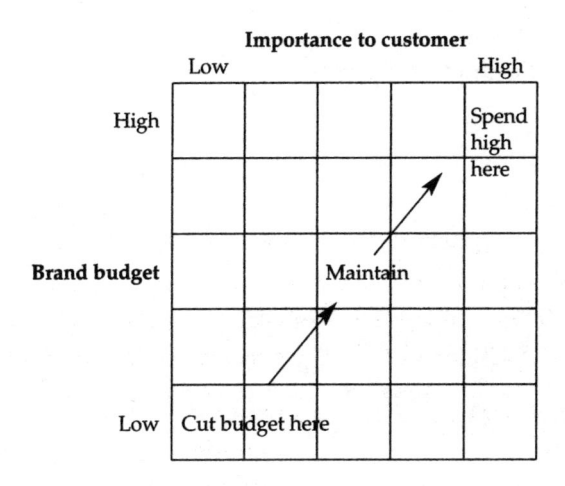

```
                    Importance to customer
              Low                         High
                                          ┌──────┐
   High    │    │    │    │    │ Spend high here │
                                          
                                    ↗
   Brand budget          Maintain
                      ↗

   Low    │ Cut budget here │
```

Figure 13. Brand alignment

## Product management

Figure 14 is a useful format to evaluate products. High turnover, low contribution products are usually 'traffic builders', pulling custom through the system. 'Top performers' deliver volume and profit and should receive top billing. 'Problems' are highlighted for attention.

261

## THURSDAY

|  | | |
|---|---|---|
| Turnover per square metre ↑ | Traffic builders | Top performers |
| | Problems (marginal zone) | Acceptable performers |

→ Contribution per square metre

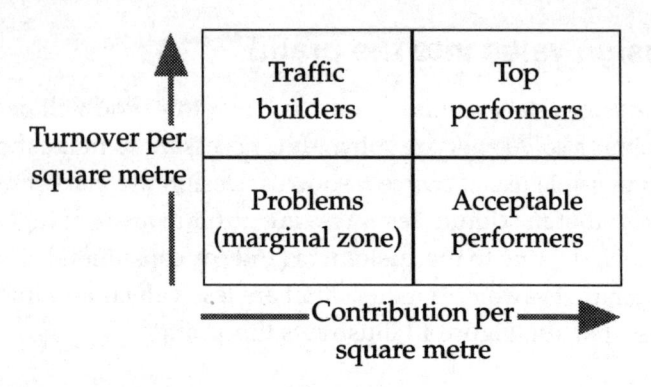

Figure 14. Product evaluator

Complete a product evaluator for your product range:

- Are the 'top performers' receiving the attention they deserve?
- If you have 'problem' products, how can they be adjusted to improve their performance? Should they be retired and the customers migrated away to other products?

## Logistics management

Logistics is a crucial element in modern marketing. If the supply channel is inadequate, staff will be unable to deliver good customer service. If they do not have appropriate tools, resources and products they cannot do the job.

Week Three

# THURSDAY

## Customer service

Good customer service is rare and, therefore, differentiating. Recruit people who like your brand and who are like the brand and you will be a long way towards achieving this objective.

> Virgin employes young, streetwise people. Waterstones employ people who love books.

All staff should know the importance of keeping good customers. Make sure they know the marketing cost of gaining new custom (customer acquisition cost). Service quality often revolves around a moment of truth during the service transaction, during which customers are gained or lost forever.

> A well known marketer, speaks movingly of when his father died. The hospital (contrary to the more common anecdotes in the press) treated his father and family with great respect and professionalism. Following the inevitable ending the hospital handed over his fathers belongings: in a bin liner. Look for moments of truth. Look out for bin liners.

## Five golden rules for great customer service

1 Structure the business around customer value and manage customers for profit, not volume.
2 The first customer contact should be the best point of contact. Put your best people in contact with your customers, not the worst.
3 Always keep your promises.
4 Centralise service to single points of contact.
5 Make sure your star customers get star service.

## Summary

The brand is moving into alignment with its aspirations, its audience and its marketing mix. We know now where it is going and how it is going to get there. It has yet to speak and that is what we will be going at next.

# FRIDAY

Week Three

# When the brand speaks

## Preparing the brand messages

Before diving into the field of marketing communications we can examine communication and consider Marshal McLuhan's famous diktat: 'The medium is the message'. You progress to how to utilise communications to build brand equity. Then we shall cover media and the tools that can be used to promote your brand and incentivise your customers.

## What is communication?

> The ability to communicate with one another more effectively than any other animal is the essence of being human. Because we have language we can think . . . or is it the other way around?

Understanding the process of communication involves the mind analysing itself. It is unsurprising that progress has been slow. It is useful to view communication from the perspective of the response, rather than the output, because it is not the performance of the communicator that matters but the results achieved. Feedback is the essence of the process. If a communication produces the right response, all is well. If not, the process is repeated and, if necessary, varied until it does.

Understanding how advertising works is as complex as understanding why a novel is good or bad. Fortunately, this is not an imperative in brand management because your task is to measure its output: its level of persuasiveness.

Week Three

# FRIDAY

## The medium and the message

The medium is the message. Of course this is true. They coexist within a communication: the medium is the context of a message and the message is the content. Non-verbal signals (body language) provide a context for communication. They are more important than words because the meanings of words are verified by the context in which they are received.

Try telling someone you hate them while smiling warmly. Then tell them you love them with a snarl. See?

It follows that brand messages need to be positioned correctly for context and content. Lucozade, originally, was positioned as a drink to make sick people healthy. Later it was repositioned as a fitness drink to help healthy people stay healthy. It remains a health drink, but the message has been re-framed. The positive context works better because health protection and well-being fit our current culture more than health recovery.

> A successful advertisement compared Christmas trees to cut flowers. The advertisement pointed out that the deteriotation of both commences when they are cut and that the advertised Christmas trees were always sold on the day they were cut. This advertisment caught customers' attention because of the association and because it was relevant (consumers only take notice of Christmas tree commercials when they want one, i.e. at Christmas) . The result was measurable both in sales of the product (short term effect) and in the brand equities of quality and service (long term effect).

# FRIDAY

Sometimes advertising is too clever and customers fail to link the advertisement to the product. If the audience love your advertisement, are they transferring this emotion to your brand? The sales figures will tell you the answer.

Your task in relation to communication boils down to: 'What do we want to say, with what, to whom?' The work you have already completed on positioning your brand has prepared you well for this.

## Building brand equity

Effective communication builds the equity of your brand. To achieve this, powerful objectives, strategies and tactics need to be determined.

## Communication objectives

Communication objectives aim to build awareness, understanding and perception of the brand. They create influence. They should inform changing attitudes and preferences. Examples can be to:

- increase sales volume
- persuade customers to try out the product
- increase weight or frequency of purchase
- build brand loyalty
- widen product/service usage
- create interest in the brand
- develop awareness and preference towards the brand
- direct attention away from price increases or other bad news

Week Three

# FRIDAY

- win preference down the trade channel
- define user differences to build sales range

Strictly speaking, sales gains are not a communication objective but a marketing objective (communication does not earn money – it spends it). In actuality, this is unrealistic. Of course you will judge your promotional results against sales performance. If the equity of your brand grows, it will be reflected in increased sales.

Choose two or three of the communication objectives listed above and turn them into precise, measureable outputs for your brand, for example, 'By 31 March, our top ten clients will make us their preferred supplier and order 30 per cent more than 31 March last year.'

With clear objectives you can describe precise outputs that can be measured and tracked. The list below specifies the key result areas.

*Evaluating advertising:*

- Is it relevant to its audience?
- Does it specifically attract sales?
- Does it build brand values?
- Is it memorable, distinctive and on strategy?
- Is it positive and action oriented?

## Communications strategy

An effective communications strategy will cover the following areas:

**1** Brand essence

Week Three

# FRIDAY

2 Brand positioning
3 Integration
4 Creative treatment
5 Selection of media and tools
6 Push and pull strategies
7 Burst and drip advertising

*Brand essence and positioning*

Your brand essence and positioning are in place. They will appear in the copy strategy that you will develop shortly. Your copy strategy will be used to direct operations.

*Integration*

A key consideration must be how to ensure that messages are integrated to deliver a sufficient degree of coherence. Failure here can result in your target audience receiving messages that are contradictory and confusing.

*Creative treatment*

The essence of the creative treatment is in your positioning statement. This will need to be translated into a briefing document.

*Selection of media and tools*

Media and tool selection is covered in the next section.

*Push and pull strategies*

A major strategic consideration is the promotion of the brand identity and reputation of the business. Strategies to attract customers or consumers are often called pull strategies. These centre on the pulling power of the brand, developed by talking to customers and consumers. Strategies to win distribution and trade battles are sometimes called push strategies. These focus on the drive down the trade channels through to the point of purchase. You need both.

Week Three

# FRIDAY

*Burst and drip advertising*
You will need to decide whether you are going to hit hard by squeezing a large proportion of budget into a short period of time or whether you will space your campaign out over a longer period. The most common approach is to use bursts of intense advertising at peak periods with a much lower intensity of effort throughout the remainder of the planned period (burst and drip).

## Tactical development

This work is normally carried out by an advertising agency. The information covered in this section provides you with an overview of the creative techniques they may employ.

This is the fun part of marketing communications. It involves devices such as logos and signatures, characters like Lara Croft, memorable slogans, for example, 'A Mars a day helps you work rest and play' and clever packaging like the special jars and bottles of Bovril and Heinz Salad Cream. Inspirational use of these devices can create a strong presence down the trade channels as well as in promotional work.

The message you design needs to persuade your audience, not yourself. The required outcome is to persuade your target audience to behave the way that you want them to. Agencies employ a wide range of techniques to ensure that your message is powerfully received. Some of the most common are outlined below.

*Metaphors and metonymy*
A metaphor is a story that illustrates a point. Stories are frequently used in advertising to engage attention.

# FRIDAY
*Week Three*

Metonymy utilises one aspect of an item to emphasise the whole. The 'Cream of Boddingtons' campaign is an excellent example of this.

*Memorability*
Memorability is essential. Repetition is memorable. Being first is memorable. Who was the first person to climb Mount Everest? Who was the second?

> **Golden rule**
> Awareness of a brand is useless in itself. The awareness needs to be linked to relevance and preference. Brands need to progress to a customer's shopping list.

*Word power*
Frost damage results from broken freezer bags, but describing frost damage as Freezer Burn has sold many more bags. Acid rain probably won more research funds than pollution ever did.

*Endorsement*
A famous German advertisement compared a group of grafitti sprayers to a dog peeing up a wall. The young audience roared with laughter – the graffiti artists were laughed at by their peer group and the incidence of graffiti damage shrank. Successful advertising needs powerful endorsement because it supplies a reason to believe. Brands utilise endorsement to link themselves to believable sources and become endorsements themselves for their sub-brands. In some countries, Nestlé sells KitKat and in others KitKat sells Nestlé.

*Positive thinking and talking*

A traditional rule of advertising is to avoid negative statements.

In your mind's eye picture a cuddly toy. Now picture not a cuddly toy. Can you do that? If you recalled a picture of another cuddly toy you have got the point. Negatives are language constructs with no tangible reality and so they are hard to conceptualise. Consequently, advertising your brand as not poisonous will associate it with poison in the mind of your target audience.

## Copy strategy and briefing

This document guides policy and protects the equity of the brand, ensuring long-term consistency. It also keeps campaign work on strategy. Use it to make clear what you want, leaving enough room for creativity to flourish. Avoid jargon and consultant speak – it gets in the way of communication. Much poor advertising occurs because clients fail to communicate their wants clearly. Reject any creative work which fails to conform to the plan.

A well-written copy strategy will contain the following elements:

> - *Brand integrity*: the key characteristics of the brand. This section will specify the brand anatomy, its personality and essence. Your brand identity statement has done this job already. Make sure that intellectual property is legally protected and that there is clarity about who owns what.

## FRIDAY

Week Three

- *Background*: illustrate previous work that has been done. Give enough background to make it clear where the brand has come from.
- *Brand Positioning*: use the statement that you have already prepared.
- *What is the advertising hoping to achieve?*: turn your objectives into output, i.e. what you expect to happen as a result of the communication campaign. Spell it out.
- *The target markets*: write a description of your target audience in plain but warm words. You need to like them to sell to them. Avoid words like contemporary and relevant as in 'Making the brand contemporary and relevant!' Say, 'We need to demonstrate that the brand is up to date and in touch with its audience.' Remember, your audience may include decision makers, influencers and buyers, in addition to end users.

  Be prepared to make sacrifices, i.e. deliberately giving up some consumer opportunities in order to be compelling to the remainder. The choice lies between taking a broad or a narrow position. A broad position may lead you to miss completely.
- *The proof*: this is your endorsement or substantiation – the proof that what you are saying is true. This is drawn from your positioning statement.
- *Tone of voice*: this is drawn from your brand identity statement.

Write a copy strategy for your brand, following the format shown above.

# Week Three
## FRIDAY

## Selecting media and tools

*A useful distinction between communication methods*
Communication can be directed towards individuals as in direct marketing or towards groups of individuals as in advertising. The first is very personal (and potentially intrusive if you get it wrong). The second is much more likely to create discussion (word of mouth in the jargon). The two communication methods are not in competition because they produce entirely different results. One-to-many communication can make you famous whereas one-to-one builds relationships. The table below lists some of the options available.

| Media | Tools |
| --- | --- |
| Advertising | Sales promotion and sampling |
| • Display and classified | Merchandising and packaging |
| • Terrestrial television | Customer service |
| • Satellite and cable | Public relations |
| • Video | Direct marketing |
| • Press, print | Personal selling |
| • Cinema | Exhibitions, demonstrations, events |
| • Outdoor | Sponsorship |
| • Radio | Product placement |
| • Cyberspace | Relationship marketing |
| • Ambient | Guerrilla marketing |

## Media buying and advertising

Buying media is best left to specialists When choosing advertising and media agencies a good place to start is the

Week Three

# FRIDAY

Incorporated Society of British Advertisers (ISBA) who will advise on best practice and agency selection.

## Selecting tools

There are a variety of tools available to you.

*Sales promotion*

Sales promotion is a skill in its own right, offering as much scope for ingenuity and brand development as advertising. Furthermore, the £8 billion UK spend far exceeds all the money spent on advertising. Substantial investment here needs to be supported by a specialist agency. Sales promotion splits into four types:

1 *Price promotions*: common examples are 'cash back' and 'no VAT'.
2 *Value promotions*: these include such things as larger packs and consumer games and competitions.
3 *Now or later*: this can be applied to both price and value promotions. The offer can be given immediately at purchase or delayed by the means of coupon collection, etc. Levels of offer redemption can be an unknown quantity in delayed promotions and this can be catastrophic. Sales promotion disasters fill the black museums of marketing.

### Viral

Viral marketing is a term coined to describe the success of Hotmail in advertising its free service on its e-mail banner. This action was largely responsible for 12 million new customers. This is because an e-mail

# Week Three
# FRIDAY

> message can be exponential. In other words, e-mail users gossip by posting items attachments to one another. One young lady sent a saucy e-mail to her boyfriend who promptly copied in his friends. This ungentlemanly act reportedly led to 10 million readers within a number of days.
>
> **Buzz**
> Similar to viral but outside the internet. Using clever ideas that will spread by word of mouth.

4 *Sales promotion strategy*: 'What do you want to achieve, with what?' is the question that underpins effective sales promotions. What outcome will be linked to what mechanic (i.e. competition, special offer)? There is no limit to the creative cunning that can be used.

> Reggie the Bath Duck is an example of a mechanic employed by a hotel chain. He inhabited guests' bathrooms and an accompanying text invited guests to float him in the bath or send him free of charge to a friend or a child. The objective, to build referrals from established guests, was a great success.

A key to building value into sales promotions is the creative use of partnerships. A promotional specialist might buy surplus tickets from an airline at a low price and sell them on to a marketer who produces an offer that requires the winner to travel free but with a friend. Of course the friend must pay the standard price and so the cost of the flight is recovered. Everyone wins.

# FRIDAY

*Week Three*

## Public relations

Public Relations (PR) specialists play a vital role in many marketing operations. Marketing PR is a term sometimes used to identify PR activities that are built into the marketing plan.

> The announcement by Heinz that they might have to remove Salad Cream from their list created an outpouring of love for the brand. This is marketing PR in action.

## Design agencies

Design has an important role to play in identity management, packaging and elsewhere. For many brands, design is as important as advertising. For example, a retail store is by far the most important advertising message from the retailer. If the shopping environment and experience is poor they fail.

## Personal selling

Skilled personal selling, when backed by promotional material, is far more effective for a small target audience than advertising can ever be. It is dependent, however, on the ability and skills of the salesperson. In this instance, recruitment and training enter the marketing mix.

A marketing campaign might be designed as follows:

- *Leader (first wave)*: advertise nationally on local radio to build awareness.
- *Middle (second wave)*: sales promotion to provide added incentives.
- *End (final wave)*: direct mail to build loyalty.

Review the media and marketing tools covered above and decide how the promotional campaign for your brand should be structured.

## Timetable and budget

The only logical approach is to decide what you need to achieve and whether the result will be a justifiable return on the investment.

## Controls and contingency

It makes sense to keep some funds in reserve to reinforce success. Controls should include variance analysis against the budget. Individual agencies should be tasked with monitoring their own performances, although the use of a specialist as a third-party analyst ensures objectivity. Sales uplifts should be included. Put them in a separate section because they are influenced by circumstances detached from this plan.

Focus groups, tracking studies (more about these tomorrow) and recall tests can be used. Most importantly, if your objectives are specific and measurable it will be possible to monitor and evaluate them effectively.

## Summary

The world of marketing communications is vast, with hosts of specialists and terrifying costs. This chapter has considered the most important issues involved, i.e. the messages the brand needs to send out to its audience and the media and tools that can be used to carry them.

# SATURDAY

# Managing the plan

- review of the process
- preparing, managing and presenting the plan
- concluding thoughts

## Completing the plan

You are now at the final stage of the brand planning process – pulling your brand plan together. Once you have a finalised brand plan, you need to move from concept to action by completing a project plan. You may need to present your plan to senior managers and so today you shall cover a suggested format for this purpose. Finally, you will need to finalise tracking procedures to measure results and make changes.

## Completing your brand plan

By now, the key elements established by your analysis should have directed you towards a clear identity and positioning for your brand. Over the last two days you have

Week Three

# SATURDAY

worked through possible vector strategies, hopefully making some selections, and pinpointed the key issues driving your product, logistic and communication plans. Your decisions concerning the growth drivers and vectors for your brand, made in the context of your brand identity and positioning, comprise your brand plan. The complete process is summarised in Figure 18.

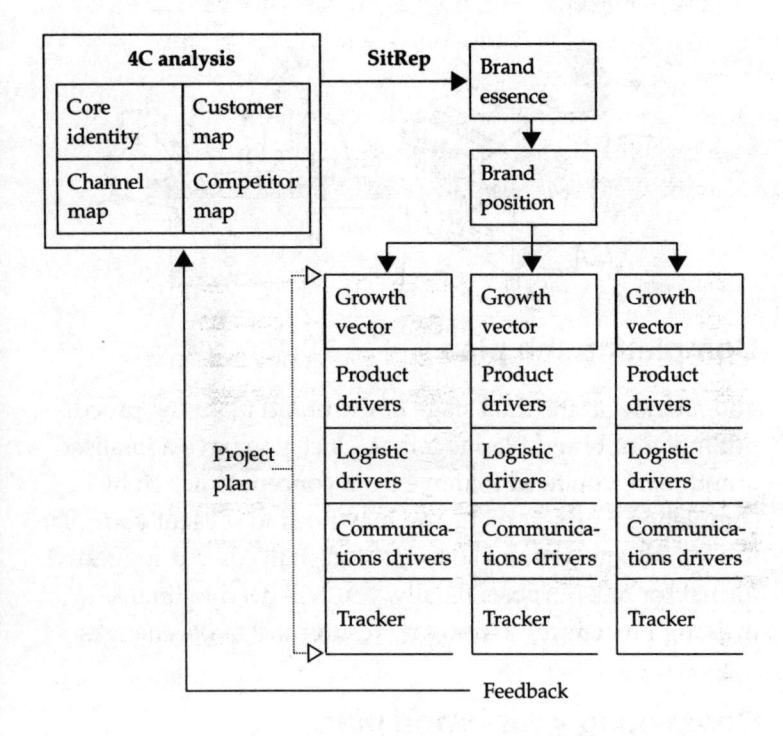

Figure 18. The planning process

Remember, the brand identity must be a consistent beacon throughout your plan. Your brand must be represented in harmony with its identity in everything you do, from defining your growth strategies to point of sale. In other words, the brand must behave how you designed it to.

The positioning of your brand is the focus of the plan. This is what the brand says when it speaks. Just as with good literature, your brand's dialogue must always be true to character. If it was Boddingtons it would say 'creamy' in an amusing, Mancunian manner. If it was Nike it would be living for sport and behaving a touch dangerously. Your brand's positioning must inform all three growth drivers: products and services, logistics and communications.

> If Rolls Royce is positioned as the ultimate car, its product specification and price will be premium, its channels will be exclusive and will deliver outstanding service and its communications will be limited to a selected, exclusive media.

The growth vectors are your chosen growth strategies, selected from all the possible routes. Avoid choosing dozens. Two will be a challenge for most brands.

The growth drivers in your plan are the focal points of your marketing mix.

## Products

For each growth vector you need to map out a product plan over 12 months, covering financial forecasts, product specifications, packaging and a pricing plan. Your sales forecast should be based on historical data in relation to an average month. Remember to smooth out the bumps that were the result of one-off events. Adjust the results to take account of your forecast for the next year's trading, including predicted consumer spending, inflation and predicted changes in your business sector, especially price increases. Then adjust the result for seasonal changes, mirroring the historical record from last year. Finally, add your growth projection. Be bold but not crazy. Rampaging growth is extremely hard to manage.

## Logistics

You will need to consider logistics in relation to your products, distribution and channels and quality. Using your product plan, make certain that you can make or buy the necessary components required to meet your product plan. In other words, can you get the right products to the right people at the right price, place and time? Adjust the product plan only if you are certain that the logistics are unattainable. Remember that quality is a vital equity and your customers' perception of the quality of your brand must be protected at all times. Refer to your channel analysis from Tuesday.

## Communications

Your copy strategy for your brand specifies what the brand will say, to whom and with what proof. You will need to make your decisions about what media and tools to use. Use either advertising, sponsorship, PR or the sales team, backed with appropriate literature, to start the campaign.

# SATURDAY

Week Three

Use promotional tools, such as sales promotions to support the campaign later on and consider direct approaches to build and reinforce loyalty towards the end. Seasonality will be a vital factor in timing the campaign to support the major sales drives. Use bursts of activity at key periods and space some spending out over the remaining time as reminders. If a big budget is to be spent, make certain that professional help is used. Even if you are spending a small budget, remember that the media world is a jungle and think twice about entering without a guide.

## Integration

The three pieces of work, which selected the drivers of the brand strategy (Product, Logistical and Communication drivers), should be mapped out onto a calendar and carefully matched to ensure that the product plan is delivered by the logistics and communication plans. Finally, all of it should support and deliver the brand's positioning.

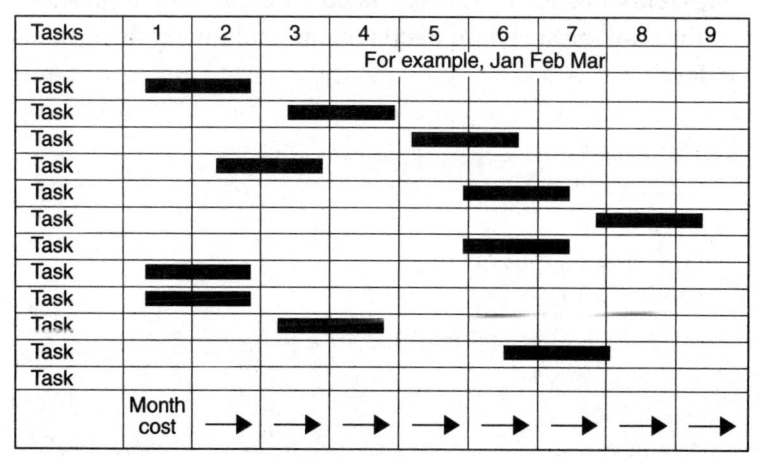

| Tasks | 1 | 2 | 3 | 4 | 5 | 6 | 7 | 8 | 9 |
|-------|---|---|---|---|---|---|---|---|---|
|       |   |   |   | For example, Jan Feb Mar |   |   |   |   |   |
| Task  | ■ |   |   |   |   |   |   |   |   |
| Task  |   |   | ■ |   |   |   |   |   |   |
| Task  |   |   |   |   | ■ |   |   |   |   |
| Task  |   | ■ |   |   |   |   |   |   |   |
| Task  |   |   |   |   |   | ■ |   |   |   |
| Task  |   |   |   |   |   |   |   | ■ |   |
| Task  |   |   |   |   |   | ■ |   |   |   |
| Task  | ■ |   |   |   |   |   |   |   |   |
| Task  | ■ |   |   |   |   |   |   |   |   |
| Task  |   |   | ■ |   |   |   |   |   |   |
| Task  |   |   |   |   |   | ■ |   |   |   |
| Task  |   |   |   |   |   |   |   |   |   |
|       | Month cost | → | → | → | → | → | → | → | → |

Figure 19. The Gantt chart

Week Three

# SATURDAY

Named after its creator, the Gantt chart is a good way to chart the product, logistic and communication tasks. Make a list of the tasks down the left-hand side and mark the calendar section with a line indicating the completion time for each task. For big brands, the three components will need separate charts. The various tasks can be costed downwards on the calendar, giving a monthly total expenditure that can be added up to establish the full year's expenditure.

## Creating a formal Plan

The Gantt chart and diary objectives form your working documents. However you will probably need to create a formal document for presentation to senior management. Formal marketing plans have a tendency to make a grand entrance and a mouse-like exit. Cupboards everywhere are full of them. Workable planning lies in the processes explained in this book. If you need a formal plan to present to the bank or the board keep it simple following the format below:

**Introduction**
1 Objectives
2 Strategy
3 Elements (the mix)
4 Programme
5 Budget (cost of plan and outcome)
6 Responsibility
7 Controls
**Summary**

# Week Three
## SATURDAY

Finally, make sure you have complied with company procedures and that lead times are taken fully into account. Go back through your arguments. Have you made a strong case? What are the key points? Concentrate on the strongest two or three points and justify them with well thought out arguments.

## Review of the marketing planning process

The work you have completed today has produced a project plan and a formal presentation document with which you are well armed to win the commitment and resources you need to live your ideas. You have now completed the full planning process and have created a powerful plan for your brand. Congratulations!

## Summary

*Quality*
Consistancy and quality are the hallmark of great brands. A Mars Bar is always a Mars Bar. It does not vary in quality, the taste is consistantly the same. Quality is relative and perceived. Relative because it is relatively better than its competitors and perceived because its quality resides in the perception of its consumers. It is only great quality if they believe it. Branding cannot offer protection for shoddy work.

*What if it all goes wrong?*
A brand is like a bubble. It can grow and become all encompassing but it can also burst. There is evidence to suggest that the best response, if things go wrong, is to own up. The public will forgive and forget errors but not

Week Three

# SATURDAY

mendacity. For many years, Marks & Spencer made a virtue out of mistakes when they inevitably occurred. A faulty product would be massively advertised. 'It is no good! Send it back for a full refund, our apologies and all sorts of goodies!' The results were invariably brand-reinforcing and very positive. What a great company! Brands can, and do, recover from disaster.

*What never to do*

> **How to kill brands dead**
> - Bring out innumerable line extensions that do not fit the brand and which the consumers do not want.
> - Cut prices and devalue them, stripping out value and profit for reinvestment.
> - Bring in a brand manager with little or no experience and watch him or her change everything just for the sake of it, before leaving to get another job.
> - Focus everything on this month's performance and to hell with the longer run.
> - Spend a fortune on research and then run the same boring advertisements as everyone else.
> - Make a plan that faithfully records the past and ignores what might happen next.
> - Do nothing until you have run some focus groups and then do everything they say.

*Think for yourself*
Marketing today is less about communicating effectively and more about developing good ideas that stand out from the incessant noise of saturation broadcasting, tedious direct

# SATURDAY

mail and intrusive telephone calls. The best way to build customer relations is by being interesting enough to attract their attention.

*Playing a different tune*

Every business segment or category has rules. These rules are often unspoken, for example, serious newspapers are broadsheet and popular ones tabloid. If they are valued by your customers, then breaking them is risky. Many of the big gains in business, however, come from ignoring these rules.

Good luck!

# Direct Marketing

**DEE TWOMEY**

**WEEK FOUR**

# C O N T E N T S

# Week Four

| | | |
|---|---|---|
| **Introduction** | | 291 |
| **Sunday** | Customers, competitors and capability | 292 |
| **Monday** | Planning your strategy and setting objectives | 304 |
| **Tuesday** | Finding and keeping the right customers | 315 |
| **Wednesday** | Building and using your marketing database | 329 |
| **Thursday** | Selecting the right media | 343 |
| **Friday** | Creating and executing campaigns | 355 |
| **Saturday** | Measurement and management of success | 366 |

## Acknowledgements

*To my three fine sons Louis, George and Joe*

Thanks to Sighle, my mum, for her extraordinary kindness.
Special thanks to Mark, ever the voice of reason.

Thanks also to the many professional enthusiasts who have shared their wisdom along the way. It's been fun.

# INTRODUCTION

*Week Four*

Direct marketing has seen a sustained and dramatic rise in importance. Over the last year alone, expenditure grew by 10 per cent on all forms of direct marketing. You would be hard pressed to find an organisation or industry that is not using direct marketing to help achieve its aims. This sector is now worth over £11 billion, according to the Direct Marketing Association (census 2001/02). Skilled direct marketers are very much in demand.

The term direct marketing is a convenient shorthand for the process of recording information about an individual's responses to plan, target and implement marketing activity, in order to win and keep customers.

Computing power has allowed direct marketing to evolve. Instead of running blanket advertising campaigns designed for the typical customer, you can now develop a dialogue with a real individual and track what happens over time.

Technology continues to move direct marketing forward. Call centre spend now exceeds spend on direct mail and internet integration has become a vital consideration.

Add direct marketing skills to your portfolio and become a key player in the business of acquiring, developing and retaining customers.

Your journey to direct marketing success will take you through seven crucial steps, from taking stock of your current situation through to measuring the results of your carefully managed plans and campaigns.

Week Four

# S U N D A Y

# Customers, competitors and capability

Prepare yourself for a stimulating week, tackling the concepts and practicalities of direct marketing. Today you will take stock of your customers, competitors and your own organisation's direct marketing capability. This forms a solid knowledge base upon which you can develop your strategies and campaigns.

## What is direct marketing?

Ask ten different marketing practitioners and you will get ten different answers to this question, for instance:

- 'It's the same thing as database marketing.'
- 'It's like ordinary marketing only it's direct to the customer whether by post, over the phone or on the net.'
- 'It's a sales channel instead of a traditional sales force.'
- 'Call it response marketing and you've summed it up.'

These statements contain some truth, but they are misleading because they do not tell the whole truth. The overriding trademark of direct marketing compared to traditional marketing is that it uses information about customers and prospects at an individual level.

The distinguishing features of direct marketing are:

Week Four

# SUNDAY

> - Customer's insights are based upon individual data.
> - All communication is designed to get a response.
> - Marketing databases facilitate interaction and personalisation.
> - Every aspect of a direct marketing campaign can be tested.
> - Results can be accurately measured.
> - Strategies are based on both customer acquisition and, importantly, on customer retention.

Acquiring a new customer can cost ten times more than keeping an existing customer. Therefore, it makes financial sense to encourage loyalty.

Whether your target customers are consumers or businesses, direct marketing works in the same way.

LOYALTY LADDER

ADVOCATE
CUSTOMER
PROSPECT
SUSPECT

Week Four

# SUNDAY

A wide variety of marketing activity is considered to be direct marketing if it involves a response mechanism, including direct mail, telemarketing, TV and press advertising, web banner ads, door drops and inserts.

Take direct mail as an example and you can see the importance of direct marketing. The Direct Mail Information Service reports that expenditure on direct mail has increased by 150 per cent over the last ten years. Within this time, volumes have doubled with over 4.9 million items mailed in the year 2001, with a split of 75 per cent consumer and 25 per cent business. This activity is worth £2,228 million in the UK alone. It is big and it is growing.

## Taking stock of customers, competitors and capability

Before you start planning, build up your knowledge of:

- *Your customers*: everything you do depends on understanding customers. To develop an effective strategy you must know who your customers are now and who they might be in the future.
- *Your capability*: you need to be sure of what you can and cannot achieve. An audit of your current direct marketing capability is essential.
- *Your competitors*: your customers are not just influenced by your company. They make choices by comparing your company with its competitors. You need to provide a compelling reason for customers to choose you and to stay loyal.

Week Four

# S U N D A Y

## Get to know your customers

Recent research shows that only half of businesses have the ability to analyse the value of individual customers. Around ten per cent of businesses do not know precisely how many customers they have. Many cannot identify why they lose customers or which customers they are most likely to lose next.

To win in direct marketing, having a good understanding of your customers will put you ahead of the pack.

## The right customers

Consider that not all customers are equal. Some will help you and others will hinder you. Like good friends, you should choose your customers carefully.

# Week Four

## SUNDAY

| Good customers | Bad customers |
|---|---|
| High value | Low value |
| Cross-range buyers | Single purchase |
| Open to offers | Responders who never buy |
| Easy to maintain | Persistent complainers |
| Brand respecters | Fraudsters |
| Repeat buyers | High-risk customers |
| Positive opinion leaders | Negative opinion leaders |
| Loyal | Switchers |

Of course the definition of good and bad customers depends on your market. Try to create a definition of your good and bad customers.

## Customer knowledge

Answer these ten critical questions to gain insights into the profile and behaviour of your customers.

1. Who are your customers?
2. What do they buy?
3. When do they buy?
4. How do they buy?
5. Why do they buy?
6. What do they want?
7. Are they satisfied?
8. Are they promotionally responsive?
9. Are they likely to switch?
10. What are they worth?

## What are they worth?

One of the key differences between a good and bad customer is the value they represent to your organisation. There are various ways to assess customer value. The most popular are:

# SUNDAY

- Pareto 80:20 analysis
- recency, frequency, monetary value
- lifetime value

*Pareto 80:20*

You may be familiar with Pareto's 80:20 rule. Applied to business the rule states that 80 per cent of sales are generated by 20 per cent of customers.

The Pareto principle is enlightening. While the ratio may vary for different businesses, the principle is the same. This should alert you to the fact that a few customers are holding your whole organisation together.

Here are some examples for the consumer goods market:

| | | |
|---|---|---|
| Spreadable margarine | 5% customers | 65% sales |
| Canned beer | 15% adults | 90% sales |
| Washing powder | 35% customers | 65% sales |

Week Four
# SUNDAY

By undertaking a Pareto analysis of customers, you have taken an important step towards knowing which customers to target. Recency, frequency and monetary value (RFM) calculations and customer lifetime value (LTV) provide further insights.

*Recency, frequency and monetary value*
The RFM model uses information about past buying behaviour to draw conclusions about customer value. This model was largely developed to assess the relative value of customers buying from catalogues. Key questions are:

- How long ago did they buy?
- How often do they buy?
- How much do they spend?

Look at two book club customers:

| RFM attribute | Mr Eve | Ms Adam |
|---|---|---|
| Recency | Six months ago | This month |
| Frequency | Every three months | Monthly |
| Monetary value | £25 | £10 |

In one year Ms Adam spends £120, while Mr Eve only spends £50, despite having a higher order value.

A combination of recency, frequency and monetary value can be used to create a score for each customer, based upon their past behaviour. The score you develop should reflect the relative value of customers to your particular business. As a general guide, frequency has the greatest impact on customer value as follows:

| Factor | Weighting |
|---|---|
| Recency | Multiply by 2 |
| Frequency | Multiply by 3 |
| Monetary value | Multiply by 1 |

*Lifetime value*

The lifetime value (LTV) model is used to calculate the total worth of a customer for the duration of that time they are your customer.

Using LTV is helpful because:

- A customer is worth much more than their initial purchase or Year 1 value.
- Customer acquisition costs can be offset against future revenues.
- Likely retention rates must be forecast.
- It encourages strategic planning.
- Every organisation must consider what a 'lifetime' means to them – do customers stay for 25 years or three months?
- Future conditions may change, so assumptions can be made clear and varied to test financial sensitivity.

*Simple LTV formula*

LTV can be calculated by:

Average spend (or profit) per purchase × Number of purchases per customer lifetime = LTV.

*Complex LTV formula*

LTV is a forecast of future revenue and thus the value of such 'future' revenue should be discounted back to today's prices. This creates what the accountants call Net Present Value (NPV).

---

**Lifetime value model**

|   |   | Year 1 | Year 2 | Year 3 |
|---|---|--------|--------|--------|
| A | Number of customers | 1000 | 500 | 275 |
| B | Retention rate (% kept into next year) | 50% | 55% | 60% |
| C | Sales per annum per customer | £600 | £600 | £600 |
| D | Total sales (A × C) | £600,000 | £300,000 | £165,000 |
| **Contribution** | | | | |
| E | Net profit @ 20% (D × 20%) | £120,000 | £60,000 | £33,000 |
| **Discounted contribution** | | | | |
| F | Discount rate @ 10% p.a. | 1 | 1.10 | 1.21 |
| G | NPV contribution (E × F) | £120,000 | £54,545 | £27,273 |
| H | Cumulative NPV contribution | £120,000 | £174,545 | £201,818 |
| I | Lifetime value @ NPV for each new customer (H ÷ A in Year 1) | £120 | £174.55 | £201.82 |

---

In this example, 1000 new customers provide a lifetime value of £201 profit each within 3 years.

Use Pareto, RFM and LTV models to help you decide which customers are right for your business.

## Understanding your company's capability

With a clear focus on the right customers, you can really make an impact. However, you need to understand your company's current capability. Get a clear view by answering these ten vital questions. Ask your planners, sales force, agencies, call centre and marketing team. But remember to qualify anecdotal evidence with hard facts.

> 1. What market position does your company hold?
> 2. How does your brand and product compare to the opposition?
> 3. How many stages are there in the sales process?
> 4. What media do you use and why?
> 5. What marketing database capability exists?
> 6. How is direct marketing structured and resourced?
> 7. Is direct marketing represented at Board level?
> 8. What budget is available?
> 9. How do plans get approved?
> 10. What direct marketing expertise is available?

The better you know your current set up, the better placed you are to capitalise upon it and improve it. If a radical overhaul is not possible, be realistic about what you can achieve. The beauty of direct marketing is that you can introduce improvements over time.

## Tuning in to your competitors

It is unusual to have no direct competitors. In fact, your customer may also be your competitor's customer at another time or for another product or service. Where customers can choose between several suppliers, what share of customer spend does your company have on that category of goods? If you had to answer the ten critical customer questions for your competitors' customers, how would your answers differ?

# SUNDAY

Think about how your market will change in future. Which products, regions, services, sectors and channels are going to become more important? Will there be more competition or less? Greater demand or a shrinking market? Where possible, develop predictions about how your competitors may behave in future and how this will impact upon your own situation.

You can access a wealth of information from the professional institutes, via the internet, from public libraries and from your market research department. Companies like Thomson Intermedia and Neilsen Media Research provide a monitoring service covering competitors' TV, press, internet, direct mail and door drop activity.

Remember that your direct marketing activity does not happen in a vacuum. Consider how your competitors do their marketing. To be heard above the noise, you need to be clear about what you have to offer and be clever about how you construct your campaigns.

It is far easier to be successful if you can offer something different and better than the competition. The difference may be:

- brand image
- technical superiority
- innovation
- value for money
- quality of product
- consistency of service delivery
- geographic coverage
- speed of delivery
- customer service

# SUNDAY

*Week Four*

If there is truly no difference between what you can offer to customers and what your competitors offer, then why should anyone choose you? Identify your company's distinctive competence before you begin to develop your direct marketing strategy. Then the fun can really begin.

## Summary

Today you have learnt about the essential features of direct marketing. Direct marketing focuses on marketing to individual customers and prospects. Pareto, RFM and LTV models allow you to identify the right customers to target.

Remember that customer retention is a key strategic goal over and above customer acquisition. This is due to the commercial value of keeping the customers that you have won.

Having reached conclusions about your customers, competitors and direct marketing capability, you are now in a good position to tackle strategic planning and objective setting.

Week Four

# MONDAY

# Planning your strategy and setting objectives

Today you will learn how to develop a direct marketing plan by identifying issues, setting objectives and deciding on strategy. Planning is a crucial stage of direct marketing. It requires clear thinking and creativity to come up with the right approach.

## The importance of planning

There is an old business saying: 'People don't plan to fail, they fail to plan.'

These warning signs indicate poor planning:

- Lack of clarity about the targets to be achieved.
- Inappropriate strategies for the market or organisation.
- Confused messages and policies.
- Unachievable time-scales and unclear responsibilities.

Good planning is apparent when:

- Everyone is clear about their role and company mission.
- The strategy fits the situation.
- Every element of the campaign supports the overall message.
- The action plan is realistic with clear interim deadlines.

Week Four

# MONDAY

## Situational analysis

Start with a situational analysis. It allows you to consolidate the information you have on your own capability, customers, competitors and the market place. This entails defining your organisation aims, compiling a SWOT analysis and identifying issues.

## Organisation aims

Start by writing down the broad aims or mission of your organisation. This may be very easy or very difficult, depending upon the volatility of your market and the clarity of your company's mission. Here are some examples of organisation aims:

- To be the leading online banking company.
- To provide the highest quality business travel experience.
- To be amongst the top three electronic component manufacturers.

Once you have clarified why your company exists and whom it serves, you can perform a SWOT analysis.

## SWOT up

Organise the information you have gathered about your customers, capability and competitors into a SWOT analysis as discussed in the first week of this book.

## Identify the real issues

From the SWOT analysis, decide which things are the fundamental issues and challenges.

For the mobile telecoms company, issues might include:

- The need for detailed research and database analysis to gain understanding of customers.
- Improvement in speed of product development and launch.
- The need to increase customer loyalty.

Take care to make the issues as precise as possible. Use available research, management information and the customer database to prioritise the key issues. By understanding where you are now, you can plan for where you want to be tomorrow.

Week Four

# MONDAY

## Destination, direction and delivery

Let's turn to the main elements of the planning process.

| Destination | Objective | Where do you want to get to? |
| Direction | Strategy | How will you get there? |
| Delivery | Plan | What steps will you take to get there? |

Your objective is the destination you want to reach. The strategy you select is the one that you feel gives you the best chance of getting there. Detailed action plans are then required to deliver the strategy.

## Setting objectives

The higher you go within an organisation, the more you will be called upon to set objectives and strategy, and the less time you will have to handle implementation of plans. The most common types of corporate goals are:

- to grow market share
- to increase sales
- to improve profits
- to reduce costs

Within these company goals, the role direct marketing plays will vary and can result in these broad objectives:

Week Four

# MONDAY

- To find new customers.
- To retain customers for longer.
- To attract non-users and/or competitors' customers.
- To increase the frequency of purchase.
- To increase average order values.
- To introduce differential pricing.
- To reduce costs of acquiring and servicing customers.
- To generate incremental sales from existing customers.
- To introduce or exploit certain distribution channels.

## Golden rules for setting objectives

Unless you are specific about your destination, how will you know when you have got there? Set precise objectives. Check them against the SMART criteria we discussed in Week Two of this book.

Here are a couple of SMART objectives:

- We will increase online sales from our core sports catalogue from £700 to £780 million by year end.
- We will increase our business customer base from 4000 to 6000 by 2010.

Your objective represents your destination. Now that you know where you are going, how will you get there?

Week Four

# MONDAY

## Strategic direction

Consider the marketplace and your organisation's position within it. Decide how you will compete for business.

There are many strategic choices to be made, starting with deciding which markets (or market segments) to compete in and then how to compete.

## Which markets? What profit?

Choose which markets (or segments within a market) to compete in by assessing the opportunity they represent. Consider the impact of alternatives by using the PROFIT model:

- **P** Potential – market size and growth
- **R** Risk – degree of risk and chance of success
- **O** Obstructions – market accessibility and barriers to entry
- **F** Fit – appropriateness and fit with your business
- **I** Investment – scale of investment required
- **T** Turnover – revenue and profit available

Your choices can be summarised by looking at which markets you will compete in and with which products.

|         |          | **Products**       |                     |
|---------|----------|--------------------|---------------------|
|         |          | Existing           | New                 |
| **Markets** | Existing | Market penetration | Product development |
|         | New      | Market extension   | Diversification     |

Week Four

# MONDAY

## Strategic choices

Work through the strategic dimensions listed here to decide upon your direct marketing strategy.

- Existing or new markets.
- Acquire new customers or retain existing customers.
- Retain, develop, replace or create entirely new brand.
- Target customers or prospects and current segments, select segments or new segments.
- Convert competitors' customers or attract non-users.
- Increase order value (up-sell) or increase customer value (cross-sell).
- Build the customer database or maintain and utilise it.
- Refine media focus or expand media coverage.
- Communicate with customers more often or less often.
- Distribute exclusively directly to the customer or via wholesale, retail, agents, company salesperson or dovetail with these channels.
- Position competitive offering based on quality, price, speed, size, reach, accessibility, service, range or image.
- Promote existing product, develop, extend range, replace or update.
- Price as high or low cost, select terms and payment methods.
- Innovate to be a trailblazer or competent follower.
- Sell via a one-stage or two-stage process (i.e. order now versus send for information).
- Attract responses in person, by internet, phone or coupon.
- Promote via telemarketing, direct mail, TV, press, inserts, door drops, web banner ads and links or e-mail.

Week Four

# M O N D A Y

Having read this list you will realise that these are not all absolute choices between one approach and another. It is possible, even desirable, to adopt a strategy of retaining existing customers while planning to acquire new customers.

Even the most successful business, with a high degree of customer loyalty, will experience a natural attrition. This happens as existing consumers move, change their lifestyle or pass away and as business customers move, merge, rationalise or cease trading.

## Strategic difference

Compared to other facets of marketing, direct marketing strategy usually encompasses:

- market segmentation
- customer acquisition strategy
- customer retention strategy
- database building and utilisation
- targeted media selection
- testing

Week Four

# MONDAY

Make certain that your strategy includes these important aspects.

Be sure that every issue you have identified in the situational analysis is addressed through your strategy. Involve key players in the process and stimulate fresh thinking and creative solutions.

## Turning dreams into reality

Once you have decided on your strategic approach, you must develop a campaign plan to bring your strategy to life. We will explain targeting, databases, media and campaign planning in the next chapters. At this stage, you need to know that a campaign plan clearly lays out what must be done, when and by whom. The plan is the mechanism through which you can deliver your strategy and achieve your direct marketing goals.

## Writing your direct marketing strategy

To gain agreement to your strategic approach, write a succinct report. Within it, explain why you recommend this particular direction, how it will work, what it will cost and what the payback will be. The format of this report should include the following sections.

*An overview*
- *Executive summary*: one-page précis of objectives, issues, strategy, budget and financial justification.

*Background*
- *Terms of reference*: who has commissioned the report, its

purpose, sources of information and background.
- *Situational analysis*: brief review of the market, company, capability, customers and competitors.
- *Learnings from past campaigns*: conclusions from past activity based on analysis of facts, not hearsay.
- *Issues*: the major obstacles facing the business.

*Objectives, recommended strategy and campaigns*
- *Objectives*: SMART aims, often expressed as profit or sales revenue, numbers of new customers, registrations on to loyalty schemes or websites, often covering a three-year period.
- *Strategic recommendation*: the overall strategic approach to be adopted, together with the budget requirement, covering the chosen market, acquisition and retention, research and analysis, database and media.
- *Operational campaign plan*: detailed action plans for Year 1 and outline actions for Years 2–3, showing how the strategy will be implemented, including responsibilities, deadlines and interim targets.

*Contingencies, financials and assumptions*
- *Contingencies*: anticipated action if you do not meet or exceed plan targets, if market conditions change, if regulations change, if competitors take certain actions.
- *Budget*: the budget required to implement the campaign, broken down by activity type.
- *Financial justification*: showing the cost-benefit of the strategy. Typically including a return on investment (ROI) and lifetime value analysis.
- *Assumptions*: setting out the judgements that have been made to develop the plan, e.g. interest rates, attrition rates, response rates.

*Detailed analysis, schedules and projections*
- *Appendices*: includes all the detailed analysis to support the conclusions of the strategy, campaign time-scales, media schedules and detailed response and conversion projections.

## Summary

Today you have found out about setting objectives and developing a direct marketing strategy. Remember to:

- Develop your plans based on an understanding of your company's aims and situation.
- Complete a SWOT analysis and identify the key issues.
- Get SMART by setting objectives which are specific, measurable, accurate and aspirational, realistic and time-bound.
- Select the strategic direction that can deliver your company to its chosen destination.
- Ensure that your strategy includes research and analysis, acquisition, retention, database development, segmentation and targeted media.
- Bring your strategy to life with an operational campaign plan.
- Put your strategy in writing to gain agreement and get the go-ahead from your organisation.

Time spent planning is rarely wasted. It means you are well placed to develop alternatives if problems arise. It also means that you can exploit opportunities as they arise. Preparation is the direct marketer's friend.

**TUESDAY**

# Finding and keeping the right customers

You now know how to assess customer value through techniques such as Pareto 80:20, lifetime value and recency frequency and monetary value analysis. Yet how do you find and keep the right customers? Segmentation and targeting provide the solution.

## How does segmentation help?

Direct marketing is all about communicating with individuals on a personal basis. However, how can you make sense of large volumes of data to target customers and potential customers? Segmentation allows you to divide up your market into customer groups or segments. Customers within a segment are similar to each other and dissimilar to other groups of customers in other segments.

Week Four
# TUESDAY

Segmentation then, is used to understand individual customers in the market place and to group them together to form distinct segments which are identifiable, accessible and substantial.

At its simplest, a consumer segmentation may be:

- non-user
- competitor's customer
- low-value customer
- high-value customer

For business markets, simple segmentation may be:

- small company
- medium company
- large company

In business markets, segmentation is often used to make selling more cost effective by prioritising the companies that require regular face-to-face salespeople and that can be served better by telesales and direct distribution.

## How to segment

Market segmentation involves finding out the key drivers that distinguish one group of customers from another.

The key drivers of consumer market segmentation tend to be:

1 Geo-demographic – who they are: age, gender, class, location
2 Lifestyle – how they live: income, occupation,

# TUESDAY

family/household composition, interests
3 Attitudinal – why they buy: motivation to select your product, e.g. price, image, application, benefit
4 Transactional – what, how and how much they buy

The key drivers of business segmentation are:

1 Company size – by turnover, employees, growth
2 Industry sector – nature of business, market place
3 Company location – geographic location and environment
4 Purchases and people – products bought, value and method of purchase, buying policy and role in decision-making process

Statistical modelling techniques can be used to isolate the key drivers and to identify customer clusters or groups. Alternatively, you can use off-the-shelf segmentation classification systems.

# TUESDAY

## Off-the-peg segmentation systems

Ready-made segmentation systems can be extremely useful where you have limited data on your prospects and customers.

Geo-demographic consumer systems use individual Census data such as age and home ownership, to classify postcodes into neighbourhood types. The resulting segments are self-explanatory: for example: well off, white-collar families with older children. By providing a customer list with postcodes, you can classify which segment your customers belong to. Consumer segmentation products include:

- Acorn from CACI, UK geo-demographic founder.
- Cameo from EuroDirect.
- Mosaic from Experian.
- Prizm and Psycl£ from Claritas.

Specialist products also exist: for instance, Scottish Acorn, Financial Mosaic and Cameo Property.

Basic business segmentation can be achieved using information about limited and public companies, made available through Companies House classifications:

- Standard Industry Code (SIC) classification by industry sector.
- Size of company.

Segmentation, whether bespoke or off the shelf, helps to make sense of customers and prospects in the marketplace. It allows you to decide which segments to target within your campaigns.

Week Four

# T U E S D A Y

## What is targeting?

Forget the need for a bow and arrow, with 'targeting' you aim for the target by reaching the right customers, in the right place, with the right message and at the right time.

Targeting is the process of identifying and reaching specific individuals in order to attract and retain them as customers. All targeting is designed to elicit a response in the most cost-effective manner.

## The importance of targeting

When developing a direct marketing campaign, in addition to the product or service by segment, you need to consider:

1 Targeting
2 Offer
3 Timing
4 Creative (design and copywriting treatment)
5 Response mechanism

These factors are ranked in priority order, following the test

Week Four

# TUESDAY

results of an extensive consumer campaign (study by Ogilvy and Mather), and experience of other campaigns supports this ranking. A change of creative or response device can create a small improvement in results. Targeting, however, can account for an improvement of six times the response, comparing the best to worst performing list of names and addresses.

Remember this if your senior manager critiques your next planned campaign. It is human nature for creative concepts to spark off opinions from just about everyone. Nevertheless, while creative treatments are important, targeting has the greatest impact on results.

## Who will you target?

Create a target profile that describes who you are targeting. Consider the following targeting dimensions for consumers and businesses.

*Consumer*

- Which segment?
- Status – prospect or customer.
- Value – high, medium or low value.
- Products and services used.
- Geodemographic profile – age, gender, location.
- Lifestage – e.g. young family, retired.
- Attitudes – e.g. brand loyal or not.
- Lifestyle – e.g. struggling to survive or wealthy professional.

Week Four

# TUESDAY

*Business-to-business*

Many of the consumer dimensions still apply. Also consider:

- Role – decision maker, influencer, gatekeeper.
- Past contact – none, responded, had appointment.
- Company type – plc, ltd, partnership, sole trader.
- Sector – industry sector.
- Location type – high street, industrial park or campus.

## Golden rules of targeting

- Ensure your targeting supports your strategy.
- Describe your target profile as fully as possible, highlighting the most important customer attributes.
- Specify who you do not want to attract, as well as who you do.
- Create a targeting shorthand so that it can be understood, e.g. committed online purchasers.
- Get scientific – use all the research and database analysis at your disposal.
- Assess your choices of media, offer, timing, format and creative through your prospects' eyes.
- Do not pay twice to reach the same people – eliminate potential duplicates.
- Establish benchmark performance levels or controls and monitor results against these controls.

## Types of targeting

Direct marketing is all about communicating with individuals. All media carries a call to action in order to encourage target customers to respond. Then we can gather individual data and make a sale. There are two types of targeting:

1 *Personalised targeting*: where you have individual's name and address records either on your database or from a bought-in list. For targeting using individual data, typical media are direct mail, telemarketing, e-mail and mobile short message service (SMS) text messaging.
2 *Broad-scale targeting*: where you do not have individual data – yet. When targeting without individual data, typical media are TV, press, door drops, internet banner ads and hyperlinks, directory listings and in-store point of sale.

## Personalised targeting

With a prospect and customer database, you can select the individuals you want to target with personalised communications. You can also make selections from external lists for prospecting purposes. Profiling and cloning techniques can help you to target more precisely.

Week Four

# TUESDAY

*Database selections*

Accurate database targeting relies on the ability to select the target customer group that you have defined. This means that the data you hold for individuals must reflect the criteria for your target.

Take the example of a direct music business. It has a new boxed jazz collection available on CD. It wants to target high spending customers who love jazz. To be able to do so their database must record:

- Which individuals have bought (as opposed to simply enquired).
- Whether the CDs they have bought include jazz (all CD titles must be categorised by type of music).
- What they have spent by type of music and in total (sales over time must be grouped by customer, not simply recorded per mailshot or per product).

*Exclude the bad, mad and sad*

When defining the selections, make sure you state the exclusions you want.

Potential exclusions:

- Opt outs – consumers asking not to be contacted, i.e. 'Do not mail me' and 'Unsubscribe' responses.
- Unacceptable credit scores.
- Incomplete name and address.
- Gone aways – where mail and e-mail is undeliverable.
- Mail, fax, phone or e-mail preference service suppressions (separate list of people who do not

# Week Four
# TUESDAY

> want to be contacted for marketing purposes).
> - Deceased – bereavement register and mortality suppressions (compiled from the Register of Births and Deaths).
> - Postcodes outside of the catchment area.

The exact exclusions will depend on the nature of your business and the campaign.

*Using lists for targeting*

When you need to find new customers, you can make use of consumer and business lists. Data including name, address, phone number, fax and e-mail can be obtained, normally on a rental basis. There are many types of lists:

> - consumer lifestyle lists, such as Consodata and Experian.
> - magazine subscriber lists.
> - business lists.
> - catalogue customers.
> - event attendees lists.

Selection criteria can be set in exactly the same way as your own database.

*Profiling and cloning*

Profiling is the process of identifying the discriminating characteristics of your customers. For example, a financial services company selling home insurance can carry out statistical modelling work to compare the characteristics of customers and unconverted enquirers. It may find that uptake improves if the person is aged 30–50, owns their own home and lives in leafy suburbs.

Week Four

## TUESDAY

The company can use this information to improve its targeting and performance by:

- Identifying unconverted enquirers matching the profile and offering further incentives to buy.
- Amending the media schedule to advertise in press titles which target the right audience.
- Making selections from external lists.

*Profiling service*
Many lifestyle list suppliers provide a valuable profiling service. Supply them with your campaign data, showing respondents and customers. They will be able to identify the discriminating characteristics between customers and non-buyers. They can also identify prospects that have the same characteristics as your customers – targeting lookalike individuals is known as cloning.

## Broad-scale targeting

You might wonder why you would ever do anything other than personalised communications within your direct marketing plan. After all, direct marketing is all about individual data, so why use broad-scale media at all? There are certain situations where broad-scale targeting is appropriate. For example where:

- There is no database yet, for instance, with a new business venture.
- There are no repeat purchases and new customers are hard to identify, e.g. wedding services.

Week Four

# TUESDAY

> - Your product or service has a mass audience, thus non-personalised media is the most cost-effective route, e.g. for utilities.
> - There is no other way to identify your target audience and you require prospects to take part in a hand-raising exercise, e.g. insurance claims assessors finding people who have had a recent accident.

Select the media that provides sufficient coverage of your target audience for the least cost, based on your target profile. You can test the uplift created by integrating media.

Once you have decided on which media to use, maximise your targeting within each media.

---

**TV** Choose the right service, channels, days and programmes

**Radio** Select the most appropriate stations, timing, programmes and format

**Newspapers** Choose the papers, regional editions, pages, formats and positions that are appropriate, on the right days with the right offer

**Magazines** Advertise in the appropriate edition, with the right features at the right time

**Inserts** Target as for papers and magazines, but you will have more flexibility to target specific geographic regions

**Door drops** Identify the postcodes with a high percentage of households that match your target profile

Week Four

# TUESDAY

> **Internet banner ads and hyperlinks** Identify the suitable online communities, websites and portals, with the right content and advertise at the right time
>
> **Directory listings and adverts** Select the crucial directories and advertise in relevant regional or business versions, both hard copy and online or CD format
>
> **In-store point of sale** Choose the right stores, shoppers, timing, location and make the right offer
>
> **On-pack offers** Appeal to loyal or potential customers by using the right pack variants with the right offers

The offer, timing, format and creative treatment must all have a strong appeal to the people you want to attract. An example of good broad-scale targeting is promotion of kids' holiday clubs, targeted at parents via inserts in school newsletters and sent out just before the school holidays.

Broad-scale targeting generates responses from individual enquirers and customers which can be used for future, personalised targeting.

# TUESDAY

## Summary

- Segmentation allows you to simplify complex customer and marketplace information and to develop strategies and plans. Segments must be identifiable, accessible and substantial. You can build your own or use off-the-shelf segmentation systems.
- Profiling allows you to identify the distinguishing attributes of your customers. Cloning is the identification of prospects that match that profile.
- Precise targeting is vital for the success of your direct marketing activity. Having no individual data is not an excuse; even with broadscale media you can employ targeting techniques.
- When developing target profiles, it is crucial to ensure that your targeting supports your strategy and that you are clear which customers you need to avoid as well as attract.

# Building and using your marketing database

Direct marketing is often referred to as database marketing because of the pivotal role that the database plays in directing and controlling personal communications. Direct marketing strategy is incomplete if it does not provide direction on how the marketing database is to be built and used to achieve the organisation's aims. Understanding your customers, segmentation and targeting are all possible with the marketing database.

## What is a marketing database?

A marketing database is the engine that drives direct marketing forward. It is a set of computer files where data about individuals can be stored, accessed, analysed and retrieved to support direct marketing communications, which are designed to acquire and retain customers.

## Use your database strategically

- Assess market penetration and your customer profile compared to the market generally.
- Understand the relative value of your customers.
- Segment your customers and prospects into distinct groups.
- Build a detailed profile of customers by segment.
- Analyse the relative success of different campaigns.

# Week Four
## WEDNESDAY

- Test new initiatives and assess likely take-up.
- Forecast future sales, profit and return on investment.

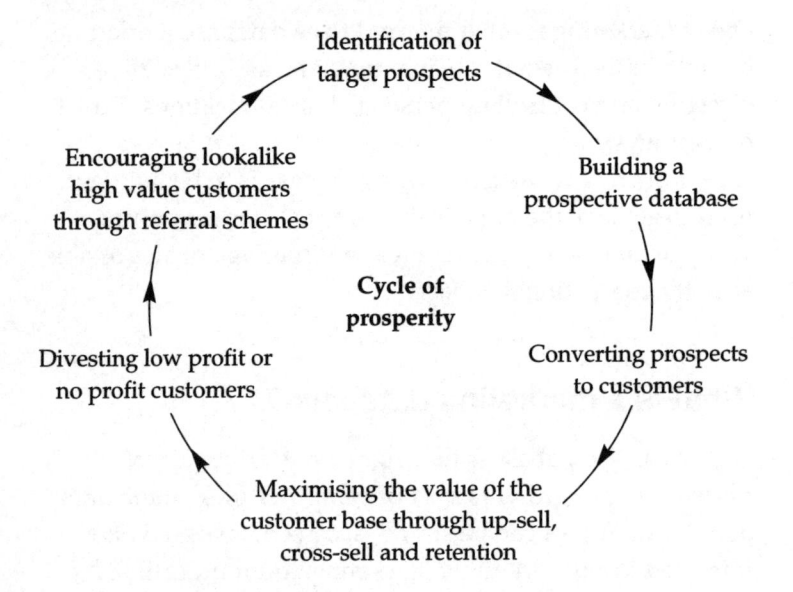

**Cycle of prosperity**

- Identification of target prospects
- Building a prospective database
- Converting prospects to customers
- Maximising the value of the customer base through up-sell, cross-sell and retention
- Divesting low profit or no profit customers
- Encouraging lookalike high value customers through referral schemes

## Use your database operationally

- Select target customers and prospects for campaigns.
- Manage magazine or membership subscriptions.
- Control loyalty and reward schemes.
- Prioritise outbound telephone call lists by warmth of the prospect.
- Generate sales from existing customers.
- Run automated e-mail messages to Web enquirers and buyers.
- Automate fulfilment of enquirer packs.

# WEDNESDAY

## Technological rate of development

The rate of change for computing technology is fast. Very fast. Hardware and software systems, which are used to run marketing databases, are developing in speed and functionality. It is becoming possible to store, process and access customer data in larger and larger volumes and at faster and faster speeds.

Due to computing development, a fully-functioning marketing database is within the reach of even small or cash-poor organisations. A marketing database system can be yours for the price of a software package and a personal computer (PC).

Complex businesses with millions of customers must have an equally sophisticated marketing database.

## Not just a pretty system

Ask the IT experts about what comprises a marketing database and they will invariably say 'hardware' and 'software'. Hardware is the physical computer kit that the system runs on. Software is the programming code that controls the way the system operates and allows your database application to work.

The IT experts are right, yet there is another vital element without which the hardware and software will go to waste: the data.

Data is vital to the effective running of a marketing database system. If you place as much emphasis on data generation, management and use as you do on computer kit, you will be rewarded.

Week Four

# WEDNESDAY

## Structured or relational

There are two main software design types for databases:

1 Structured
2 Relational

Structured databases have a prescribed format into which the data fits. Examples are flat files and hierarchical files. In a flat file, data is held in a series of packages in a long line or string. Hierarchical files are structured much like a family tree with data branches for each family linked to their parents. Again the structure is rigid. Structured databases are effective where data is simple and fairly static, where reporting requirements are unlikely to change and where cost of development is critical.

Relational databases, on the other hand, are flexible. Data need only be input once and is stored in tables linked by ID numbers. The customer ID number is known as the URN or unique reference number. Relational databases can access data to report on any combination of variables with great flexibility. A database set up in Microsoft Access is a relational database.

If data is complex, changes rapidly and requirements cannot be entirely predicted, a relational database works well. The majority of marketing databases are relational.

Organisations implement their marketing databases in different ways, from a single PC to an enterprise-wide system.

## Popular software

There are many software suppliers, ranging from Siebel and Peoplesoft to small-scale databases written in Microsoft Access. Popular systems include: Goldmine, Maximiser, Customer Focus, Mailbrain, ACT! and Outlook. For small companies, shareware is another option. Database shareware can be downloaded from the Web for a minimal registration cost. Additional functionality can be provided through specialist software. Products exist for address management, mail sorting, mass customisation of e-mails and data validation and de-duplication of information.

## What makes a good database?

- Flexible data storage, management, reporting and selection.
- Customer-centric view with complete contact and purchase histories for individuals, including campaigns and responses.
- Fast performance for search enquiries, input, data loads, selections and reports.
- Validation of records, address management and de-duplication of information.
- Capable of supporting personalised direct marketing communications, whether website registrations and broadcast emails, telemarketing, direct mail and mobile SMS text messaging.
- Tools for analysis and testing, including profiling, scoring, segmentation, tests versus control group.

Week Four
# WEDNESDAY

## Creating a marketing database

It can be simple to set up a database. Then again, it can be the most complex and demanding project that you have ever been called upon to complete. The degree of difficulty depends on the complexity of the system, the expertise at your disposal, the level of integration with other systems and the number and diversity of the users.

Perhaps that is why, having analysed numerous database projects that succeeded or failed, Arthur Hughes, the American database expert, advocates:

- Think small and fast – implement within a year at maximum.
- Keep an eye on the bottom line – calculate return on investment upfront and aim for that defined outcome.

Week Four

# WEDNESDAY

- Use a multi-skilled team with a strong leader.
- View requirements from the customers' perspective.

*Source: Journal of Database Marketing Vol 5, 1998*

## Successful database projects

To be successful requires strong project management skills and a good mix of technical IT and direct marketing expertise.

*Step 1 Project set up*

- Appoint a project manager and cross-functional team – the team will develop and implement the project, monitoring progress and taking steps to keep it on track.
- Develop a detailed project plan showing all the tasks involved plus responsibilities, interim deadlines and critical path.
- Agree the budget for the project – set up and ongoing costs.
- Set an implementation deadline and agree targets for return on investment with the Board before proceeding further.

*Step 2 Requirements gathering*

- Communicate with users, direct marketers and IT staff so they are aware of the project and know how to provide input.
- Conduct a data audit to understand data sources, quality, volumes and processing requirements.
- Compile a business requirements specification, detailing the needs that the database system must satisfy.

# Week Four
# WEDNESDAY

*Step 3 System development*

- Decide to build the database in-house or outsource.
- If outsourced, put the work out to tender, obtain proposals and references from three short-listed suppliers – agree contracts with the preferred partner.
- Clarify ongoing support required for the project.
- Obtain a functional specification from your IT developers to confirm the technical specification for the system.
- The developers will design the system and build it.

*Step 4 Testing and deploying*

- Provide dummy data for the system developers.
- Conduct user acceptance testing to ensure the system works.
- Load current data, mapping input files to the new fields.
- Consider parallel running of the old and new system during the transition period.
- Consider phasing in the adoption of the system by user group.
- Conduct user-training, provide a user manual and help desk.
- Roll out the complete system; endorse it with a communications programme to explain the benefits to users.

*Step 5 Ongoing management*

- Begin ongoing data management activities to keep data accurate and up to date.

# WEDNESDAY

- Administer access levels, security safeguards and backups.
- Utilise the system for strategic planning and campaigns.
- Undertake a formal review of the system and take action to achieve financial targets.

## Data – the vital ingredient

In order to have accurate and up-to-date information, you must actively manage your data. There is nothing worse than receiving a prospecting call from a company when you have been their customer for the last year. Multiple mailings to the same person waste money and lack credibility. Misspelt names and addresses are irritating and make for poor relationships.

Like the conductor of a great orchestra, the direct marketer must create database music from diverse data sources and data uses.

## Data sources

Data sources will vary depending on your business but could include:

- telephone enquiries
- applications
- web registrations
- loyalty scheme data
- external lists
- member-get-member referrals

# Week Four
## WEDNESDAY

- responses to campaigns
- exhibition enquiries
- coupon redemptions
- sales transaction records

## Don't I know you?

Typically, a consumer database will hold information on name, address and contact details, demographics, lifestyle, purchase and promotional history, suppression status and segment. Business data is similar but has the added complication of:

- Parent and subsidiary company relationships.
- Different company names within the same group.
- Groups of individuals who make buying decisions, including the ultimate decision maker, influencer, gatekeeper and buyer.

## Data decay

Remember that your perfect customer or prospect data will not remain accurate without continual refreshment.

| **Consumer markets** 6% of people move house each year | **Business markets** 35% of business data decays in a year |
|---|---|

## Data gremlins

Try to avoid these data gremlins which beset so many databases:

# WEDNESDAY

- Out-of-date information used to classify whether the individual has made an enquiry or purchased.
- Duplicate customer records.
- Poor quality addresses.
- Customer name fields containing comments about the person's attitude or likelihood of buying.
- Failure to suppress people who have asked not to be contacted.

## Data guardians

Your data is more likely to be accurate if you have guardians to look after it:

- Adopt a data culture where everyone who handles data actively helps to ensure it is accurate.
- Have system rules governing the completeness and quality of new data, including mandatory input fields and selections from drop-down boxes.

# Week Four
## WEDNESDAY

- Have strict criteria for the quality of data you buy in from cold lists and rigorously check compliance.
- Use the Postcode Address File (PAF), available from the Royal Mail on CD, to validate any of the UK's 27 million addresses and correct poor-quality addresses.
- Have systems to accurately de-duplicate customer and enquirer records through merge-purge programmes.
- Ensure that you have a complete contact and response history for individual customers.
- Suppress people who do not want to be contacted from your direct marketing communications.

There are several external files that can be used to clean your data. Clean and accurate data reduces wastage and improves your response and conversion rates.

# WEDNESDAY

| Data cleaning | External file |
| --- | --- |
| Addresses | Postcode address file (PAF) or address management software |
| Deceased | Mortality file, e.g. Smee & Ford, Bereavement Register |
| Movers | Electoral Roll confirms name and address Royal Mail National Change of Address File (NCOA) for redirections; REaD Goneaways File for non-delivered mail |
| No interest | Mailing preference service, telephone preference service, fax preference service and the e-mail preference service |
| Credit risk | Experian and Equifax credit scoring |
| Business change | Companies House data on changes to businesses |

## Summary

Developing and using your marketing database is an important strategic concern. The database is the powerhouse of direct marketing. Hardware, software and data are the key components.

Rapid technological advances continue to open doors for direct marketers, increasing what it is possible to achieve while decreasing costs. Relational marketing databases are very common and offer great flexibility, but structured databases can be appropriate for straightforward applications. Typically, marketing databases are either part of an enterprise-wide CRM system, operate as a stand-alone system taking data feeds from back-office functions or are provided as simple PC-based systems.

Week Four

# WEDNESDAY

Setting up a marketing database from scratch requires a clear vision of how the database will support your business, a precise statement of requirements and an upfront payback model. Strong project management skills are also necessary to make it happen.

Data management is a vital function to ensure an effective marketing database, not least because of the rate of data decay. Avoid data gremlins, such as duplicate records and rely on data guardians to safeguard the integrity of your information. Suppression files are readily available and can save you embarrassment, time and money.

Week Four

# THURSDAY

# Selecting the right media

You know your marketplace. You have analysed how the market divides into different customer groups or segments. You have selected the customers and prospects that you will target with a distinctive offer that sets you apart from the competition. Your database is in good shape to support your activity and to allow an ongoing dialogue with prospects and customers. Now it is time to get to grips with the media choices available to you.

## How direct marketers spend their money

Media is the name given to the communications channels available to you, from TV to telemarketing. Spend on direct marketing media has more than trebled since the DMA first began its census in 1994, from £4.1 billion to £11 billion today.

The most used media, ranked in order of importance are:

1 Telemarketing
2 Direct mail
3 TV
4 Door to door
5 Inserts
6 Field marketing
7 National press advertising
8 New media
9 Magazine display
10 Contract magazines
11 Radio
12 Regional display advertising

**13** Outdoor/transport
**14** Cinema

*Source: The DMA Research Centre 2002 Advertising Association.*

Telemarketing is currently the leading direct marketing medium by spend. Spend on direct mail continues to increase, despite the advent of new media and the use of TV as a direct-response medium. The database takes a pivotal role in communications and it is an important budgetary consideration.

## Media evaluation

There are many media choices available to the direct marketer. To make sensible decisions remember to FISH:

- *Fit*: which media fits your target profile?
- *Influence*: is it the right media to influence what target customers think, feel and do in order to get a response?
- *Scale*: can you reach enough of your target audience?
- *Hit*: is it the best channel in terms of cost per hit, i.e. cost per coverage, cost per response and cost per sale?

# THURSDAY

Week Four

## Budgeting for media

Costs can vary quite widely. This information is provided as a general guide. Always check the costs when planning campaigns and watch out for media inflation.

| Guide to costs for direct marketing media | |
|---|---|
| **Media** | **Cost per thousand (CPT)** |
| **TV** | |
| National and regional direct response TV | £5–10 |
| **National press** | |
| Tabloid, for a 25cm × four-column, mono advert | £5 |
| Broadsheet, for a 25cm × four column, mono advert | £20 |
| **New media** | |
| Internet banner advert, cost is per thousand page impressions | £15 |
| **Inserts** | |
| In national press/consumer titles, for A5 size, colour printed insert, media cost includes print | £40 |
| **Door-to-door** | |
| With targeting by area and neighbourhood type, for an A5 size, colour printed leaflet, cost includes print | £55 |

# Week Four
## THURSDAY

| | |
|---|---|
| **Direct mail** | |
| Well targeted direct mail, including printing, personalisation and enclosing, from 50p per mail pack | £500 |
| **Telemarketing** | |
| Inbound call handling, from £2 a call | £2,000 |
| Outbound call competition, from £2.50 a call | £2,500 |
| **Field marketing** | |
| Salesperson face-to-face appointment | £50–200 per appointment |

Note: Guide prices exclude VAT and are based upon information from the Institute of Direct Marketing.

Remember that media costs are one element of campaign costs. Ensure that, where appropriate, you also budget for:

- Agency fees.
- Design, copy, artwork, Web animations, lists and print production where not included in media costs.
- Response handling, data capture, fulfilment materials and incentives.
- Freephone, freepost and business reply postage.
- Couriers and deliveries.
- Insurance, redemption indemnity costs.
- Legal fees.
- Direct marketing operation overheads.

## Response rates by media

The number of potential customers that respond to a campaign can vary dramatically. Here is a general guide, but find out the norms for your business. Accurate

Week Four

# THURSDAY

## Budgeting for media

Costs can vary quite widely. This information is provided as a general guide. Always check the costs when planning campaigns and watch out for media inflation.

| Guide to costs for direct marketing media | |
|---|---|
| **Media** | **Cost per thousand (CPT)** |
| **TV** <br> National and regional direct response TV | £5–10 |
| **National press** <br> Tabloid, for a 25cm × four-column, mono advert <br> Broadsheet, for a 25cm × four column, mono advert | £5 <br> £20 |
| **New media** <br> Internet banner advert, cost is per thousand page impressions | £15 |
| **Inserts** <br> In national press/consumer titles, for A5 size, colour printed insert, media cost includes print | £40 |
| **Door-to-door** <br> With targeting by area and neighbourhood type, for an A5 size, colour printed leaflet, cost includes print | £55 |

| | |
|---|---|
| **Direct mail**<br>Well targeted direct mail, including printing, personalisation and enclosing, from 50p per mail pack | £500 |
| **Telemarketing**<br>Inbound call handling, from £2 a call<br>Outbound call competition, from £2.50 a call | £2,000<br>£2,500 |
| **Field marketing**<br>Salesperson face-to-face appointment | £50–200 per appointment |

Note: Guide prices exclude VAT and are based upon information from the Institute of Direct Marketing.

Remember that media costs are one element of campaign costs. Ensure that, where appropriate, you also budget for:

- Agency fees.
- Design, copy, artwork, Web animations, lists and print production where not included in media costs.
- Response handling, data capture, fulfilment materials and incentives.
- Freephone, freepost and business reply postage.
- Couriers and deliveries.
- Insurance, redemption indemnity costs.
- Legal fees.
- Direct marketing operation overheads.

## Response rates by media

The number of potential customers that respond to a campaign can vary dramatically. Here is a general guide, but find out the norms for your business. Accurate targeting and media selection, together with a compelling proposition, will encourage prospects to act and act now.

### Guide to response rates by direct marketing media

| Media | Response rate | Response volume |
|---|---|---|
| Face-to-face calling | 10–30% | 10–30 per 100 appointments |
| Outbound telemarketing | 5–10% | 5–10 per 100 completed calls |
| Direct mail | 1–4% | 1–4 per 100 mailed |
| Door-to-door | 0.2% | 2 per 1,000 households |
| New media banner ads | 0.1–0.5% | 1–5 per 1,000 web surfers viewing ad |
| Loose inserts | 0.1–0.5% | 1–5 per 1,000 readers |
| National press | 0.075% | 7.5 out of 10,000 readers |
| TV | 0.05% | 5 out of 10,000 viewers |

Note: Response rates are provided for guidance only, based upon information from The Institute of Direct Marketing. Response rates vary widely depending on the product, targeting, offer, timing, creative treatment and response mechanism.

Remember that cost management and media selection must go hand in hand.

## Pros and cons by media

Which media should you use within your direct marketing campaigns? The answer depends on who you are targeting and what you want them to think, feel and do. Let's take each of the core media in turn.

# THURSDAY

*Outbound telemarketing*

| Plus | Minus |
|---|---|
| • Personalised and can readily pre-qualify contacts (call first to identify the right person)<br>• Infinitely testable<br>• Quick to deploy | • Expensive cost/contact<br>• Difficult to contact certain people: 5 per cent households without phones, ex-directory numbers, business numbers using voicemail, mobiles<br>• Lacks visual stimulus<br>• Can be viewed as intrusive |

Good for generating business appointments, converting enquirers, persuading waiverers and taking orders.

*Direct mail*

| Plus | Minus |
|---|---|
| • Personalised and infinitely targetable and controllable<br>• Less expensive than telemarketing and face-to-face<br>• Can convey detailed and complex information<br>• Can include reply-paid cards, vouchers and pre-completed forms | • More costly than door drops<br>• Requires data management skills<br>• Can be high wastage due to small percentage response<br>• Data errors in name and address production lack professionalism |

Widely used where individual records of customers and prospects are available on the database or via external lists.

# THURSDAY

*TV*

| Plus | Minus |
|---|---|
| • Excellent for creating awareness, influencing hearts and minds and building brands<br>• Great for reaching large audiences<br>• Good where hand raising is required<br>• Can work for niche markets where programming matches targeting | • Not personalised<br>• Can only convey a small amount of information<br>• Expensive production costs<br>• Needs memorable phone number and Web address<br>• Limited ability to target<br>• Increasingly fragmented audiences not reflected in advertising cost reductions |

Used where a mass audience exists, where niche audiences match target profile, and where self-identification is required.

*Door-to-door*

| Plus | Minus |
|---|---|
| • Far cheaper than direct mail for mass markets<br>• Can select by household, e.g. within a store catchment area<br>• Can provide trial samples | • Can only target by household, not by person<br>• High wastage due to low % response<br>• Can aggravate customers if prospects are offered a better deal |

Used for mass markets; small businesses can target precisely, by walking from house-to-house, door-dropping certain households e.g. driveways needing repair.

## Week Four
# THURSDAY

*Loose inserts*

| Plus | Minus |
|---|---|
| • Greater scope than press ad for use of colour, different formats, different printing techniques, e.g. scratchcard and use of regional tests<br>• Good for postal responses, e.g. used for photo film envelopes | • Not personalised, less control over who reads insert<br>• More expensive than press ads<br>• Insert can be lost or messages diluted amongst other companies' inserts |

Widely used where target profile and readership profile match. Higher costs of inserts versus press ads can be offset by increased response.

*Face-to-face calling*

| Plus | Minus |
|---|---|
| • Primary media for high cost business-to-business and consumer purchases<br>• Can build rapport with multiple decision makers<br>• Allows a two-way dialogue and the opportunity to overcome objections by providing more information | • Very expensive compared to other media<br>• Needs phone and database support to work well<br>• Cannot reach mass audiences this way<br>• Requires skilled salespeople |

Used for high cost sales. Normally an essential part of the business-to-business media mix.

## Week Four
# THURSDAY

*National press*

**Plus**
- Cost-effective media where offering has broad appeal
- Can create an impact and be persuasive
- Allows more scope for testing than TV
- Can use advertorials – ad and editorial combined
- Unlike TV, can also offer postal response route

**Minus**
- Not personalised
- High fixed cost per ad, run risk of low response levels
- Best times to advertise are also best times for competitors to advertise – message can be diluted alongside competitor ads
- Not good for narrow or local market segments

Used where a mass audience exists, used for one-stage and two-stage sales, heavily used for financial services.

*Web banner ads*

**Plus**
- Low production costs
- Can use free banner ad exchange schemes or negotiate charges per click through
- Get more than a response, link to website with data collection and online ordering
- It is discreet for sensitive services

**Minus**
- Certain sections of society do not have Web access
- Click throughs may not result in sales
- Banner ads are relatively expensive versus press
- Your success is reliant on the ability of the supplier to drive traffic to their site and your website to convert visits into sales

Used by a broad range of companies to reach target audiences and drive traffic to their websites. Flexible and quick to deploy.

## Other media choices

The media that we have focused upon is where most of the money gets spent, but it is not the complete picture. Think about the appropriate way to reach your target market. Be open minded and also consider:

- *Magazine display*: similar advantages to press, but allows more refined targeting.
- *Outdoor/transport*: can target by journeys and traveller type.
- *Radio*: similar to TV, opportunities for sponsorship and competitions as well as response advertising.
- *Regional press*: useful for local services.
- *Contract magazines*: important for many companies, including the AA and Saga.
- *Cinema*: used for local services and targeted campaigns. Can align age of target audience with film certificate ratings.
- *Website*: excellent vehicle for interaction with potential customers, can capture detailed information and take online orders.
- *E-mail*: low cost compared to direct mail because no print or postage. Can include links to campaign landing-pages and websites.
- *SMS mobile text messaging*: can convey simple messages. Provides immediate response mechanism.
- *Exhibitions*: often used for generating leads for business-to-business products and services, also used for certain consumer audiences, e.g. weddings, crafts, home décor.
- *On-pack*: used in conjunction with promotions to attract trialists and gain data on existing customers.
- *In-pack*: allows collection of data on customers, used for consumer goods, can also include money-off vouchers and collect-and-claim offers.

# THURSDAY

- *In-store point of sale*: for collection of data on customers and competitor customers, especially used for consumer goods.

## Media medley

Reaching the right customers entails selecting the most appropriate and cost-effective media. It is important to appreciate that many media can work together. As a direct marketer, you need to be able to blend different media for maximum impact.

Consider the case of a new consumer utilities provider. At launch the business uses broad-scale advertising to generate awareness and responses for customer acquisition. DRTV and national press will form the media platform. The contact centre will handle phone and website responses. Fulfilment will be carried out by e-mail and direct mail.

As the customer base grows, the business will focus on customer retention and cross-sell opportunities via direct mail and e-mail. It will use telemarketing and internet banner advertising to top up the customer bank by acquiring new customers from the potential switchers in the market.

## Media know-how

Make good use of the resources at your disposal to help you with media selection and targeting:

- media packs provide audience profiles and statistics
- expertise of consultants and media planners
- competitor media behaviour and claimed successes
- your company's past campaign performance

Week Four

# THURSDAY

## Summary

Getting to grips with media involves an understanding of broad-scale and personalised media choices. Media selection requires you to FISH. This means assessing the Fit with your target market, the Influence that media can make, the Scale of coverage required and the cost per Hit. Cost management and media selection are two sides of the same coin.

In practice, most direct marketers blend a variety of different media in order to achieve their objectives. You must do this to maximise the overall response, playing to the strengths of each media to exploit its full potential.

# Creating and executing campaigns

The creation and delivery of direct marketing campaigns may be one of the most stimulating roles that you are called upon to perform. There is something for everyone because this job requires the skills of the:

- analyst
- producer
- psychologist
- entrepreneur
- logistics manager
- wordsmith
- artist
- lawyer

## Why does my company need a campaign?

Direct marketing campaigns bring your choice of strategic direction alive through operational plans which allow you to reach your destination.

Your organisation may run a single direct marketing campaign during the year, or a multitude of campaigns at different times, focusing on different products and services. Whichever it is, campaigns are about tangible actions and delivery of results.

## Campaign development

All that you have learned and achieved so far is of value when drawing up a campaign plan. You know where you are now. You have already decided where you want to be and you have set objectives. The strategic direction you plan to take has also been mapped out. Now you need to make it happen. For each strategy you need to set out a series of actions.

The good news is that you have already tackled three important areas which will form part of your plan:

- segmentation and targeting
- the marketing database
- media selection

## Allowable marketing costs

Before you become absorbed in elaborate plans or entrepreneurial deals, you need to be sure of your budget. Set an allowable marketing cost to decide an acceptable and appropriate direct marketing budget to get the company to its destination and achieve the required sales or profit level.

Week Four

# FRIDAY

Take the sales targets you set for direct marketing activity. Then, based on the required level of return on investment (ROI), calculate acceptable direct marketing costs. For example:

| | |
|---|---|
| Sales target | £1,000,000 |
| ROI | 20:1, i.e. spend £1, get £20 in sales revenue |
| Budget | £1,000,000 ÷ 20 = |
| | £50,000 allowable direct marketing spend |

You must also decide how to split the budget between:

- Acquisition campaigns or retention campaigns.
- Building your database or managing and using your data.
- Use of broad-scale or personalised media.
- Generating responses or converting responses into sales.

Having established your budget, you must get creative to gain maximum punch for every direct marketing pound.

## What product and service are you offering?

Consider product features and benefits, price and what differentiates the product from competitor products. Will you develop the product, replace it, enhance it, customise it or change delivery, maintenance or payment options?

## Do you need any research and database analysis?

You have learned a great deal by analysing your customers, capability and competitors and by completing a SWOT

Week Four

# FRIDAY

analysis. Are there any gaps in your knowledge? Decide whether you will obtain information by further database analysis, by analysing published research or by commissioning new research.

## Which markets and segments will you compete in?

Your strategy will explain which markets and segments you will operate in at a broad level. Now add some detail. Define each segment, its size, profile and value.

## What is your proposition?

Your product or service has many features; it is used in different ways and offers different benefits. You need to provide a compelling reason for customers to choose you and to stay loyal. Is it the same proposition for all segments or is it different? Will you use added offers or incentives?

| Why should I choose you? | Answer this and you have an overall proposition. |
| --- | --- |
| What's the big deal here? | Answer this and you have an offer. |

## How will you find and acquire new customers?

What is your specific target profile for new customers? Where will you find new customers? Will you use cold lists, advertise in the press or ask existing customers to introduce a friend?

# FRIDAY

## How will you retain existing customers and sell more?

Which customers will you focus your efforts on? What reinforcement and incentives will you provide to motivate them to stay loyal? Will you offer preferential rates, special recognition, membership rewards, collect-and-claim schemes, points programmes or added-value services?

## How will you build and use your database?

Does your database have enough records already or do you need to find mechanisms to collect customer and prospect data? Will you profile and clone your data to identify lookalike prospects from external lists? What selections will you make for acquisition and retention campaigns? What mail, phone or e-mail lists will you need to trigger automatically, such as renewals due, subscriptions overdue or appointment follow up? What reports and campaign evaluation will you require?

## What about targeting and media selection?

Your acquisition and retention campaigns must specify your target prospect profile and target customer profile by segment. Who exactly will you select and who will you avoid? Which specific media will you use to attract new customers? Which specific media will you use to keep existing customers? How many people can you reach by each of the selected media? What format will your message take, for example, advert position and size, contents of mail pack, length and structure of outbound phone call? How many responses and sales do you forecast?

## What tests will you run?

Testing is covered on Saturday in greater detail. For now, consider what you need to test. Remember the campaign factors listed in priority order on page 319. Here are the figures showing the impact these factors can have upon performance.

*Difference between best and worst performance by factor*

| Factor | Impact on response |
| --- | --- |
| Targeting | × 6 |
| Offer | × 3 |
| Timing | × 2 |
| Creative and format | × 1.35 |
| Response mechanism | × 1.2 |

Remember that, after your product or service, the most important thing to test is targeting.

## What about timing?

When will you run the campaign? Do you want to create a big impact in a short space of time or can you spread activity throughout the year? Is there a good time for people to act? Consider timing at a top level and in detail – seasonality, peaks and troughs, contract renewal cycle, company budget year and accounting year end, annual renewals month and date, birth date and age triggers, day of the week, time of day and stated preference for best time to call.

## Which creative treatment will provoke a response?

You know the product or service that you are promoting.

# FRIDAY

Week Four

You have decided on the proposition that makes your product distinct from the competition and provides a compelling reason for your target audience to take action. How will you explain what you have to offer in words and pictures (and sounds if you are using the phone, radio, TV or the internet)?

What hooks can you use to gain interest and what likely objections must you overcome?

| Hooks | Objections |
| --- | --- |
| Save money | Too cheap |
| Make money | Too expensive |
| Quick and easy | Takes too long |
| Reliable and fewer problems | Don't want it |
| Feel good | Don't know you |
| More prestigious | Don't like you |
| Well-known brand | Don't believe you |

Build a mental picture of the people you are targeting. Think in their language. For example, is a savings product 'extra cash' or 'an intelligent investment'?

# FRIDAY

Determine how you will adapt the overall campaign theme to maximise the response potential of each media and play to the strengths that each media has in the communications mix.

## What response mechanism and call to action is appropriate?

All direct marketing communications must include a call to action. Having conveyed your selling message, you need to let potential customers know what you want them to do next.

Your call to action might be one of the following:

- 'Call free on 0800 123 456 for an immediate quote.'
- 'Just clip the coupon for 50p off your next purchase.'
- 'Fax back to request an engineer's appointment.'
- 'Click here for even more savings.'
- 'Sign the pre-approved form and return, postage free.'

Freephone and freepost response options tend to uplift response.

Broadcast media relies on memorable phone numbers or website addresses. Business communications often use Web links and fax-backs, as well as phone lines. Direct mail can include a phone number, voucher, website address and a personalised postal coupon or application.

The secret is to match the preferences of your customers. Provide the response mechanisms that work best for each media. Give incentives for responding. Test the impact that offering a 'choice' of response channel has on uplifting overall response.

## Convert responses into sales

When developing your campaign, consider how you will apportion your budget between generating responses and converting those responses into sales. Too many organisations fail to put enough thought into how they will convert responses into sales. Do not be one of them.

Consider how to maximise the value of each response with:

- Immediate and professional handling of inbound phone calls, faxes, e-mails and applications.
- Campaign landing pages within your website with easy navigation for placing orders.
- Communications that reinforce the original proposition and provide incentives to act now.

This applies whether your company has a one- or two-stage sales process. One-stage is where the customer places an order in response to your direct marketing. Two-stage is where you generate initial enquiries that then become sales. At every stage you require a strong call to action clearly stating what customers should do next and providing reasons to act now.

To close the sale you can use:

- deadlines for applications
- reminders
- bonuses and preferential rates for early responses
- money-back guarantee if not satisfied
- extra incentives, such as initial month free, free warranty

Week Four

# FRIDAY

## Keep it legal

Direct marketers need to be mindful of the laws that govern their business. Complying with the law is not optional – you must make sure that you operate within the law or you will face the consequences.

Codes of practice exist to provide helpful guidance on required standards:

- The Direct Marketing Authority Code of Practice.
- The British Codes for Advertising and Sales Promotions.

## Data protection fundamentals

Compliance with the Data Protection Act (DPA) is fundamental for direct marketers. The Act states that personal data must be fairly and lawfully obtained, used for the purpose it was given, securely processed and that explicit permission must be sought for collection of sensitive data. Safeguards are also required where data is transferred to non-EU countries. Make sure that you comply. For example:

- Are you registered under the DPA?
- Does your direct mail and e-mail allow recipients to opt out?
- Do your inbound phone calls ask for permission to retain information for marketing purposes?
- Does your website have an unmissable privacy policy?
- Do you ask for permission to collect 'sensitive' data, such as race, religion and health?

Week Four

# FRIDAY

Guidance can be obtained from the Information Commissioner for Data Protection.

Remember, while codes of practice provide valuable guidance, there is no substitute for professional legal advice. Ensure that your company lawyer is involved in your plans and formally approves your direct marketing adverts, scripts and materials.

## Summary

Direct marketing campaigns bring your strategy to life, delivering the results you require. Make certain that you set a sensible budget and have specific actions for:

- your product or service
- extra research or analysis
- segmentation
- your proposition
- acquisition of new customers
- retention of existing customers
- the database
- targeting and media
- testing
- creative treatment
- generating responses
- converting responses into sales

With detailed schedules for developing the campaign and planned timings for all activities and communications, you remain in control.

Week Four

## SATURDAY

# Measurement and management of success

By now you will be familiar with the features of direct marketing. You know that:

- An understanding of customers is based upon individual data.
- All communication is designed to get a response.
- Interaction and personalisation is facilitated by a marketing database.
- Strategies are based on both customer acquisition and, importantly, on customer retention.
- Every aspect of a direct marketing campaign can be tested.
- Results can be accurately measured.

The latter two aspects of testing and measurement are explored in more detail today.

## The three Rs – record, review and refine

The beauty of direct marketing is that it is accountable. When you have sound strategies and campaigns that hit the mark, your achievements are clear for all to see. Even better, you do not have to gamble your entire budget on one course of action.

# SATURDAY

*Week Four*

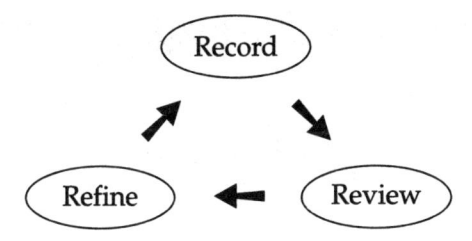

```
        Record
       ↗      ↘
   Refine  ←  Review
```

You can build a successful direct marketing platform by testing different options and backing those that work best. Then you can strive to beat the top performing campaigns.

Results are recorded, reviewed and refined in a circle of continuous improvement. Let's look at each of the three Rs in turn.

## Recording individual data

With accurate information to draw upon, you are in control. You can use the data to ensure you reach your direct marketing destination.

*Get the basics right*
Ensure you use separate fields to record each element of a person's name and address, including their postcode. Unless address variables are separated, you will be hampered when you want to verify them and de-duplicate or personalise communications.

*Record results at an individual level*
Log responses and sales by individual person. You can measure not just the overall campaign, but drill down for further insights.

*Track data sources*
Make sure that you know where new data originates from. Give source codes to your own data, bought-in lists and general enquiries. This way you can track the best performing data sources.

*Note the campaign code*
Use campaign codes as a shorthand to describe when the campaign ran, who was targeted, what media was used and which test was used.

Make sure campaign codes are accurately recorded when responses are received. For example, by printing them on press response coupons, asking inbound callers and making campaign codes a mandatory part of data input.

*Record the financial as well as the physical*
Make life easy for yourself. Keep accurate records of the actual campaign costs for all activities, broken down into sub-campaigns and test cells. Many companies keep strict records of the number of responses and sales, but fail to apply standards to the way they calculate and apportion costs. It can be very difficult to backtrack and review historic performance if you do not keep a precise log of costs as you go along.

## Reviewing and measuring results

There is an old business saying: 'What gets measured gets done'. There are certain standard measures that are useful when reviewing results – make good use of them.

*Overall measures of success*
Senior management's interest in direct marketing is top line: 'Did we hit forecast, on time and within budget?'

# SATURDAY

Week Four

Key measures are:

- Return on Investment (ROI) – profit/spend and sales/spend.
- Sales turnover – total sales revenue.
- Profit contribution – sales less costs (goods sold, distribution and direct marketing).
- Market share – % sales, by volume or value

*Tools in the box*
The direct marketer has a raft of additional, useful measures which include:

- standard campaign measures
- customer measures
- database measures
- media measures

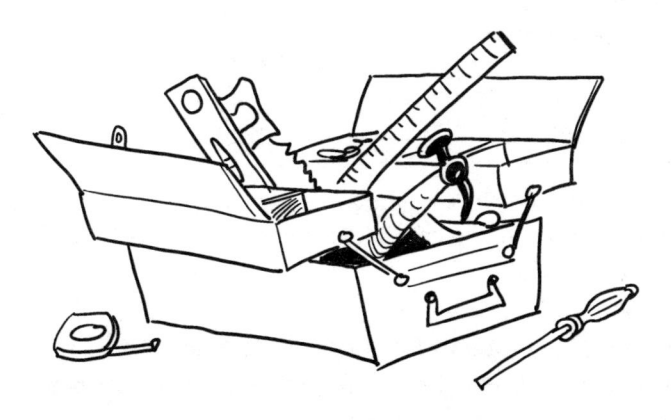

*Standard campaign measures*

| Response rate | = (number of responses/audience) × 100 |
| Cost per response (CPR) | = cost/number responses |
| Conversion rate | = (number of sales/number of responses) × 100 |
| Cost per sale (CPS) | = cost/number of sales |
| Average order value (AOV) | = value of sales/number of sales |

Take a campaign:

| Costs | £10,000 |
| Audience | 20,000 |
| Number of responses | 1000 |
| Number of sales | 250 |
| Sales value | £50,000 |

The campaign results are:

| Response rate | 5% |
| Cost per response | £10 |
| Conversion rate | 25% |
| Cost per sale | £40 |
| Average order value | £200 |

*Customer measures*

As well as measuring campaign responses, measure results at a customer level.

- volume of prospects and customers acquired
- customer base growth rate, i.e. % volume increase
- customer repeat purchase rate, i.e. % cross-sales

## SATURDAY

- attrition rate, i.e. % customers lost per annum
- retention rate, i.e. % customers kept per annum

Remember to use the measures of customer value which were covered at the outset:

- pareto 80:20 customer value
- recency, frequency and monetary value
- customer lifetime value

*Monitor timing*
Response tracking and forecasting is essential when you have an in-house contact centre, sales team or fulfilment team. Measure responses over time by media and use this for staffpower planning and stock management.

If you know that 100 per cent of the responses to a campaign are received within three months, but 80 per cent are received in a week, you do not have to wait long to know if your campaign will be a success. After just one week, you will have a very clear idea.

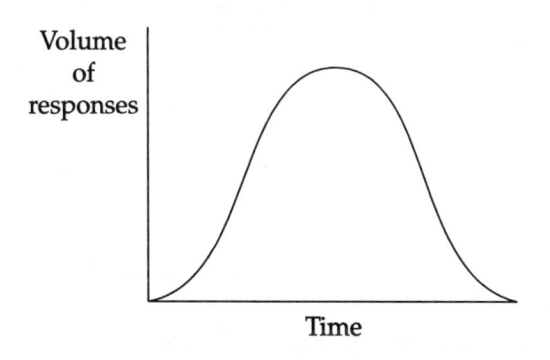

**Response curve**

# SATURDAY

Monitor the impact of other timing measures to maximise your effectiveness. For instance, work out the ideal timing to issue advance renewal notices and reminders. Some companies have found that older customers like to make buying decisions well before the renewal deadline, while younger ones will respond up to the final whistle.

## Specific media measures

The standard campaign measures are widely used across all media. In addition, there are some terms peculiar to the media they are measuring.

## Telemarketing

- Calls answered – the % of calls answered.
- Calls abandoned – the % of calls received where the caller hangs up before they get put through.
- Average time to answer – waiting time in seconds.
- Call duration – average length of call.
- % of calls completed – outbound calls where the contact person was available and the call was completed.
- % supervised transfers – % of calls where the caller had to be referred to a second tier of support in order to answer their query.

## Direct mail

- % of goneaways – percentage of packs that could not be delivered.
- % of response by mailing cell.

# SATURDAY
*Week Four*

## Direct response TV

- Opportunities to see (OTS) is used to measure the actual audience achieved during a TV campaign compared to forecasts.
- Responses are measured by creative treatment and per channel or station, per daypart, per position within the commercial break, by frequency shown and by length of commercial.

## Database

- Total customer and prospect records.
- Recency of records – when last updated.
- Field occupancy rates – % of records where data is complete.
- Rate of data decay – % of data on the database that becomes out of date within a year.
- % opt out – number of customer records where you must not make further marketing contact.

## National press advertising

- OTS is used to measure the average number of times a reader will see an advert.
- Response as a % of circulation and also by position.
- Share of voice – percentage of ad spend versus competitors.

# Week Four
# SATURDAY

*Inserts*

- Response per distribution type – solus, shared.
- Response per insert type – loose, bound-in, tipped-on (glued), in-pack.

*Door-to-door*

- Response as a % of households targeted.
- % penetration of targets by postcode – showing percentage of targets that will be hit by selecting specific postcodes.

*Field marketing*

- Hot, warm and cold sales leads.
- Number of appointments, proposals, tenders.
- Cost per appointment.

*Web*

- Site visit – customer visit to a website.
- Average length of visit – time spent viewing and interacting with your website.
- Referring site – which other site has the visitor clicked on to reach your website, i.e. the source of your website traffic?
- Page impressions – number of times the page has been viewed.
- Registrations – number of visitors supplying data.
- Average basket value – average spend per customer per visit.

Week Four

# SATURDAY

*Add research for greater insights*

Direct marketing measures explain what has happened, research can explain why. Use it to supplement your understanding of:

- The reasons why people did or did not buy.
- Attitudes to your company, products and services in comparison to the competition.
- Customer satisfaction and commitment to your company.

## Refining for continuous improvement

To be a good direct marketer you need to do two things:

1 Pre-empt the results that you might get by planning for contingencies
2 Embrace the need to continually beat your results – use a cycle of testing and roll out of improvements

*Contingency planning*
Be ready for the unexpected:

- Constantly monitor results versus forecast during each campaign.
- Set aside part of your direct marketing budget to allow room for manoeuvre if results do not turn out as expected.
- Plan for contingencies, such as responses being higher or lower than target.
- Decide what steps you will take if you need to improve conversion rates or increase average order values.

## Week Four
# SATURDAY

*Testing, testing, 1, 2, 3 . . .*
It is vital to construct robust tests, measure their relative performance and incorporate the learning into future campaigns. Not only does it move your organisation forward, it is also very rewarding.

*How do you go about testing?*

- Establish your current best direct marketing performer by media. This is your 'Control'.
- Decide how much budget to put into your previously tried and tested campaigns and how much into your tests in order to find new campaigns.
- Try to beat the control. Remember to test the most critical factors first and set SMART performance targets. After your product or service, the factors to test are:
  - targeting
  - offer
  - timing
  - creative and format
  - response mechanism
- Assess roll-out potential of each test to help you decide where to focus your efforts.
- Although creative is a lower priority, changing the creative treatment and format can have a significant impact where there is little room to further improve the targeting, offer or timing.
- Make sure that you only test one variable at a time. If you change more than one thing, you will not know with any certainty which factor produced the change in results. Construct a test matrix to control this process.

# SATURDAY

> - Take care to make sure that the results you get are statistically significant and inspire confidence. Achieving 20 responses instead of ten is a 100 per cent uplift, but do you really want to base future plans on the behaviour of just 20 respondents?

Refer to your company accountant, statistician or planner. Your organisation may even have a look-up table that sets out the volumes required for certain tests. If you do not have any of these, find out what scale of results will allow you and your senior managers to make decisions and agree this prior to testing.

*Test matrix*

This example shows a test matrix for a direct mail campaign, where list sources and creative treatment are tested.

| Test cell | List | Creative | Test quantity | Roll-out quantity |
|---|---|---|---|---|
| 1 | A – Control list | Control pack | 10,000 | 50,000 |
| 2 | A – Control list | New pack | 10,000 | 50,000 |
| 3 | B | Control pack | 10,000 | 40,000 |
| 4 | C | Control pack | 10,000 | 70,000 |

Cell 1 uses the best performing list and mail pack. It is our control. To assess performance of the lists, compare the alternative test cells 3 and 4 with cell 1. To assess the performance of the creative, compare the new pack in cell 2 to cell 1. As you can see, the test matrix allows us to test different factors while only altering one variable at a time.

*Propensity to respond or buy*
Employ the information you have gained from running campaigns and develop a scoring model of respondents and buyers. Identify the attributes that are predictive of success. Utilise this information to select the most responsive targets and to avoid those unlikely to respond. This will increase the cost-efficiency of your activity.

*Sanity check your segmentation*
Analyse the groups of prospects and customers on your database. Use this knowledge to guide future activity.

Have any of these individuals moved from one segment to another? For example, have any lapsed customers been reactivated? If so, what campaigns are now appropriate for them?

Does the information gleaned from campaigns support your segmentation of the market or does your segmentation now need revision? For instance, if you have one segment which now accounts for 50 per cent of your records, it could be further sub-divided to ensure that activity remains relevant to individual customers and prospects. Again, statistical modelling techniques can help to develop a meaningful customer segmentation.

## Summary

Recording and reviewing results enables you to refine your direct marketing strategy and campaigns. Use the raft of measurement tools to evaluate your strategy. Refine activity by contingency planning and by running tests, which can be rolled out as part of a continuous improvement cycle.

Week Four

# SATURDAY

The three Rs are a feature of direct marketing. They lead to greater success, greater profit and greater recognition for you.

## Direct marketing round-up

Lord Leverhulme is famously reported as saying:

> *'Half the money I spend on advertising is wasted, the trouble is I don't know which half.'*

He was not a direct marketer or he would have been able to account for every penny.

By being creative, in the broad sense of the word, you can maximise the punch for your pound. You will know precisely what impact your expenditure has made upon customer lifetime values, turnover and profit.

Technology will continue to be an enabling factor for acquisition and retention strategies. New messaging innovations will provide alternative media channels for direct communications. The rapid uptake in internet usage presents increasing scope for the direct marketer to interact with prospects and customers in a responsive environment.

With direct marketing you can give your customers what they want and enjoy commercial success.

# Free Publicity for your Business

**GUY CLAPPERTON**

**WEEK FIVE**

# CONTENTS

# Week Five

| | | |
|---|---|---|
| **Introduction** | | 383 |
| **Sunday** | Getting started | 384 |
| **Monday** | Structuring your press release | 397 |
| **Tuesday** | Who does what in a magazine? | 410 |
| **Wednesday** | Following up your press release | 422 |
| **Thursday** | Sustaining relations with the press | 436 |
| **Friday** | Non-press PR | 446 |
| **Saturday** | Conclusions and coping with problems | 456 |

# Week Five
# INTRODUCTION

You may be very happy with your business and satisfied that it provides a valuable service. That is fine and healthy, but getting people to hear about your business is another thing. We all know of businesses that would do very well indeed if only their potential customers were aware of them. However, at the start up stage, money for advertisements and marketing is in short supply.

With the help of this week you should be able to start tapping into a vast free resource – the press and other means – to get your company noticed for nothing, or at least for very little. This kind of publicity is not intended to last until you become the size of ICI, but it should get you off to a good start.

- Setting your expectations.
- Learning how to put a press release together.
- Tracking what happens to a press release once it leaves your desk.
- Learning how the press works and thinks.
- Working on non-press related PR and marketing.
- Coping when things go wrong.

This week is not designed to perform miracles. If you have nothing interesting to say it won't transform a dull operation into something riveting. But if you know you have a story in there somewhere then hopefully this week will help you to find it, and more importantly it will help you sort out what you want from it. You will understand a bit about the press process and why some releases work and some do not, and what you are likely to achieve by sending a good one out – not just the coverage but the stuff that comes afterwards.

Week Five

# SUNDAY

# Getting started

Why are you reading this? The obvious answer is because you want free publicity for your business or organisation, but there is more to the question than that. What are your objectives? Presumably you believe that a higher press profile will offer more in terms of business benefits, but is that really right?

Let us look at some examples. Suppose that you own a building company and you want more clients. You really do not want to get into the habit of cold-calling or door-to-door sales. You might think that a report in the local paper would be a good idea, and you might be right – but hang on, ask around a bit first. How many of your friends have ever hired a builder because they saw an article in the local paper? Come to think of it, how does a builder become newsworthy unless something goes wrong?

The point here is that you need to manage your expectations and, above all, set sensible objectives for your publicity work. Many small businesses and charities perceive themselves as failing in their publicity, not because nobody is paying any attention, but because their sales do not increase directly as a result.

Now, back to the builder. He gets himself a little coverage in the local press – we will worry about the story later, for the moment assume that it is positive. It happens a couple of times and so he builds up a little book of cuttings. Then, when he is visiting a potential client and they ask about references, he gives them a few names

# SUNDAY

Week Five

and the cuttings book. This helps to sway them in their choice of company towards him, rather than to his competitors.

Later the builder's business is expanding and he wants to get financing for growth. As well as the due diligence and checks that any other company has to go through with his business plan and financial forecasts, he also has his cuttings book. This helps as collateral. Of course, another type of business – a restaurant, a sports shop – will have customers coming in who have read about the place.

Therefore, before you plough into your press and PR campaign it is worth thinking through your objectives. Give yourself a yardstick to measure against and you will stand some chance of success. If you miss that step, how will you measure your success?

Week Five

# SUNDAY

## Myths exploded

While we are on the subject of expectations it is worth outlining a few of the things that will not, or at least should not, happen to any story you might release to the press.

- Few newspapers or magazines will publish your press release verbatim.
- No self-respecting journalist will allow you to vet the story prior to publication.
- You cannot dictate where your story appears in a publication.
- You cannot guarantee placement of your story.
- If a competitor has a strong angle on your story and is in a position to put it to the reporter, there is nothing you can do about it unless it is factually wrong.
- You cannot 'buy' editorial coverage.

The first of the items on the list, about publishing press releases verbatim, will vary from paper to paper. Young reporters have it drummed into them that they must add some value to everything that they publish. There would be no point in two newspapers running the same thing word for word anyway; they would look plain silly.

Different newspapers will be looking for different things in a story. If you owned a small chain of CD shops, for example, you might tell the local press and a few of the music press that you were opening a new branch. The local paper would be interested in the local angle: the new jobs and maybe a continuing story about a retail area recovering from a slump;

# SUNDAY

the music press might be more interested in any specialities you were offering in terms of niche or minority music.

Information on all of these possible angles should appear in your press release, but expect any interested journalists to pick out the bits that will appeal to their readers, to focus on them and to expand them by talking to you and other people for more detail.

### The extremely local group

The vast majority of the press will use a press release as a starting point but there are a handful of exceptions. Small local papers in particular will often use releases from local groups and charities verbatim as long as they are written well enough, otherwise they may be binned. So regardless of whether you expect your copy to go in word for word, write it as if it were for publication.

# Week Five
# SUNDAY

Vetting copy, and for the purposes of this book every article that is submitted by a journalist to his or her editor is 'copy', is something that major stars can do because they can refuse to do interviews otherwise. If you want a Madonna interview and, for example, she insists on copy approval, then the only way you can get the interview is to agree to her wishes. If your subject is technical and you need to ensure that the journalist has understood some of the more complex issues, you may be able to have your copy published in its original form.

However, these are rare examples. If a small business or charity tries to insist on verbatim press releases, they will get short shrift from the papers. There are four basic reasons for this:

- There is freedom of the press in the Western world – this might sound portentous but it is something in which journalists believe passionately.
- Asking a journalist to allow you copy approval means they have to remember who needs to see articles first and who does not. The most efficient and fair way of handling the issue is to apply one rule universally.
- Nine times out of ten, people try to water down their quotes during the approval process – the result is a blander story, which is exactly what the journalist and editor do not want.
- There is not enough time!

## SUNDAY

Week Five

If, in spite of this, you still want to try for copy approval, at least tell the journalist in advance. However, provided that the journalist has been honest about their profession and the fact that they are interviewing you, they can print anything if it is true and accurate.

It is disappointing if you do not get the placement on the page that you think you deserve, but asking for a specific page or complaining when you do not get it, can make you look naïve and even amateurish. Journalists have to see the whole newspaper or magazine in context, and if you complain your story may not appear at all. However, do not worry, this does not necessarily mean that you have wasted your time, as we shall discover later on.

Of more concern is when either a competitor or a well-versed journalist gets hold of a story that you were hoping would put a positive gloss on your company, and it ends up backfiring. Say that you are moving into new offices and you decide to issue a press release. However, the journalist either

# Week Five
## SUNDAY

knows or is told by his contacts that you are only moving because you have had to let half your sales force go and you had to find somewhere cheaper. If the story is accurate there is nothing you can do about it, except make sure that you put forward your side of things and hope for balanced coverage. Obviously, if circumstances are that extreme you should think carefully about whether to write a release or not. A less clear-cut case might be if you had won a major contract and the news story focused on how the previous supplier had lost the contract, relegating you to the last paragraph. It happens and, if the story is true, you have to live with it.

Finally, the point about buying editorial; do not try to bribe journalists and do not assume that taking them for a beer or for lunch will guarantee you any coverage. Furthermore, if you advertise in the paper do not expect to automatically get a write-up.

# Week Five

## SUNDAY

## Angles

All of the above might sound a little negative, but if you are going to play the publicity game then there is nothing wrong with learning a few of the rules.

By now you should have started to work out exactly what you want to achieve from any press coverage, and you will know a few of the howlers to avoid. Now for the fun stuff – what to put in your release.

A useful first step is to start reading papers and magazines and specifically the publications in which you want your company to appear. Look not so much at who else they are covering, but at how they are covering them. Take a fictional example of the magazines *Audio Retailers' Monthly* and *Audio Product Buyer*. They have both covered the launch of a new superwidget. It is the same story but the first paragraph in *Audio Retailers' Monthly* reads:

> Dealers will be able to get a lot out of Frank Smith Sound's new Superwidget in the form of joint marketing budget, add-on services and a generous mark-up. Demand should be strong and point of sale materials will be on offer as standard, with all products available on a sale or return basis.

# SUNDAY

Now look at the product buyer's magazine:

> A gap in the market has been filled by Frank Smith Sound's Superwidget, which is guaranteed to make your sound even sharper. Plug it into your music centre and it enhances the quality of all of your cassette recordings to make them sound like minidiscs, and all for under £400 . . .

You can see the difference immediately. The retailer's interest in the product is purely commercial and they focus on that element. The end customer wants to know what it does and how much it costs. Your job is to familiarise yourself with the needs of the readers of each of your target publications and construct a press release that tells each editor and journalist what they need to know. If you wanted to get into the above publications you might want to write separate releases, one for the trade press and another for the consumer. For the moment we will try to put one together for both. It might start:

> Frank Smith Computing has released the Superwidget, a plug-in device for Audio systems that diminishes hiss and sharpens signals. Using the latest in technology it is supported by a dealer programme that will include generous discounts and point of sale material. Demand is expected to be high for this new product.

Later on we shall show why you would not want to write a release with so many passive verbs in it, but for the moment let us focus on content rather than style. Certainly our release begins with all of the essential facts for both magazines. However, consider the competition; you might be up against another 50 releases in any given day, which is around 700 per week, and the magazines have, say, about 20 news slots available per month. All the release says so far, in essence, is that Frank Smith Sound is going to make an audio product. No kidding.

## The hook

What the release lacks so far is a hook – something that is going to make it stand out. This can take any number of forms. Let us think about the product itself and put some ideas down:

# SUNDAY

> Frustrated by hearing hiss on your favourite audio tapes every time you listen to one? No worries – the Superwidget from Frank Smith Sound will clean them up as they play – and if you're a retailer we'll help you tell your customers how they can get this useful gadget up and running for under £300.

It is still not wildly thrilling, but it does start by identifying a need that many readers and editors will recognise, and in the next sentence it tells you how you can get help. Then, by introducing price and dealer support, the story starts to emerge in a form that will be interesting and digestible to any editor who might be interested in the product.

Your hook can take any shape. If you are providing jobs in a deprived area, then that is a hook in its own right. Another example is if you are setting up a new business in response to some sort of crisis – a number of small companies gained press coverage when farmers set them up in response to the British Foot and Mouth crisis of 2000/2001; many companies received attention in the late 1990s by sticking the 'E-Commerce' tag on to their business. It can be a small thing, for example, a promotion you are running or if you are a charity, a new appeal. Your aim is to answer the question 'Why should I tell the readers this?' If this remains unanswered, then you may be dead in the water.

# SUNDAY

Week Five

Finding a book should not actually be difficult. Consider the following list.

- Has something actually happened? An event makes a hook easier, although it is not essential – if you want to do a release about your new dominance in your market you might find nothing has happened except a good balance sheet for the month. Present it well and it may still attract coverage.
- Has anything related happened? Consider that if your balance sheet has improved, someone else's may have suffered: 'Frank Smith Widgets overtakes John's Gadgets' might make a better hook than 'Widget Sales Increase'. Of if not, 'Frank Smith Widgets Grows Market by 30 per Cent' – and make it a story about how your marketing is getting more new customers in.
- There may be an event outside your business of which you could take advantage for your releases.

# SUNDAY

> People in safety equipment might want to piggyback the fireworks around November the fifth, for example.
> - Jobs being saved.
> - Jobs being created.
> - Influx of money into a business – whether from an outside investor or increased sales.

Try making your own list that will help your business – it is surprisingly easy.

## Summary

You now have an idea of your objectives, you understand a little about how the press works and you know how not to appear a time waster. You have given some thought to presenting your press announcement with an interesting opening to avoid looking like another ordinary company doing day-to-day business. As an exercise you could try to draft more of the press release about the Superwidget or write an opening paragraph for your own product, company or other organisation.

Tomorrow we shall have a go at writing the rest of the press release.

Week Five

# MONDAY

# Structuring your press release

The first thing you need to do is to draw a triangle. Or better still, make a pyramid out of plasticine or something similar. Now rub out the bottom of the triangle or take a bit of the plasticine off with a knife, cleanly. On the drawing, draw the bottom line to make a smaller triangle. The shape you have in front of you is still a triangle. It is smaller, but it remains easy to identify as a triangle or pyramid.

This is the model to bear in mind when you are writing your press release because most journalists will miss out the bottom bit when they receive it. And if the release is going to get used at all, the journalist still needs to know what they are getting and the bare bones of the story you are trying to tell.

*PYRAMID STRUCTURE WORKED BEFORE...*

We can work on an example. The basic story is that your motorcycle repair shop has opened a new branch in Leicester. The 'hook' will be, say, that Leicester's bikers have been previously under-resourced and yours is the first such establishment to open there. The release reads:

## Week Five

# MONDAY

### Leicester bikers reprieved

After years of travelling 7 miles to get their motorbikes repaired, Leicester bikers can breathe a sigh of relief as Jordan's Repairs opens a new branch at the heart of their city. It opens on 29$^{th}$ February and racing legend Murray Walker will attend the day, subject to working commitments.

Owner Jim Jordan has taken on five mechanics to run the shop, which will build on the success of his three existing branches in Hull, Manchester and London. 'A business like this stands or falls on the quality of its staff,' he says. 'We have a very low failure rate and I'm pleased to be bringing that to Leicester with the new premises.'

Jordan, 38, started the business in 1985 when he couldn't find a decent mechanic to take care of the Harley-Davidson he had inherited when his father died. Attached to an uncle's garage at the time, he found he had to move into new premises and take on staff quickly when word spread to other vintage bike owners in the area. 'It was stunning,' he says. 'I almost grew too quickly, it was a pretty hairy time.'

He made the decision to service all bikes only after trading for 10 years. 'It was getting to the stage where we were going to expand or we weren't, and I decided we were – but there are only so many Harleys to go around.' He misses the specialist days but has enjoyed a fast track to the top of his business.

# MONDAY

Now try a little experiment. Ask a friend to read the first paragraph of the release. Get another friend to read the first two paragraphs. Get another to read the first three. Each person should, in theory, be convinced that they know all they need to, and that they have read a complete – albeit short – news story.

Now try doing the same with the news pages in your newspaper – not the features, which work differently, but the news items. They should all work in the same way because journalists are trained to write like this. The reason for this is that if they write too much, the sub-editor will need to do some cutting and, to make the job easier, they always cut from the bottom.

Note also that there are some quotes in the release. These will be used rarely; journalists normally want their own quotes from you and not something you have prefabricated for a press release. However, if the journalist is on a deadline and the paper is due to go to the printers and another story has fallen through, the easier you make it for them to use your release, the better.

Therefore, structurally:

- Think 'pyramid'.
- Put essentials in at the top and expand upon them.
- Assume journalists will be too busy to read beyond your first paragraphs.
- Put some usable quotes in there but avoid clichés like 'commitment to quality' and 'game of two halves' etc.
- Bear in mind that people will cut from the bottom – so no summary paragraph!

Week Five

# MONDAY

## Where are we going with this?

You now have the basic shape of a press release, although of course there are releases which work while breaking the rules and others which follow the rules and are badly written. There is a brief sermon on good English and grammar at the end of this chapter. Some press releases, however, fail to achieve any positive publicity simply because they are sent to the wrong place.

A case in point is in the cartoon. By all means it is an exaggerated, slightly flippant example, but it makes the point. You need to think about targeting your press release in exactly the right way.

# MONDAY

*Week Five*

## Possible objectives

Not all press releases are designed to get stories into print – incredible but true! You might have any one of the following as your objective and a subtly different approach is needed for each:

- coverage of a story
- getting quoted in reaction to a story
- getting into a feature which covers your general business area
- general profile building
- damage limitation or cover-up

In the first of those cases, you need to make it clear what has happened and why it is interesting. In the second, focus on the personality of the staff member you want the journalist to call (and they will want to speak to someone to get their own quotes – forget any notion of their using only the press released quotes, those are to attract attention only). In the third, again the profile of the personality is more interesting. You need to think 'Am I writing something time-sensitive' and, if so, 'Will they remember me in a month?' The more hooks you give them to call you under any of these circumstances, the better your public profile will build. The last objective will be fully covered towards the end of this chapter.

# MONDAY

## The media

Yesterday we touched on some of the different sorts of media and their needs, for example, the trade versus the mainstream press. It is worth considering some of the different types of press that you might encounter and what to bear in mind when approaching them.

*National press*

The nationals are understandably the most difficult press to penetrate because they get thousands of releases from everyone. Your story, if it is going to get anywhere, will need national interest. That does not mean your customers need to come from far and wide but maybe, for example, you have done something innovative in your business from which other companies can benefit. In the late 1990s and in early 2000 many companies got coverage because they were selling electronically, no matter where they were based. Nevertheless, do consider, when putting your release together for the nationals, that the 'hook' needs to be a big one.

*Local press*

For the local press you need to stress the local angle and, in many ways, you need to tell the reader why this *is not* in the nationals. Think job creation, think local customers, think local publicity events and stunts and put these as the hook in the first paragraph.

*Consumer press*

When a journalist says 'consumer press' he or she does not mean a magazine that does consumer campaigns, but something that goes to the consumer and is sold on high street newsstands and in newsagents. Think carefully about

# MONDAY

whether your release should go to these papers and magazines and whether they write about the sort of issues you are promoting. Remember the bike repair shop at the beginning of this chapter? The owner repairs bikes and blokes ride bikes, but is *Esquire* likely to take the story? Or would it be better to approach a biking magazine?

The consumer press will want to know why their readers would want to buy your product, donate to your charity or whatever – make sure that you tell them. In the first paragraph.

*Trade and professional press*
If you sell to businesses or are a charity looking for business sponsorship, then consider the trade and professional press as well as, or instead of, the consumer press. These are the publications that nobody outside the field would ever bother to read; *Design Week* for designers, *Packaging Week* for people in logistics, *Draper's Record* for people in curtains. If you are in the relevant field then you are probably reading at least one of these anyway. These types of publications will be easier to get into (although these things are relative) and if you are well informed about your subject, you might become someone they can call upon for comment.

The value of this last point is, of course, up to you. If you want a higher profile among your peers then make sure the press is well aware of who you are and where they can get hold of you. If you are too busy running the business then you can be more low-key.

Week Five

# MONDAY

## Single or multiple releases?

A key question for the first-time press release writer is whether to write a single press release to cover all of the various branches of the press. Ultimately the answer will depend on how much time you wish to spend on writing, but some factors to bear in mind would include:

- If you are selling anything to the trade and want to interest the trade press, you may want to include details (such as mark-up) that they would not want the end customer to see. Granted, the trade press can call up for the extra details but there is the chance they may not bother.
- With the specialist press you can get a lot more technical – a motoring magazine will want a lot more information on what is under the bonnet than, say, a general magazine.
- The story might not be appreciably different for the various publications though – if you can not work out the different angles, do not kid yourself, just send one really well-written release off.

## Information overload

How much of this glorious prose should you spray upon an unsuspecting world and how flowery should you make your opening sentences? The basic answer is two pages maximum and not flowery at all. There is an issue about the amount of information that a journalist needs in order to write a story; some want to see buckets of research that they will never use and others want to know the basics, write the

Week Five

# MONDAY

piece up and move on to the next thing. If you have some technical information, put the details on a separate paper so the journalist can refer to it when they need to, rather than wade through a longer release.

Additional information you can usefully attach to a release would include:

- Pictures of anyone quoted – use decent ones, preferably taken by a professional. A statement that photography is available on request will be fine if you are concerned about budget.
- Company backgrounder that can be kept on file, or a paragraph at the end of the release. Make sure this is visibly separate from the main release.

- Your business card or that of someone in marketing.
- OK, OK, your corporate mouse mat. Or a pen with your number on it. If you *must.*

### Format

A word about the physical shape of your press release. Anything more elaborate than this is likely to look like overkill:
- A4 paper
- your letterhead or at least logo
- double spaced
- Aameaningful headline
- contact details at the bottom – phone number and e-mail

Week Five

# MONDAY

## Cover-ups

We will finish today with the trick question we started with. You will no doubt have spotted it. No? Well, go back to the original dummy release we drafted – the one about the motorcycle repair shop. There is an inconsistency in it, which a journalist worth his or her salt will spot immediately.

SPOT THE DIFFERENCE

Look at it again. The business, when it specialised in Harley-Davidsons, was growing dramatically – 'It was stunning . . . I almost grew too quickly, it was a pretty hairy time,' says our release. Then after 10 years there is a change: 'He made the decision to service all bikes only after trading for 10 years.' It was getting to the stage where we were going to expand or we weren't, and I decided we were – but there are only so many Harleys to go around.' What happened during that first ten years? Did the Harley-Davidson market really dry up, did the original staff of specialist mechanics leave, or what? There is a definite sense of something being glossed over here.

Week Five

# MONDAY

A good journalist will always want to look between the lines and see whether there is a story you are trying to avoid telling them. If not, fine – do not make it look as though there is. If there is another story, have a contingency plan ready if you get questions about it – preferably one that does not involve slamming the phone down.

In the same press release there was another howler – the mention of Murray Walker's appearance. This is fine in itself, but consider this: will the journalist want to come and get a picture of the estimable Mr Walker, rather than run a story in advance? You will not get your story into the paper twice. If you accept that a paper will find a celebrity more of a draw than your press release, would it be better to send an invitation to the paper and offer drinks on the day?

What could we have done?

There would have been two solutions to avoiding letting the journalist think he or she had got ahead of the repair company in this case:

- Come straight out with it and tell them what happened. How about 'When the original Harley-Davidson specialist mechanics left to form their own company, Jim decided to broaden the company and has succeeded spectacularly'. Nobody is about to use hype like 'spectacularly' in the newspapers or magazines without checking for themselves, and probably not then either. However, they are unlikely to read anything too negative into this sort of up-front comment about a growing business.

# MONDAY

- Just do not mention it: the reader came to the press release not knowing about the original speciality in Harleys, so they are not likely to miss it if it does not appear.

## Summary

Today you should have started thinking about:

- the structure of the release
- the objective of the release
- the market for the release
- how much to put in the release
- enclosures
- second sources of comment for your release
- a final thought about whether a release is right every time

Tomorrow we shall concentrate on where you should send your press release.

# Who does what in a magazine?

If you are writing a press release or cold-calling a newsdesk with a story, then you will want to speak to the editor, right? Wrong. You will get passed around an internal phone system by assorted underlings and they are not just being protective – well, some of them are – but want to ensure that you get through to the right person without wasting your time or anyone else's. Unfortunately, insisting on speaking to the editor will make you sound pompous or naïve.

## What people do

Before you approach a paper or magazine it is worth developing a basic understanding of what the various individuals do.

*Editorial assistant*
This is the person who chases invoices internally and

ensures the smooth running of the office – frequently he or she will also order the stationery and file the press releases into an archive, assuming there is one.

They are also frequently the editor's first line of defence when filtering calls, and often have the power to put your call through or not. Editorial assistants also tend to open the post – the individual on the envelope is rarely the actual recipient. The editorial assistant opens everything in most places and might pick out some of the more interesting stuff to pass on to someone else; mostly though, the 100 plus releases each day will go into a slush pile for fillers – whether fillers means the 'news in brief' section, news items that get put in when a better story falls through or other emergency uses.

Treat editorial assistants well. They may sound as though they are on the bottom rung, but they are the most likely person to call you if you are a new contact to the magazine – and if they write about you, their prose will not look any different to the reader than that of the editor.

*Reporter*
The reporter's job does what it says on the tin – a reporter talks to people and writes, and that is about it. Feature writer, news correspondent and all of the 'general' writing jobs are a subset of reporter.

*Chief reporter*
A number of magazines and newspapers have chief reporters and other specialist correspondents. This tends to mean that the editor wants to promote them beyond the 'reporter' tag but that the reporter did not want to start commissioning work and managing budgets.

# Week Five
# TUESDAY

*Features editor*

For the person pitching ideas to an editorial team, the features editor is one of the key people to get to know. He or she commissions the longer pieces which are likely to be less time-sensitive and more issue than news driven. You might be able to get a list of forward features from the features editor or from the ad department; you can then pitch your company as a contact when they are going to write something relevant.

*Section editor*

There is a variation on features editor in larger magazines that expect to have many features to plough through or which require specialist input. They have section editors, for example, on *Management Today* for its various sections, and the consumer press has them – *GQ* will have a style editor and a travel editor. However, watch out – many of these editors are freelancers rather than in-house staff and so press releases addressed to them at the publication will end up in the editorial assistant's lap.

*News editor*

The news editor commissions and edits the news section, usually found at the front of a newspaper or magazine. On the nationals, this job will be divided among a number of people and there will be a foreign news editor, a business editor and so forth. Smaller publications will have a smaller staff. This would be your contact for time-sensitive releases.

*Editor*

By now you will be wondering what the editor does. He or she is responsible for the overall shape and feel of the publication. They will do some writing and, of course, some

# Week Five
## TUESDAY

editing and proofing of pages, but they are really more like a managing director than a coalface worker, in most instances.

Obviously, in the really small instances, for example, niche newsletters, the editor might do a lot more – page layouts, production work, etc. However, for publications of any size the editor's main skills will be in people management and delegating to the right member of staff.

*Sub-editor*

A common misconception is that the sub-editor is the person just below the editor. Not so. The subs are the people who take pieces of writing or 'copy', to use the jargon, and turn it into a style that is consistent with the rest of the magazine or newspaper. A contributor might have referred to a company as 'they', for example, when the house style is 'it'; all of these and more general points will be picked up by the subs.

*Production editor*

The production editor controls the subs and will liaise with outside agencies, such as printers, repro houses and perhaps picture agencies, to ensure that the publication actually happens. He or she will write headlines (for which the reporters will invariably get the complaints) and cut copy ruthlessly until stories fit a page design, or cajole reporters and commissioning editors into writing more until they fill the length.

We are talking 'seriously important' person here and the readers should hardly be aware of them.

*Art editor*

The art editor is responsible for page layouts and commissioning photographers and illustrators. Expect to

# Week Five
# TUESDAY

hear from them only if you are doing an interview and they want to commission their own pictures.

*Contributing editor*

This is a bit of a catch-all job title which many magazines use for different types of contributor. Contributing editors may contribute nothing or anything – it is impossible to tell simply from the magazine's masthead.

*Publisher*

The publisher has next to no direct influence on a magazine's contents since his or her job is purely commercial. It is ultimately the publisher's job to ensure that a publication is in profit for as much time as possible and this is achieved by keeping salaries under control and chivvying the advertising team to keep the cash coming in. If you had an idea that involved marketing or a promotion, rather than simply a press release, the publisher's office is the best one to try – other than that the publisher should not be visible to anyone outside the publishing company.

*Advertising manager*

The advertising and editorial departments should always be separate. However, the editorial department on a magazine will ensure that the advertising team has an idea of what is coming so that they can send out the 'features list'. For instance, if there is a big movie round-up coming in November, the advertising team can get some film-related advertising sales moving.

This is why the advertising and marketing departments are useful to contact for a media pack. This will contain demographic information on who buys the magazine and where it is targeted, the tone and a forward features list if

## TUESDAY

one is available. This is not a substitute for reading the magazine, but it is a useful addendum.

*The freelance journalist*
Not all of the pages of a magazine are filled by the staff, and the freelance journalist will write many articles and is often a good contact to cultivate. He or she is free to pitch ideas into more than one magazine or newspaper and will have a good idea of what is coming up in their section of the market; on the other hand freelance journalists do not have the power to commission anything, so please, please do not plague them with 'Are you publishing this?' calls after sending in a release.

*Your contact*
From the above list you will have been able to work out who *will not* be in touch about your release unless there is a query over a spelling or a need for a photo. So how do you know who is going to get in touch? The answer is of course, you do not and indeed nobody might, but if they do then it is worth cultivating them. The vast majority of newsdesks and features staff will divide companies up among themselves and it will be their job to 'follow' your organisation. Assuming this happens and they deem you important enough, expect periodic calls to find out what is going in. Some contacts find this annoying but then they asked for the attention in the first place – and they forget that this can be an excellent opportunity to bin the release they were about to send off and let the journalist think they found out about it by themselves!

Week Five

# TUESDAY

### Jargon

By now you might be a little confused and so here are some definitions.

**Advertorial**: An advertisement written to look like editorial – you will pay through the nose to get these in.
**Backgrounder**: Set of documents or a single document giving company details such as turnover, history, key personnel biographies – whatever you think will be relevant.
**Copy**: Any piece of writing by a staff or freelance journalist.
**Dog-leg**: Article shaped like a dog leg, put around an advert.

> **Feature**: A long article, not usually driven directly by news.
> **Masthead**: The list of who does what that every magazine will publish. Also known as the 'flannel panel'.

## Approaching the team

If you want to get your name around the editorial office, the people to speak to are the reporters, features editors and news editors, yes? Well, maybe yes and maybe no. Many magazines will open all of their press releases centrally and so only the editorial assistant and news editor or whoever sifts them will actually see the releases. Therefore, multiple copies of a single release are out; a single, well-written release on a pertinent subject will have the same effect.

> **A word about advertising**
>
> There is a handful of local, small newspapers that will offer companies editorial coverage only if they advertise with them. They are in the minority and the readers will quickly gather that they are being offered advertising copy and may dismiss it as biased. By all means advertise in the newspaper or magazine that you are targeting. You will be able to dictate exactly what the readers see in your advert, which will not happen in the editorial section; you will be offered a specific place in the paper and, of course, you will pay for it. However, do not expect this to influence your coverage on the editorial pages – many journalists pride themselves on ignoring any cajoling from the

Week Five

# TUESDAY

> advertising department to 'give this bloke some space, he's spending a fortune with us', and trying to apply pressure commercially may inspire contempt rather than get results.

## The contacts list

Although it might be pleasant if you had the time to write individual letters to every journalist who might be interested in writing about your piece, in reality you are going to have to target a list of people and monitor your responses.

Depending on how big you want your list to be, there are a number of ways to build it up. The simplest but most time-consuming is to decide which publications you wish to target, call them up and ask to whom you should send press releases and start sending them. The arguments in favour of this are:

- it is cheap
- you remain in total control

The arguments against are:

- You may not know all of the publications you need to target.
- You will not be aware of new magazine launches in your area.
- It is time-consuming.

If you are only aiming at a very small niche, it is possible to build your own thorough list. If you sell only to the trade, for

Week Five

# TUESDAY

example, you will want the trade press and no one else to be aware of you, so you can target a handful of publications.

The alternatives for building your contacts list are as follows:

- *Buy or borrow a directory*: *Willings, Brad* and a number of others will be available through your library.
- *Get a professional directory on CD*: Pims, Mediadisk and others are available. This is the point at which the exercise starts to cost serious money.
- *Use a press release distribution source from the internet*: www.responsesource.co.uk is one of the better ones. This will distribute your press releases to registered journalists on the site and will also inform you when a journalist is writing something on which you could usefully comment, and give contact details for the journalist. This one costs.
- *Use a PR company*: anything from the sole trader to the multinational. This will not be particularly cheap, but if you are just beginning you might find the smaller companies cost you less than using your own time on PR when you should be out meeting clients. Always check the contract to see what you are getting in return for your cash.

### The exclusive

A number of journalists dream of breaking an exclusive – the story they know that they, and only they, have discovered. By all means consider giving them an exclusive if they want one, but remember:

Week Five
# TUESDAY

- You are effectively playing the competition off against each other. Can you afford to alienate the rest of the press like that?
- Once you have agreed to an exclusive, do not give it to anyone else – people do this and then wonder why the first paper will not talk to them again.
- You will need to decide whether you want to build a relationship with a journalist that warrants the exclusive status of your story – it is one thing becoming chums with the editor of *Needlework International*, but when they move to another paper you will have to start again with their replacement.
- Please, please make sure you have something worth saying when you go exclusive. Some features are exclusive because nobody else is interested enough to print them.

Above all, if an exclusive is on offer make sure it is precisely that. Do not be like the person who once called a journalist to offer some 'exclusive research' on which her client was doing a series of one-to-one interviews the following week – the word 'series' immediately told the writer in question that these were far from exclusives, 'exclusive' was just being used as a buzzword to get him interested.

In fact it might be worth going through your press release or invitation with a red pen, finding anything that looks like a buzzword in any industry and taking them out before you think about sending anything off.

# T U E S D A Y

## Summary

Today you have found out about:

- who does what on a newspaper and magazine
- the issues surrounding the targeting of your press releases
- the issues about targeting individuals
- how to build a contacts list
- the issues surrounding exclusivity

Tomorrow we shall look at what happens once the press release is dispatched.

Week Five
# WEDNESDAY

# Following up your press release

So far, you will have written your press release and the right journalist should have received it. You sit and wait for either the press release to run in the paper or for the follow-up call to arrive. Nothing happens. So, what do you do?

### The PR follow-up from hell

Many inexperienced PRs or PRs coerced by their clients think that it is an excellent idea to follow up every press release with a bright, breezy call to the journalist. Either they can charge the client for their time on the phone or their client is pushing them for a personal response from the journalist(s) in question. Or, as some seasoned reporters suspect, the senior PRs decide that the best way to train an office junior is to let them come face to face with hostile journalists early on.

The follow-up call tends to run something along the lines of:

PR: Hello, I'm calling about a press release we sent on my client.
Journalist: How long ago was this?
PR: About 3 weeks ago.

Typically, at this stage the journalist will either be patient and explain that he or she receives 50 or more releases each day and could not possibly remember any individual one, or becomes irritated because it is the third similar call that day and slams the phone down.

## Week Five

# WEDNESDAY

The choices open to you when nobody appears to be paying any attention are straightforward enough.

- follow up with a phone call
- follow up with another press release
- try to arrange a meeting with the journalist
- hire a PR agency

The last option we will not cover here because this book is about free PR – in reality, consider hiring an agency when the job of PR is getting out of hand. We will discuss the first three.

## The follow-up call

One of the trickiest areas in do-it-yourself PR is the same as in any other area of PR – how to frame a follow-up call if you think that your press communication has been ignored. The difficulties are as follows:

Week Five

# WEDNESDAY

- If the journalist or editor did not find your piece inspiring there is often very little more to be said.
- If an interesting piece was simply overlooked then there is still not going to be a lot to add. Even if it was scintillating, it is going to be too old to be any use for next week's issue or the one after.
- Publications receive too many unfocused calls about why press releases were not used. At worst, the caller will sound like a moaner.

The answer is to treat the call as you would any other business call. This means that not only do you need to know what you are going to say, but you need an objective – a reason for making the call in the first place. These might include:

- Finding out if there are any other relevant pieces coming up; maybe they are doing a round-up of new businesses in their area, maybe there is a small traders' supplement – find out if there are any unobvious ways in which you can get involved.
- Getting a better idea of what the paper is after – sounding as though you are interested in them rather than interested in any coverage you might get is always a plus!
- Finding out whether any reporter in particular covers your business area; if you are in retail, does the paper have a specific retail correspondent, if you are in farming does the paper use a regular agricultural correspondent etc.?
- Arranging a meeting so that the editor or journalist

## WEDNESDAY

Week Five

can get a better idea of what you do and vice versa – if you persuade someone to come and meet you, be sure you have something interesting to say!

### A useful hint

If you are going to follow up the press release, be prepared to be rebuffed. It was an unsolicited communication after all, and if you received a follow-up call for every unlooked-for business approach, you would presumably not be very pleased. It is always worth checking when the paper or magazine comes out and making an educated guess about when they go to press – avoid calling at that time as if your life depended on it.

Week Five

# WEDNESDAY

## The follow-up press release

If you want to send another press release, then the follow-up call can be a good means of paving the way for it. Try to find out whether there was something inherently wrong with your item. If it is 'not a strong angle' then try to do something about that if you can, provided you do not stretch a story into something that it is not. Look at your own initial release objectively and assess whether it was:

- brief
- to the point
- clear in its 'hook'
- tailored for your target publication

You will have thought so at the time or you would not have sent it off. Now that you have had some cooling off time, think again – you might be surprised.

## Try to arrange a meeting with the journalist

There is overlap here with the follow-up call on our list, but it can be worth meeting journalists in order to get a more personal idea of what they need from you before they can write something.

### The journalist's week

Like any other business, newspapers and magazine shave a pretty rigid production cycle. You would not expect the *Evening Standard* to miss the midday

Week Five

# WEDNESDAY

edition because something was happening internally at the paper, nor would you want a midday *Guardian* because they were running a bit behind that day.

Bearing this in mind, it is clear that the papers and magazines must adhere to their deadlines strictly and unforgivingly. So when you put your call in, the first thing to ask is whether it is convenient to talk – if it is a weekly and you have hit 'press day', the day when everything has to be in, then nobody will have the time to talk to you. On the other hand they will notice if you are courteous enough to ask before launching in to your diatribe.

And of course if you can get an idea of when press day actually happens (or press week for a monthly), you can probably work out when they put the newspapers together. Time your releases so that they arrive on the right desk on that day rather than several days before, getting forgotten in the process.

Week Five
# WEDNESDAY

People get very nervous about meeting the press. They think that they are going to be quoted out of context – and if you are the Chancellor of the Exchequer and admit casually that you would love to raise income tax by 98 per cent for everyone earning over £20,000, you are probably right. For the most part, though, misquotes and bad press relations happen because of misunderstandings. Let us look at a few ways of heading these off.

*Pre-knowledge and preconceptions*
A statement that can be fatal to a meeting between a journalist – particularly a young journalist – and a businessperson is the assumption that when the journalist confirms that he or she has read the backgrounder, he or she actually means it. Journalists can be as insecure as anyone else and will frequently be unwilling to admit that they have not got a clue about your business.

Obviously, it can be frustrating if the journalist appears not to know what you are talking about – there is a myth that journalists have access to vast amounts of exclusive research materials and the time to do something about it. This used to be truer than it is now; given the advent of the internet as a popular communication medium, most people have access to the Web and research facilities as good as any journalist.

The good news is that you can add to the research available to the journalist by putting a good press area on your website. Ideally this should include:

- Recent press releases.
- Press release archive if you have been trading for a while.

# WEDNESDAY

- Corporate backgrounder – never, ever assume someone knows what you do for a living.
- High-resolution pictures of key personnel and products – make it easier for journalists to use your stories if they have a slot on a news page that is lacking in pictures, whether your office is open or not.

Also bring a press pack with you, or send it to the journalist in advance.

*Press packs*

So what is a press pack? It can mean anything from a couple of press releases to a full set of recent releases, including the very latest pictures of everything. If you can do this and get the pictures on to CD, so much the better. It is worth making a check-list of everything that is desirable to include in a press pack:

- Corporate backgrounder.
- Company brochure if you have one.
- A handful of previous cuttings if any (remember to check copyright on these).
- Your business card or that of the employee assigned to deal with the press.
- The current press release (of course).
- Potted biographies of everyone quoted in the press release who is an employee of the company.
- Pictures, high resolution and preferably on CD, of everyone quoted in the release.

Week Five

# WEDNESDAY

*What to expect from a journalist*

The simple guide as to what to expect from a journalist is usually 'someone as nervous as you and with as little idea about how the meeting is going to go'. Remember the following points:

- They are after a story or usable material – this is not cynical or impersonal, it is just the job. So do not worry too much about the sales pitch.
- They will ask a lot of questions – they are trained to expect interviewees to put up some sort of front.
- Do not expect them to be uncritical – they are not customers or employees dazzled by your product, they are paid to be objective and to anticipate their readers' possible objections to your story.
- With luck they will come along with their own set of questions for you, in which case answer them – if they are coming because they like the restaurant or because they are curious about your company, they may not. So try to have a story or at least a company background to talk about for when conversation runs dry.

## The follow-up call from the journalist

So far we have assumed that your press release has hit the slush pile and been ignored. Realistically, because of the sheer number of releases flying around out there, this is the most likely outcome, at least for the first few. However, it is also possible that your piece of news will rise straight to the top of the pile and a journalist will call. This is nothing to be worried about, but there are some things to remember:

# WEDNESDAY

Week Five

- If you are not thoroughly briefed about the story, or you need to check some details, say that you are in a meeting and return the call when you have the information about you. Nobody minds you checking facts.
- If a call comes in when you are out, return it as quickly as possible. Newsworthiness dates very quickly and something a journalist was interested in on Monday might be completely forgotten by Wednesday.
- Focus on the story you want to promote by all means, but remember a journalist might be calling about something relating to your business area for another article, inspired by your release. Stick too rigidly to your script and you might exclude yourself from beneficial coverage.

*I'VE BEEN LOOKING FORWARD TO MEETING THE PRESS FOR AGES...*

## What the journalist wants

The journalist wants one thing – a good story. That is really about it. If you have this or can contribute a useful second view on another story, then you are basically in. This is actually quite a profound statement and one that many people do not seem to understand. Here are some things the journalist does *not* want:

- Platitudes.
- Irrelevant comment about things that you would rather he or she wrote about.
- A ticking off for not behaving like an extension of your marketing department. This can happen; there are people so close to their business or job that they forget a journalist has his or her own job, and is only accountable to the readers, the editor and the publishing company and to nobody else provided they have written an accurate story.

## One to one or one to many?

An alternative to the one-to-one press briefing by phone or in person is the press conference. The idea is simple: you get journalists together and give them a presentation. They then go and write the story up.

It is simple in theory, and in practice less so. Judging whether it is a good idea depends on a number of factors:

- Does your announcement have broad enough appeal to attract enough journalists to avoid embarrassment?

Week Five

# WEDNESDAY

- Is your presentation so important that your journalists will not mind all going away with substantially the same story?
- How geographically dispersed are your target publications? This will have a bearing on the venue you pick.
- Will the cost of hiring the venue and entertaining (feeding and watering preferably, unless it is a very important announcement) the journalists be justified?
- If you are going to present to a crowd, will you have to hire equipment, i.e. multimedia projector to go with your laptop?
- Are you actually any good at presenting?

Journalists will turn up to a mass briefing expecting to see other journalists, and so try to spread the net fairly wide when approaching people. A round-table discussion hints at lower numbers and you might want to consider setting up one of these instead if you know a restaurant with a private room, for example.

IT'S A LOVELY STAMP COLLECTION – REALLY – BUT WHAT ABOUT THE WATER POWERED CAR?

Week Five

# WEDNESDAY

## External PR company?

At some stage during this process you may decide that it is time to look into the possibility of using an external specialist PR company. This is where you need to have a good sense of your time and the value of PR – is the £1500 plus you will be likely to spend each month going to be worthwhile? Bear in mind that a good PR agency will track your success in the press and report back to you periodically as well. If it allows you to refocus on your core business, it could be a very sensible investment to make.

Things to ask a prospective PR company:

- If you are impressed with the directors that meet you to pitch for the account, ask whether they will be handling you personally or passing you on to the office junior.
- Make sure you have set objectives for your prospective PRs – and listen to their advice on how realistic these are.
- Ask about their results for previous clients – ask to see clippings and find out what these actually achieved.
- Check whether they have any clients in your business area – a conflict may or may not be a problem.
- Find out whether they are recruiting someone to help with the extra workload you will be putting their way, or how else they will be coping with it.
- Of course check for hidden extras and make sure periodic reviews are built into the deal.

# WEDNESDAY

Week Five

## Summary

Today we have focused on what to do when making initial contact with the press. You should be clear about:

- following up the press release
- preparing yourself for a journalist's call
- preparing a press pack
- assessing whether you need to do a press conference
- speaking carefully and not causing problems for your company

Tomorrow we shall look at maintaining a press relationship.

Week Five

# THURSDAY

# Sustaining relations with the press

By this stage you will hopefully have your proverbial foot in the press' metaphorical door. You will have seen your name in print and will be delighted to show your Hall Of Fame clipping to anyone who would care to look at it.

And you will be itching to start all over again. Except that is not quite how it works. Your ideal objective should be to become a regular participant in the press without becoming too ubiquitous. This will reassure your shareholders and your customers will become even more familiar with you. It can be a good idea to look at the following questions:

- Would you be better off forging a relationship with a single newspaper or magazine rather than trying to become friendly with many publications?
- Is your business or other activity interesting and unique enough to sustain continued coverage?
- Does your target publication often carry stories sourced from the same quarter?

## The regular commentator

If you read any sort of trade newspaper, you will probably be aware that there are a number of faces that keep cropping up time and time again whatever the subject. These proverbial 'rentaquotes' are actively promoting their business through established relationships with journalists and there is no reason why you should not join them.

Week Five

# THURSDAY

> **Step back**
>
> Before you embark on trying to become a regular press 'talking head' though, ask yourself if this is a good idea. If it is purely a matter of ego, consider doing something else that will benefit your business more directly. Reassuring shareholders and potential shareholders, as well as customers, is important; but on the other hand, if you own a small restaurant then a review in the local paper and, if you are really good, another in *Time Out*, is probably all you need beyond a listing in your local directory.

## Becoming a 'commentator'

There are no hard and fast rules about how to become a regularly quoted commentator in the press – some people seem to have the knack, others do not. However, there are a few useful guidelines, which may at least put you in the running.

*Flexibility*
As we agreed on Wednesday, you need to be flexible enough to talk about what the journalist wants to cover rather than sticking resolutely to your own script. This does not mean that you forget which company you are working for; but it does mean that you accept that a namecheck is good enough to publicise your business at this stage.

*Returning calls*
Amazing amounts of companies fail to return a journalist's call and then complain that they receive no coverage. Try to

# Week Five
## THURSDAY

bear in mind that the world of publishing and journalism is a fast one – if you do not call back quickly when someone is looking for comment to publish, your competition will.

If you have arranged a phone call at a given time with a journalist, try not to be on the phone at the appointed hour. It does happen and the journalist will soon lose interest.

*Say something interesting*

This should go without saying, but often people come out with truly bland quotes. Let us say that you or a competing company has just won a major contract and issued a press release. You are called for some feedback. The following are all equally plausible responses:

- We're very pleased to have won the contract.

Well of course you are. But who wants to print that? The

# Week Five
## THURSDAY

journalist is calling to find out something that does not go without saying.

- **The new supplier is a quality company.**

Seriously, this quote does get offered up from time to time. Once again, the journalist knows that you think or hope that you are dealing with a good company, otherwise why bother?

- **This fills a gap in our product portfolio.**

Better. We are getting an idea of why you signed the contract.

- **This replaces a contract that we lost a month ago.**

Up to you – it will certainly get reported and it is honest. If the loss of the contract was reported initially, then you have a reason for mentioning it. If not, it is probably best not to draw attention to the negative stuff – the determined journalist will ask you about it anyway.

## Off the record, unattributable

So far this week we have dealt with the 'straight' version of how to get noticed. If you are doing enough of interest and your market is not spectacularly overcrowded, you should be starting to see results. But what about this other stuff that you keep seeing reported – the 'source close to the company says' writing, and what about that call you had when you

Week Five

# T H U R S D A Y

were about to close a branch and make redundancies but had not announced it to the press?

These are where the press' 'mates' come in. Read the following section with extreme care – going into these areas can backfire spectacularly.

*Off the record*
Off the record should ideally mean precisely that. You tell a journalist something and it does not get printed. Some journalists though, particularly the younger variety, get off the record confused with 'unattributable' – and the quote ends up in the paper but without your name attached.

Assuming you are planning to go off the record and the journalist involved understands the full implications, you will need to ask yourself exactly why you want to tell a journalist something that they cannot print. There can be a number of legitimate reasons, for example:

■ 440 ■

# THURSDAY
*Week Five*

- Someone is spreading rumours about your company's performance. Your actual figures are confidential but prove the rumours to be untrue – so you want the journalist to understand you are solvent without seeing your details in print.
- The journalist has a question about a gap in your business that you know you have addressed but cannot announce yet – maybe you have taken a new member of staff on but he or she is still working notice out for the old employer, for example. The only way you can confirm you have addressed the business problem is by telling the journalist what you have done.
- You want to say something on behalf of your suppliers or customers but do not actually have their authority to do so – in which case you can either go off the record or you can keep quiet.

There are many other reasons why people go in for off the record. They might have something scurrilous to say, they might want to get a bit pally with the journalist or they might have an inflated idea of their own importance and think that going off the record will reinforce this somehow.

Overall – and you will not hear a journalist saying this often – it is probably wisest never to go off the record. If you are talking to a journalist, assume you are talking to the readers too. This eliminates any possibility of misunderstanding – more journalists have fallen out with their sources as a result of simple misunderstandings over whether they were on the record or not than most care to admit.

Week Five
# THURSDAY

*Unattributable*

You may have read newspaper and magazine reports in which 'sources close to the company' have said something, or 'friends' have said that a government minister is exhausted but pleased to be staying in the Department of Administrative affairs.

Sometimes these 'friends' or 'sources' are the person themselves who believe that the quote would damage them if it were traced back to them. This is a game that you can play with a cooperative journalist but, as with the off the record ploy, it can backfire very easily if there is a misunderstanding or if the journalist decides that getting a good story is more important than keeping you happy.

The other type of 'source' who leaks a story to the press is disgruntled employees, competitors or family members whose birthday you forgot – anyone can become a source. It is also true that if you let journalists know what is happening in other companies outside the authorised versions, you will become a source yourself – and you might be able to negotiate for a couple of 'nice' stories about your company to appear in the paper. On the other hand you might suspect (you will not know for certain) that your competitor is a 'throat' and feeding the paper stories about your company, and nothing you do or say is going to change that. It is a risk you run.

Essentially, becoming a press 'source' is a risk. If you are inclined to do it, you will do it whatever any book on the subject might advise, but do be aware of the risks. On Saturday we shall have a quick look at libel laws in case you put yourself at any legal risk or damage your personal reputation.

Week Five
## THURSDAY

## Your agenda

The other problem with talking to the press is that often you end up focused entirely on press and PR at the expense of running your business.

## Your objectives

Another trap into which a number of managers fall – particularly owner-managers, who are not accountable to anyone else – is underachieving their objectives through the press and not really noticing. This can be for a number of reasons:

# Week Five
## THURSDAY

1 No objective was actually set
2 Failure to monitor PR activity against business objective
3 Vanity taking hold after a few clippings start to appear in the local or even national press
4 Unrealistic objectives set in the first place and subsequently abandoned

On Monday we examined some strategies that should eliminate the possibility of the fourth item on that list happening. You will recall that we looked at how unlikely it was to increase your business directly as a result of a single article, and that most of the benefits would be intangible. Here is a list of realistic achievements – it is worth making your selection from this list and reviewing your actual performance against them periodically.

1 Increased visibility among your customer group
2 Building a book of press coverage to show potential clients
3 'Comfort factor' coverage for your shareholders, whether private or public

If these things are not happening, it may be worth re-evaluating your approach to publicity, or indeed focusing elsewhere.

# Week Five
## THURSDAY

## Summary

Today you should have picked up the following points:

- How to sustain contact with the press without becoming too ubiquitous.
- The difference between on the record, off the record and unattributable quotes.
- Developing your agenda as opposed to that of the journalist.
- Managing and monitoring your press coverage.
- Returning to your initial objectives to assess the coverage you will hopefully have received.

Up to now we have considered the press as a major way of reaching your target market and they are a very important channel. However, they are not the only one and you can publicise your business in other ways without spending a fortune. Tomorrow we shall move on to a different tack and look at the non-press side of public relations.

Week Five

# FRIDAY

# Non-press PR

Your business may be one that honestly would not benefit from press coverage at all. Perhaps you own a small internet bureau which, other than the odd mention in the local paper, does not have much to say to journalists – at least, not much that will get more people through the door. You may own a builders' merchant and are more interested in talking to local business than appearing in the local news, but you would like to see your brand awareness increase. There are ways of doing this that will not break the bank. Nevertheless, if you are reading this book to get strictly free publicity, then much of this chapter will be of marginal interest, since there are small costs involved.

## Websites

In the late 1990s, interest in the internet hit a peak. Everyone who wanted to get rich quick suddenly sprouted a website as if it was an extra limb. Not everybody needed one and people were frequently disappointed by the results they achieved. However, people whose sites were reasonably competent found that their brand awareness did increase somewhat. As with any other sort of publicity, websites were and are appropriate for a number of things: inert websites are suitable only for the smallest businesses; full-blown E-Commerce is essential for the larger company, particularly the retailer.

There are many books on E-Business for people who want to pursue the web side of promotion seriously; for our purposes it is worth focusing on just a few action points if you are planning to build a website.

# FRIDAY

- Never assume that people will just happen across your site – it needs to be referred to in all of your promotional material.
- Do not assume that people will not notice if you are using free web space – they will often spot this. It may not matter to your customers, but be aware of it.
- As we have said throughout, before putting anything online, into a press release or anywhere else, make sure you have something to say!
- If you are unable to build a website well yourself, consider spending money on getting someone else to do it for you – a bad site reflects badly on your business and will cost you in lost custom.
- Register with all of the search engines to make sure that people find *your* business rather than that of your competition when they are searching for something.
- Try to get hold of a relevant name ('domain names' as they are called) – the more memorable the better, and the more generic the better. If you are a builders' merchant, for example, you would be better off with www.woodwork.co.uk than www.johnswoodsupplies.co.uk because people need to know about you already before they enter the latter into their web browser.

## Free samples

Free samples are not, of course, free to the person who gives them out, but nor do they cost as much as they would to the customer if they bought them.

Week Five

# FRIDAY

Let us assume that you have a small chain of hairdressers. You have noticed that Monday is a quiet day in your branch. So, you leaflet all the local shops and some local residents to tell them that there is a half-price offer on Monday if they bring the leaflet. The leaflet does not need to be expensive, a photocopy will do.

Then again, perhaps you are a specialist food retailer or restaurant – would one of the local supermarkets allow you to stand outside and offer people free samples as they pass by? One such promotion took place in Thornton Heath, London as this book was being written – passers-by were offered a pot of freshly-cooked noodles in an authentic Chinese sauce. Provided that there is no conflict of interest, there is no reason why local businesses should not cooperate in this way.

## SMS

It can be a mistake to assume that marketing using technology basically means e-mails. Numerous companies have found that the mobile phone and the texting services available on it can be used to their advantage, as long as they keep records on their customers. One leading hairdresser chain, for example, offered a discount to anyone who downloaded their logo to their mobile phone from the website. They also ran a simpler campaign by texting customers in a given geographical area to let them know that they could have 25 per cent off a haircut on, say, Monday (assuming this was when business was slow).

Smaller businesses might want to text all of their customers in this way, and the good news is that there are very inexpensive pieces of software to allow you to do this on your computer. Just set up a list, type in your promotional message and off it goes to your customers' phones.

## Legal niceties

It is difficult to believe but just occasionally, people get caught doing illegal promotions, often without realising it. However, these things can get a little more difficult to track when you are promoting items on the internet. You might think it is a good idea to give away a free bottle of champagne to your first ten customers, and as long as you are careful where you promote you would be right. But you would have to be careful how you 'promote'. Anyone who has bought anything over the internet will be aware of the drop-down boxes that ask where you are buying from – *and if you have a website with one of those boxes you will be deemed to be actively marketing to any territories listed in there.*

This means if you offer such a promotion then you will be breaking the law anywhere that gaming or alcohol are illegal such as certain Middle East countries.

## Local alliances

Do not forget that you can also ally yourself with other non-competing businesses in related areas, and exchange publicity to each other's mutual benefit. Imagine for example that you are a business service agency (you provide secretarial support and some consultancy) and there is a stationers and computer supplier in the same business unit as you. Any of the following should be possible:

Week Five

# FRIDAY

- Exchanging leads between each other but make sure that your customers are aware that you exchange addresses – be very careful of the data protection act here.
- Keep a stack of each other's business cards and brochures to distribute to customers.
- Share the costs of occasional mailings and maybe adverts – ensuring that neither company feels that their sales message is being compromised.
- Have a link to each other on your websites with a recommendation – only a percentage will actually click through, but those that do will definitely be interested in the services on offer.

By this stage you may consider merging the companies – but halving any costs by sharing them is an option not to be missed.

Even if you do not work in the sort of business unit where you are likely to meet other businesses, remember the networking opportunities offered by other business organisations:

- Chamber of Commerce – many local branches (http://www.chamberonline.co.uk).
- Federation of Small Businesses (http://www.fsb.org.uk).
- Institute of Directors – comprising mostly small business directors (http://www.iod.com).
- Your local Training & Enterprise Council (TEC) will

# FRIDAY

Week Five

> almost certainly know of business 'clubs' (www.tec.co.uk).
> - Telework Association for flexible workers and people who work from home (www.tca.org.uk).

## The public event

You may have heard the phrase 'cheap publicity stunt' used pejoratively. No matter; use it anyway. Remember a few guidelines:

> - be tasteful
> - be decent
> - try to be unpredictable
> - be interesting
> - be relevant if possible
> - funny and visual is good

There are many public events that are tailor-made for publicising businesses and charities, many of which will carry only nominal fees for participation:

> - hiring a float at the local carnival
> - taking a stand at the local business fair
> - involvement with local schools where appropriate

Giving away promotional t-shirts will get you free advertising space on someone's body and might cost little depending on the quantities; someone standing in your local shopping centre handing out leaflets can also be inexpensive.

Week Five

# FRIDAY

We are now edging towards the paid for. If we move back to the press, without actually talking to journalists this time, there are ways of getting even more publicity.

## Internet newsgroups

Frequent internet users will be aware of Newsgroups – the discussion areas on virtually any topic, open to anyone with an appropriate internet connection. These can be useful for establishing yourself as a contact for customers, but bear some basics in mind:

- Test the water by reading the newsgroup first. Some are full of timewasters and some are full of classified adverts that no-one will acutally bother to read – you will just end up on a junk mail list.
- If you are satisfied a newsgroup contains potential customers, do not sail in with a straight advert – take part in some conversations first and demonstrate you are worth talking to and possibly buying from.
- If there are rules on a newsgroup about publishing internet addresses and price lists, respect them – you will only find your messages are erased otherwise, and you might get barred from taking part.
- Watch the time it is taking – it is very easy to get carried away on the internet and persuade yourself you are being productive.

Week Five

# F R I D A Y

## Letters pages

All local newspapers run letters pages. Frequently these are filled with correspondence from angry local residents about council decisions, followed by the councillors defending their decisions, and so it goes on. The trade press also carries letters – and not just because it is a way of filling the pages for nothing. It is worth considering writing to the press under a number of circumstances:

- You are able to write short, punchy and, preferably, witty letters.
- You have a point to make that can be established quickly.
- You want to inspire others to write in the same vein.
- You want to be seen adopting a particular cause.

The subject matter is up to you. In fact, although there is never any guarantee that your letter will be published, if it is, then apart from trimming for length, you can be certain your point will be made rather than a watered-down version from a journalist. Again, check your objectives.

- If you want to increase sales then you are limited, but you might be able to get a debate going on the prices of certain goods in general.
- If you want your company identified as a business with strong local connections then maybe something on traffic control or the preservation of a local monument or building will catch people's interest.

Week Five

# FRIDAY

The possibilities are many, but not limitless. Remember the golden rule: never think that an editor is going to let you say in a letter something that really ought to go into a paid for advertisement. That is not the idea and never has been. On the other hand, a lively correspondent can end up in a useful position, for instance if you take issue with something one of the regular columnists says and start a debate across the letters page. Columnists move on eventually and you never know, when the editor is considering a replacement he or she might think of approaching you. This would mean a regular column with your picture, your name and, conceivably, your company name every week or every month. You would have total control, bar the odd nip and tuck for length, over the content of the column.

Drawbacks to becoming a columnist:

- You might find your opinions totally riveting as might your customers – but can you tailor them to the same length every week?
- Can you actually come out with an opinion each week without boring the reader? Test yourself – think of four subjects on which you could write. Then bear in mind that this is only your first month.
- Writing takes time and if you are a small business proprietor you might not have much of that.
- Writing to a given length is a skill you will not necessarily have – how many times would you anticipate beginning a sentence with the letter 't' for example (not too many is a good response, but have you actually thought this one through seriously?)

# FRIDAY

- You might get a competitor on the letters page getting publicity by disagreeing with you!

## Summary

Today we have looked at getting publicity without the help of the press. Charity work is a possible way forward, but ideally would not be purely for the purpose of publicity, and free samples are a useful promotional idea. Publicity stunts need careful handling, but taking part in prearranged public fairs and jamborees is a positive step; alliances with other businesses could have knock-on benefits, as could the creation of a good website.

Tomorrow we will round our course off, and look at a few horror stories that demonstrate how not to do it!

Week Five

# SATURDAY

# Conclusions and coping with problems

Looking back over the week's work, you might notice that we started off fairly negatively and outlined what would be difficult or impossible to achieve. We shall now finish by looking at what happens when something goes wrong.

## When the journalist is wrong

Journalists make mistakes. So, what happens when they say something which is purely and simply wrong? If the error concerns you, your reaction will depend on a number of things:

- severity
- consequences
- duration of impact

# SATURDAY

Severity can be easy to assess and might lead you to take little or no action if the mistake is not a serious factual error. Perhaps someone has spelt your name wrongly. Does it matter? Probably not. Maybe someone has named you correctly but given you the wrong company name, which could be more serious for you but will do little long-term harm, and a quick note to the editor will almost certainly get a correction into the following issue. That is if it is worth it; consider whether you are likely to lose business as a result of the inaccuracy and whether it is therefore worth making a fuss – a correction will inevitably need to repeat the initial inaccuracy and therefore prolong your exposure to it. You need to assess how severe the mistake was and how long you want to keep it running.

### Corrections and clarifications

Many newspapers and magazines have special areas dedicated to corrections and clarifications, which are useful for editors who do not believe that their staff are invincible and perfect. *The Guardian* has such an area at the foot of its letters page, and regular readers learn to look at this to check whether anything from the previous day was in fact incorrect.

Other papers take a different view. A market researcher was surprised to find that she had told a Sunday newspaper that 8 per cent of small business owners had mobile phones. She called and asked whether they could correct the figure back to 80 per cent; they agreed to do this on the website but said that they did not run corrections in the paper, ever.

# Week Five
# SATURDAY

> The professional approach is one that builds scope for corrections into the regular structure of the paper.

Hopefully this is as severe as inaccuracies about you or your company will get. It can get unpleasant when, say, inaccurate figures are printed, or someone starts a rumour that you have gone bust and a journalist does not check their facts. Occasionally a wrong name pops into someone's head and they are on deadline and so it gets left. Once a computer company used two wholesalers – one of them had gone bust and a journalist named the wrong one in print. The same paper, a few weeks later, mentioned a managing director of a company in a piece on personnel, but accidentally put in the name of the MD of another company. Journalists are human and make mistakes.

The thing to remember is that journalists hate the fact that they have got something wrong just as much as you do. They will be angry with themselves but they will certainly acknowledge your right to some sort of correction.

Before blaming the journalist, try seeing things from the other point of view – ask yourself where things could have gone wrong:

- Were they inexperienced? If so, you might want to show some patience – in 10 years' time when they are well-established you do not want to be on their 'avoid' list.
- Were you inexperienced? If so, consider whether any misunderstanding might have come from you –

# Week Five
## SATURDAY

> and concede this when seeking a clarification. This approach is likely to keep communications open.
> - Did you make it clear that a particular comment was off the record?
> - The journalist will have a note or tapes to back them up when they believe their version of events was correct – have you?
> - Did you combine two announcements that might become confused to an outsider's mind? Large numbers of misunderstandings happen because the business owner is too close to his or her material to see things are not as clear as they might seem in someone who is intimate with the background.

## Wrong approach rather than wrong facts

Something that can be more difficult is if you feel that you have been misrepresented, but the journalist thinks that they have done the job properly. The first thing to remember is that the reporter works for the newspaper or magazine rather than for you; the fact that you got a bad review, or your quote was not first in the paper, or that your press release about a contract win ended up about the company that lost the contract, is all fair game.

There are cases, however, where you may feel that journalists have simply behaved wrongly or unethically. If you feel that the press is harassing you – and this is very unlikely unless you are a major celebrity, in which case you will have PR professionals to fall back on – you can look to the Press Complaints Commission (www.pcc.org.uk) for support.

# Week Five
## SATURDAY

There are also cases when you had something to say and were not consulted. No matter how annoyed you are about a piece of journalism, keep the following check-list by your side when you pick up the phone:

- You have made mistakes too.
- The journalist is at a disadvantage – you can use this to look for an interview opportunity or some extra coverage which you know will be positive, or you can blow your top which will not actually help you.
- If you put finger to keyboard rather than pick up the phone, they will almost certainly print your letter because journalists take the right of reply very seriously indeed.
- Consider how you would handle any other business problem and ask yourself whether you should take care of this in any other way.
- If you take a constructive attitude to a problem like this, a journalist should be silently thanking you under his or her breath.

## Libel

In extreme cases you might consider that you have been libelled. In this case, and assuming you have reasons not to approach the newspaper or magazine in question yourself, you will need to take legal advice.

Libel is an interesting legal beast. Essentially you need to prove that something that has been said in print about you is untrue and damaging – any settlement will be based on

# SATURDAY

the damage that a jury believes you to have suffered. There are exceptions to the libel law:

- Dead people cannot be libelled.
- If something is provably true it cannot by definition be libellous – although, if it has no relevance to a story, you might be able to prove that there was malice involved (e.g. if you are opening a shop, you are aged 54 and a journalist digs up a shoplifting offence committed when you were 15, you might have a case against them).
- The law does not actually say this, but vulgar abuse tends not to be actionable because it is so difficult to prove that any damage has been done. If you want to call someone a pillock, fine – a crooked pillock and you are in trouble!

Before taking any action against anyone, do take legal advice and only use legal action as a last resort. It is not a good idea to threaten legal action – if you are going to resort to it, do it. If not, it is only hot air anyway.

## Broken embargo

There are occasions on which people put a release out under embargo – with a date on it after which it may be used. Contrary to popular belief this embargo has no legal force, nor is there any way of enforcing it other than to stop communicating with the journalist in question after it has been broken, which is quite likely to be counterproductive anyway. Respecting an embargo is more or less a favour

# Week Five
## SATURDAY

with a few airs and graces, but there are a few ways of making them more secure:

> - Ask the magazine whether it would accept a press release under embargo. You will risk their publishing something purely in order to steal a march on the competition, but at least you will be covered.
> - Always mark an embargo carefully – do not let them say 'we missed the bit where it said that'.
> - Never invite a journalist to a press conference with embargoed content without warning them first. There are few things worse than turning up to a conference and finding you cannot use the content – and then having to explain this to the news editor who has probably pencilled the story in somewhere already.

## Top ten mistakes

Over the course of the week you have encountered a number of ways to manage your press relations and a number of ways that should be avoided. To round up, here, in no particular order, is a top ten of mistakes – things you should not do if you want to maintain any relations at all with the press.

1 Do not tell a journalist how to do his or her job. The amount of times that people get told what to write – usually an extension of someone's marketing policy – is far too often. Do not add to it.
2 Do not tell a journalist what they should be asking you. They know their readers.
3 Do not get upset when a journalist talks to someone

## SATURDAY
*Week Five*

about your press release or your company when you would rather they did not – it is a free country and people can talk to who they like. Look after your own comments and leave other people to worry about theirs.

4  Do not call a journalist up about a 'story they are writing for you'. That may be how you see it, but it will not be how they perceive their job. Many PR agencies make this mistake.

5  Do not call a journalist about a 3-week-old story and ask whether it was of interest – if it was, they would have called you.

6  Do not call a journalist, tell them you are an admirer of their work and then ask which papers they write for (this does happen). Likewise, do not call a journalist and tell them you would like to know a bit about them and then get their name wrong or, in extreme cases, their sex wrong.

7  Do not send e-mail attachments when a journalist has made it clear that they do not want them. Journalists differ in their preferences about receiving press releases; do keep your database up to date.

8  Do not complain when your picture does not appear to illustrate a piece after sending a passport picture into the newspaper or magazine.

9  Do not tell a journalist that they got the story wrong when they missed a sentence out of your press release.

10  Do not send the same press release into the same paper twice in the hope that if you leave the date off, they will not notice and might run the story again.

Believe it or not, all of the above do happen.

Week Five

# SATURDAY

## A word about copyright

The other thing you will need to bear in mind, if you are using or referencing other people's work, is the issue of who actually owns it. The Bern Convention, which reflects international law, says that the originator of a piece of work owns the rights unless otherwise stated. So if someone has reviewed your product it does not go without saying that you can copy and send the review to all your customers and prospects – just because it is published does not mean it is yours. Pictures, too, are subject to copyright laws – if you had a picture done for your annual report, the photographer will be within his or her rights to object severely if the same picture turns up in the press or

## SATURDAY

elsewhere. Most will negotiate for extra rights – ask first, or better still put extra uses in the initial contract.

## So when do I need to hire a PR agency?

So far we have focused mainly on free publicity, which is fine – it is what you want. There may come a time when this is just not enough. Here are a few pointers to judging when you need to think about doing something more permanent about your press relations. We touched on this on Wednesday but at the end of the week you might want to think it through in more depth – here are some signs to watch for:

- When your phone is going as much for press comment as it is for your core business.
- When your internal staff are fielding too many press calls and not selling.
- When the umpteenth journalist has asked for a media pack and you have realised you do not have one.
- When you have commissioned pictures and other services and are sure there must be better deals available.
- When you are getting coverage but want to take things to the next stage, and just do not know how to make that happen.
- When you are not important enough to get interviews in your own right but, being sneaky, you know that a good PR with some higher-profile clients will be able to persuade an editor to interview you in return for an exclusive with one of the high-fliers. You just can not do that by yourself.

# Week Five
## SATURDAY

Your decision after that is whether to hire someone internally or go for an agency (we will call the independent people 'agencies' as well, for convenience). Things to consider are:

- A single individual will leave you without cover during holidays.
- An agency might send someone high-calibre to pitch the account then send the juniors in once they have won your business.
- A single individual who underperforms is more difficult to replace than an agency.
- An agency might not prioritise you as you would wish.
- An agency can send different people to offer you different perspectives – an individual is likely to 'go native' in the end and see everything in your company's term.

## Summary

By following today's guidelines you will have a reasonable idea of libel laws. We have also covered some of the other laws relating to journalism and publishing, but please remember that this book is not intended as a substitute for legal advice. If you are in any doubt, check with your lawyer – or better still remember the mantra 'if in doubt, leave it out'.

You should now know how to react constructively when a journalist says something about you that is wrong – and it will happen if you talk to enough of them, the best journalists can make mistakes. You will also have an appreciation of copyright issues, which need to be taken seriously.

**Week Five**

# SATURDAY

## Final thoughts

You are now equipped to write your press releases, start banging the proverbial drum and get some interest going in your company. You know what you are after in terms of your publicity and you know how to measure your success.

However, we cannot offer any guarantees. If your press release is brilliant and thrilling, but so are another five and an editor has only three spare slots for news items, then it is a case of taking pot luck. If you happen to hit an editor's desk when they have just gone to press with something similar to your story that you could not possibly have known about, then you are a bit stymied. The only thing to do if you keep getting knocked back is follow up with a polite call and see whether there is anything in your approach that you could change, or whether it is just a matter of being one of a crowd of well-written but bland press releases.

We hope, however, that you find that this book is the start of something serious and that you have a flair for publicity once you have learned the moves. Even then, the next step is down to you, and once again there can be no guarantees.

Good luck!

# Consumer Behaviour

**SUSAN CAVE**

**WEEK SIX**

# CONTENTS

# Week Six

| | | |
|---|---|---|
| **Introduction** | | 471 |
| **Sunday** | Basic psychological processes | 472 |
| **Monday** | Attitudes to money | 486 |
| **Tuesday** | Purchasing | 499 |
| **Wednesday** | Different types of consumer | 513 |
| **Thursday** | Product advertising | 528 |
| **Friday** | Product retailing | 535 |
| **Saturday** | Negative effects and implications | 547 |

Week Six
# INTRODUCTION

We should all be interested in consumer behaviour, simply because we are all consumers. This is an activity that goes on constantly throughout our lives, and affects the way we think, the way we feel, the way we look, and how we spend our time. A large number of us also provide services or products to consumers. We then need to understand, from a wider perspective than our own, what influences consumer behaviour and how best to present our products.

In this week, you will find a brief introduction to basic psychological processes, attitudes towards money, purchasing behaviour, different types of consumer, the branding, advertising and retailing of products, and negative effects of consumerism.

Each day is broken down into topics, which are outlined at the start. Each topic is then presented in the form of definitions/issues, important points and implications. There are also some activities for you to try. A summary is given to recap at the end of each day.

Week Six

# S U N D A Y

# Basic psychological processes

Today you will be focusing on the psychological processes that underpin consumer behaviour. It is essential to understand these if you want to develop successful products and market them effectively. The processes that we will examine today are:

- perception and attention
- learning and memory
- motivation
- attitudes and attitude change
- the self-concept
- group processes

## Perception and attention

*Definitions/issues*
Attention is the process through which we become consciously aware of stimulation received from our surroundings. Clearly, we encounter a massive amount of information, and cannot attend to it all, therefore we have to be selective. Perception is the interpretation we place on that input. Objects and situations will be perceived in very different ways by different people as a result of these processes.

*Important points about attention*
1 We process information quite rapidly, but there is a limit to how quickly we can do this.

Week Six

## SUNDAY

2. We can generally only deal with one item or activity at a time, unless we are well-practised or items are presented to different senses (e.g., we can read a book and listen to music at the same time).
3. Choice of item to attend to depends on what is important to us, either in the short or the long term.
4. Importance may be determined by our motives or by other factors such as novelty and distinctiveness.

*Implications*

- Avoid presenting too much information at any one time ('advertising clutter').
- Use as many senses (e.g. vision, hearing) as possible to put information across.
- Find out what is important to consumers.
- Make products and advertisements novel and distinctive.

Week Six
# SUNDAY

*Important points about perception*
1 Perception is a constructive process rather than a mechanical registration of 'reality'.
2 The constructions that we build are based on previous experience, expectations and motivation.
3 Although there will be broad similarities, there will also be differences between individuals in the perceptions they construct.
4 The more ambiguous the input received, the more constructions and interpretations will differ in different people.

*Implications*

- Basic messages need to be clear and unambiguous to the intended recipients.
- It is important to identify the target group for any communications in order to achieve this.
- Some ambiguity can be useful to create interest.
- Objects and messages can be used as symbols for other things, or to evoke fantasies or memories.

## Learning and memory

*Definitions/issues*
Learning is a relatively permanent change in behaviour that is the result of experience. Changes induced by drugs, injury or ageing are excluded by this definition. Memory is the storage of information about these experiences within the individual and its retrieval from the memory stores. These processes are important in determining how long-lasting influences on our behaviour will be.

# SUNDAY

Week Six

*Important points about learning*

1 Learning is more likely if experiences are repeated.
2 Learning can occur through the **association** of two events e.g. if they are presented close together in time.
3 Learning depends on **reinforcement**: behaviours which lead to pleasant consequences are more likely to be repeated.
4 Learning can occur through the **observation** and **imitation** of the experiences of others as well as through personal experience.
5 Some people are more likely to be imitated than others.

*Implications*

- People need to encounter products and advertisements as often as possible (don't overdo this, though, as it can lead to 'advertising wearout').
- Presenting a product alongside something that is

# Week Six
# SUNDAY

> already regarded highly will enhance the esteem in which it is held.
> - Purchasing must lead to a perception of pleasant consequences if it is to be repeated.
> - The reports obtained from other people, by word of mouth or through promotions and advertisements, have a significant effect on behaviour.
> - People on whom we model ourselves will make the best promoters of products.

*Important points about memory*

1 Memory consists of both a short-term and a long-term store; not all information received gets passed on to the long-term store.
2 Information is more likely to reach the long-term store if it is repeated, vivid, personally relevant, and if it is processed in terms of meaning rather than just looked at superficially.
3 Information that fits in well with our existing interests will be better remembered because it can be slotted into the way we have organised our memory store.
4 Recall is a process of reconstructing the past, and may well be distorted.

*Implications*

> - Product information needs to be repeated, personalised and to 'make people think' (e.g. by being presented in an incomplete form) if it is to be stored in memory for any length of time.
> - Elaboration of information or products in the form of visual images, jingles or distinctive packaging will

Week Six
# SUNDAY

> assist memory processes.
> - Products and information must be made relevant to the interests of consumers, or interest must be created by the products.
> - Key information must be presented clearly so that it will be remembered accurately; what is implied may be remembered as factual.

## Motivation

*Definition/issues*

Motivation is the energising force which drives behaviour and sustains it until some goal is reached. It involves a state of **need** and goal-directed behaviour aimed at satisfying the need. Motives may be learnt or unlearnt, positive (desire for something) or negative (desire to avoid something) and conscious or unconscious. Since they make us behave in particular ways, it is important to understand what motives we have and how these can be developed.

*Important points*

1 **Biological** motives such as the need for food are common to everybody; there are, however, differences in the way that people prefer to satisfy them.
2 We also have **cognitive** motives, such as the needs for stimulation, consistency and beauty.
3 **Social** motives include the need for positive regard from others, the need to belong to groups, the need for power and the need to achieve and fulfill our aspirations.
4 **Frustration** of our needs (when efforts to reach goals are seen to be blocked) is a powerful influence on behaviour.
5 Behaviour is also determined by **values,** or overriding

principles; these vary according to the individual and according to culture.

*Implications*

- Product marketers need to find out how different groups of people prefer to satisfy their biological needs.
- Both products themselves and advertisements can capitalise on the cognitive needs such as the need for beauty in our surroundings.
- Products and advertisements can be created to appeal to our aspirations and linked with membership of desirable social groups.
- Products which offer ways of overcoming frustrations (real or manufactured) will also be regarded highly.
- The values of the target group need to be established in order to develop the right approach to marketing.
- Symbolism in advertisements may be used to appeal to unconscious motives (sexual, for example).

## Attitudes and attitude change

*Definition/issues*

An attitude is a lasting general evaluation of an object, person or issue; a like or a dislike. According to the widely accepted ABC model, it has three components:

- **affective**: a feeling or emotional response towards the attitude object;
- **behavioural:** a predisposition towards certain behaviours with respect to the attitude object;

Week Six

## SUNDAY

- **cognitive:** a set of beliefs and knowledge about the object concerned.

Our attitudes towards products and services are obviously important determinants of whether or not we will purchase them, and a prime reason for advertising is to change attitudes.

*Important points*

1 People like to maintain consistency between attitudes towards different, related objects and issues; they also like to maintain consistency between the components of a given attitude. Inconsistency creates tension and is a force for attitude change. The level of tension depends on the importance of the issue.
2 Attitudes towards a product will be determined by the combination of attitudes towards different attributes of that product, e.g. the cost and speed of a car.
3 Existing attitudes are important determinants of whether or not people will accept new information.
4 Social norms and the perceived consequences of purchase also contribute towards our attitudes to a product.
5 The process of changing attitudes must take into account several elements of the communication employed, such as the communicator, content of the message and the nature of the recipient.

*Implications*

- If people can be shown to be inconsistent in their attitudes or persuaded to change one component this will create pressure to change. Persuading green consumers that it is important to recycle as well as to conserve energy is an example of the first;

presenting new information about a product (cognitive change) or persuading them to try a sample (behavioural change) is an example of the second.
- It is essential to build on existing attitudes rather than challenging these at the outset.
- Market research needs to take into account several different attributes of a product if it is to develop products that more closely approximate consumers' ideals.
- It may be more appropriate to manipulate or appeal to social norms to produce attitude change rather than targeting individuals (as in the anti smoking campaign).
- The communicator's credibility and image must be suited to the product and the target group.
- The most effective messages in general are those which present both sides of an argument, repeat the main points and employ a moderate level of fear (if appropriate).

## Self concept

*Definition/issues*

Self concept is an organised set of perceptions about the self – it is what we think we are like rather than what we are like. It is important to our discussion of consumer behaviour because we will buy products that fit in with our view of ourselves; we also use some products to relieve our insecurities about ourselves.

# SUNDAY

Week Six

> *ACTIVITY*
>
> You can investigate your own self concept by answering the question 'Who am I'? Try to write down 20 responses to the question. When you have done this, look at the different types of attribute you have written down.

*Important points*

1 The self concept consists of three components:
   - **self image** (this includes personality traits, abilities, social roles, attitudes, motivations, and body image)
   - **self esteem** (how much we value ourselves)
   - **ideal self** (the person we would like to be).
2 The self concept is mostly social in origin and derives from the feedback we receive from others about how they perceive us.
3 Another important source of ideas is the social comparisons we make between ourselves and others.
4 The products and services that we consume (e.g. cars, houses, clothing) can also provide us with ideas about who we are (our **extended self**).
5 The self concept incorporates our gender roles as well as the other roles we play as part of our everyday life (e.g. father).
6 The **body image** – our ideas about our own body and what we see as ideal – is just as likely to be inaccurate as our ideas about our psychological attributes.

Week Six

# SUNDAY

*Implications*

- The products we buy will be used by others to evaluate us.
- Product attributes need to match some aspect of our self image or our ideal self.
- Products can be used as gifts or self-gifts to boost self-esteem ('you deserve it').
- Products are often sex-typed, ie associated with one sex only, to fit in with gender roles.
- Changing gender roles may necessitate or permit changes in advertising, e.g. male perfumes.
- Products for the body can take advantage of perceived imperfections or can focus on image as an indicator of group membership, e.g. fashion.

Week Six
## SUNDAY

# Group processes

*Definitions/issues*

This refers to the behaviours we demonstrate which are primarily the result of belonging to social groups. Very few people do not belong, or aspire, to at least one social group. Such groups can exert a powerful influence on behaviour, as anyone who has tried to go against their expectations will confirm, and this influence extends to consumer behaviour.

*Important points*

1 Social **roles** and **norms** set the standards for behaviours that are expected of people in particular positions in society (roles) or who are members of particular groups (norms).
2 Occupying multiple roles or being in several groups means that there are often conflicting expectations.
3 Group membership is an indicator of status and class: our position in society relative to other people. Consider the implications of belonging to a golf club!
4 We also aspire to belong to certain groups (**reference groups**) which influences our consumption patterns.
5 The family is probably the most important group that most people belong to.
6 The culture we live in also has common ways of behaving which may be deeply ingrained.
7 Nevertheless, there is a variety of alternative lifestyles available in modern society, with correspondingly different patterns of consumption.

# SUNDAY

*Implications*

- Standards for behaviour extend to consumption and can be used to sell products, e.g. executive cars.
- Role conflict provides marketing opportunities as in the development of the convenience food market for the working mother.
- Products need to have a status and identity linked with social groups if they are to transfer those to the consumer.
- The stage a consumer has reached in terms of the family life cycle needs to be taken into account when establishing disposable income and consumer needs.
- Cultural differences are crucial to marketers: selling items that are not part of an established way of life is likely to be an uphill struggle.
- The lifestyle of the target group of consumers needs to be established accurately before products can be successfully developed and marketed.

## Summary

Today you have looked at some basic psychological processes which are crucial to understanding consumer behaviour:

- Attracting the attention of consumers and influencing the way they perceive the information presented.
- Ensuring that the information presented is learnt and can be recalled.
- The motives, needs and values of target consumers must

## SUNDAY

be researched so that product development is appropriate to them.
- Attempts at producing attitude change can focus on information, emotion or behaviour – but must take into account existing attitudes, social norms and the nature of the communicator, message and recipient.
- Linking products with the self concept of consumers is an important feature of marketing; this has been particularly the case with sex-typed products and those linked with body image.
- Group membership creates expectations which extend to consumption of certain products or services.

Tomorrow we shall move on to examine the way that consumers think about money - and parting with it!

Week Six
# MONDAY

# Attitudes to money

The ultimate aim of consumer research is to encourage people to spend money on particular products in preference to others. In order to do this, it is important understand how people feel about money and to look at differences in spending patterns. Today's topics address these issues in the following ways:

- psychology of money, economics and pricing
- poverty and wealth
- spending, saving and borrowing
- targeting those with resources

## Psychology of money, economics and pricing

*Definitions/issues*
In modern societies, money (coins, notes, cheques and credit cards) is the way that we exchange our work for the goods and services we want, save for future needs or speculate in the hope of making more money.

*Important points*
1 Money means different things to different people; those who are employed may see it as a good thing whilst the unemployed see it as a source of worry and its absence as shameful. In general terms, males associate money with competence, financial risk-taking and management whereas females see it as a means of obtaining goods and enjoyable experiences.

# MONDAY

**Week Six**

2. The worth of different types of money may not be accurately interpreted. A coin will be seen as having less value than a note of the same denomination. Credit cards are seen as less 'real' than cash.
3. Money also has a symbolic value representing power, security, happiness and satisfaction. It is not generally acceptable as a gift (except from parents to children) since it symbolises status and seniority.
4. Expenditure on goods and services depends less on how much money we have than on how well-off we feel and what we think is likely to happen in the future. Our current income determines expenditure on food and other consumables whereas durables such as cars and major appliances are more influenced by **consumer confidence** about the future.
5. 'Spenders' are generally healthier, happier and more optimistic than self-deniers. The money-troubled are more dissatisfied with life, themselves and their relationships.
6. A fair exchange is expected when purchases are made.

# MONDAY

Consumers have an idea about an **acceptable price range** and products must fall within that to be considered for purchase. They also have a **reference price** which is the price they expect to pay for a particular product based on fairness or past price.

7 For many products price is also considered to be an indicator of the quality of the goods. Although this **market belief** is not always justified, it is a good guideline.

8 Despite this, consumers' knowledge of prices is often poor, especially for some categories of goods, e.g. coffee.

---

*ACTIVITY*

Jot down some items that you buy regularly. Note alongside each what you think the price is. Next time you make a purchase, check your estimates to see if you are exactly right, within 10% or outside that range. Which types of item were correct and which were incorrect?

---

*Implications*

- It is important to understand the subjective value that money has for your target consumers. If you want to persuade them to make purchases they must feel that they are getting value for money.
- Coins and credit cards may be used more readily than notes.
- Since money is not acceptable as a gift, goods and services can be marketed as alternatives.

# MONDAY

Week Six

- Measurement of consumer confidence is an important part of marketing. Questions such as 'do you feel better or worse financially than you did a year ago?' and 'how well-off do you expect to be in a year's time?' can be used to measure this.
- Marketing strategy can be adapted to current economic conditions. For example, Campbell's Soup Co. responded to a recession by putting soup into family size tins and cutting prices after discovering that more people were having to eat at home. They also marketed soups as sauces for home cooking.
- When new lines are introduced, products must be priced within the acceptable price range. There are exceptions: e.g. Dualit toasters priced at £100 compared to the usual range of £12–30. Marketed as catering equipment, they are stylish and indicate status and seriousness about cooking.
- Offering goods at prices that are too low may in some cases affect sales adversely as it raises doubts about quality. In one case a new cheap range of cosmetics failed to sell until the price was increased. Low-priced goods need to undermine the perception that price is associated with quality. Using quality brand names, selling in quality stores, offering warranties and employing advertisements can be used to achieve this. Konica films used the slogan 'Why pay the price if you can't see the difference?' to attract buyers away from the more expensive Kodak films.

Week Six

# MONDAY

## Poverty and wealth

*Definitions/issues*

Poverty can be defined absolutely in terms of total earnings below the amount required for maintenance of physical and mental health. It can also be defined in terms of the 10% of the population who earn the least. Wealth is objectively defined (e.g. by the Inland Revenue) on the basis of income. Subjectively most people define a wealthy person as one who has substantial savings and a lot of property rather than just a high income.

*Important points*

1 Research into the culture of poverty has shown that the poor have a **present time orientation**, meaning that short-term goals and gratification will be more important than any long-term plans. Risk-taking behaviours will be reduced.

---

### ACTIVITY

Before you read on, look at the reasons for poverty given below and see which you agree with:

- laziness — 45%
- chronic unemployment — 42%
- drink — 40%
- ill health — 36%
- too many children — 31%
- old age and loneliness — 30%
- lack of education — 29%
- lack of foresight — 21%
- deprived childhood — 16%

# MONDAY

> (The percentages given show the number of people in Britain endorsing that explanation; other European countries showed a different pattern of responses).

2 **Just world beliefs** mean that rather than blaming society, the poor are generally seen as responsible for their own fate. Such beliefs would lead to agreement with statements such as: 'In this country almost everyone can make it if they try hard enough' and 'most people on social security are lazy'.

3 A large proportion of wealth is concentrated in the hands of a relatively small number of people. In America, the wealthiest 20% have 50% of the income. Most people see this as unfair and consider the rich to be overpaid and the poor to be underpaid. There is also a **preference drift effect** whereby people consider their own standard of living as the minimum acceptable.

> *ACTIVITY*
>
> Indicate the 6 most important reasons, in order of importance, why you think some people are better off financially than others. When you have finished, compare your answers with those given below.

4 As with poverty, people offer many explanations for wealth. Most British people see the wealthy as having been lucky or helped by others (e.g. through inheritance or good schooling) rather than as having worked harder. Thus the poor are responsible for their condition but the rich are not. Richer people are also judged to have other positive

# MONDAY

attributes such as being more likeable and attractive.

5 Although most people would like to be wealthy there is no evidence that wealth is associated with happiness; it simply seems to change the nature of the person's worries. Some research indicates that those who live in advanced market democracies may experience more material satisfaction, but they are increasingly unhappy. Cultural values in many of these societies seem to be moving towards the pursuit of spiritual development rather than material gain.

6 The wealthy spend more money on services, travel and investment. They do not buy home furnishings, appliances, etc. because they are generally older than the less wealthy and already have those items. Newly wealthy people, such as lottery winners, spend money on things such as property, cars, consumer durables and travel. Most do not continue to work and they will also invest most of their new wealth.

Week Six

# MONDAY

*Implications*

- Products which target the poor need to cater for short-term needs rather than long-term goals; any investments need to be low-risk.
- The different images held by most people about the nature of rich and poor people – and the reasons for their financial condition – mean that very few will want to be seen as poor. Wherever possible, people will tend to consume in ways which put them in a positive light and make them feel better about themselves. For example, in *'The Road to Wigan Pier'* George Orwell notes that the poor people he encountered would purchase relatively expensive 'luxury' foods such as chocolate biscuits and condensed milk for these very reasons.
- Appealing to the new urge for spiritual development rather than associating products with purely material aims or even with happiness may be more successful with modern consumers.
- Products which target the wealthy need to emphasise investment and provide services. Different types of wealthy people exist and to some extent they will be interested in different products.

## Targeting those with resources

*Definitions/issues*

'It is much easier to hit a bull's eye when you can see the target'. This means that it is important to identify the people who have money (economic resources) and the time to spend it (time resources) since they will make more likely

# Week Six
# MONDAY

consumers than those who do not. How they are spending that money must also be identified.

*Important points*

1. Economic resources are identified by looking at family income. Since the early decades of the twentieth century there has been an increase in the proportion which is spent on housing and a decrease in the amount spent on food and clothing; consequently more is left over for spending on other commodities.
2. Expenditure on food and other consumables is largely determined by current income, with expenditure on durables being more affected by consumer confidence.
3. Age is another important determinant: housing is the main expenditure for the 35–44 year-old group; eating out and clothes for the 45–54 group; and health care for the 65+ group.
4. The **'up market'** is the top 25% income group, typically dual-income households who are time constrained and emphasise quality when purchasing goods or services. They buy furniture, electronic goods, tableware, tools, building materials, fine jewellery and menswear. This group is print-oriented i.e. they read newspapers and magazines rather than watch television.
5. The super-affluent group at the top end of the scale have most appliances and home furnishings already. They spend more on services such as education, travel, nannies and cleaners.
6. The **'down market'** comprises the majority of consumers world-wide. In the USA this group comprises the young, old, single and divorced consumers. They spend highly on education, prescription drugs, tobaccco, milk and

# MONDAY

Week Six

laxatives but are light users of products such as wine and Diet Pepsi.

7 The availability of credit may extend resources temporarily but in the long term they will be reduced because credit costs money. Young consumers and those with high incomes may be more inclined to borrow and people are most likely to borrow to finance education, medical bills and cars.

8 Many people feel that they do not have enough time, known as being '**time crunched**' which indicates that time is another valuable resource to consider. People have time budgets and 38% will go without sleep to try and fit in more activities. About half of the Americans surveyed indicate that they would forgo a day's pay in order to have more time with family and friends. Women, parents and minorities are the most time-crunched groups.

9 As well as working time we have **leisure time** – that time during which we have a choice about our activities – and **obligated time** which is not discretionary, involving housework, personal care and socialising.

Fred was feeling time crunched...

## Week Six

# MONDAY

*Implications*

- Knowledge of the way the income is apportioned between different areas of expenditure can be used to guide marketing strategies.
- Measures of consumer confidence can be used to forecast future demand for some goods and to plan levels of production and stocking.
- Age and income are a useful guide to the type of product and service likely to be of interest to different groups.
- The 'up market' group require quality goods and services. They are generally short of time, and will pay more for goods that are immediately available, trouble-free and where customer care is of a high standard, limiting inconvenience. Being older they are also a good market for products and services aimed at enhancing youth and health such as beauty products and health clubs. Since they have desirable property, security systems and insurances are also likely to be of interest.
- The 'down market' represent a sizeable proportion of consumers, particularly for certain types of product. They respond to marketing strategies which offer 'no frills' but still provide a stylish retail environment and treat customers with respect. 'Successful discounters have made their mark by convincing customers that they are smart and special, not poor riff-raff'. The Aldi chain of supermarkets offers low prices, a restricted range of products, charges for bags and provides a minimum of service.

## MONDAY

Week Six

- Time crunched individuals will be less willing to spend time making purchasing decisions and shopping. Making these activities easier by providing information about products, building out-of-town shopping malls so that parking is less problematic, easing congestion and queues in stores, making provision for mail-order and internet shopping, accepting different forms of payment and reducing the likelihood of post-purchase problems will all assist consumers to make their purchases speedily and efficiently.
- Obligated time can be reduced by selling labour-saving devices such as microwave ovens, dishwashers and ready meals. Hiring services such as child care, cleaners and gardeners will also help the time-crunched.
- Where leisure time is reduced it may be more intensively used. Air travel and expensive sports facilties may help such people to make the best use of their time. There may also be a move away from less intensive activities such as golf to more intensive sports such as squash.
- Some products may permit **polychronic time use** where several activities can be carried out simultaneously. Mobile phones and laptops allow people to work while they travel; exercise equipment can be fitted with lecterns so that books can be read whilst exercising.

Week Six

# MONDAY

## Summary

Today we have looked at the ways consumers spend money and use their time resources:

- As well as an objective value, money has a subjective and a symbolic value; economic stability is important to mental health and status.
- Current income and consumer confidence about the future are important determinants of both spending and marketing strategies.
- Goods must be priced within the acceptable range for the type of product; quality is associated with price so too low a price will be counterproductive.
- The poor want short-term consumable goods and the wealthy services and investments; they both want to enhance their self-esteem through their purchases.
- Up market and down market marketing require different strategies but there may be some overlap.
- The time crunched will respond to products and services which save obligated time, enable better use of leisure time and permit polychronic time use.

Tomorrow we will be looking at how consumers go through the process of purchasing.

Week Six

# TUESDAY

# Purchasing

Having established that your consumer will be prepared to part with a certain amount of money the next step is to look at what customers want to buy and how they want to buy it. You also need to consider how they feel afterwards as that will influence future purchases and the recommendations they make to others. Today we will look at:

- materialism
- psychology of purchasing
- decision-making
- purchasing behaviour

## Materialism

*Definitions/issues*
Materialism can be defined as the desire for money and possessions above everything else. Some possessions are consumable (e.g. services and perishable goods) but many are not (e.g. cars, pictures, ornaments, furniture). It is important to understand why people desire durable goods such as these.

*Important points*
1 Objects may be desired because they have an **instrumental purpose.** They may provide amusement, as in the case of music centres. Ownership of objects may give us a feeling of control over our environment – a trait readily seen in children and one that is particularly important to males.

Week Six
# TUESDAY

2. Objects also have a **symbolic purpose**, standing for the personal qualities of the owner and giving us a sense of identity. This seems to be particularly important to females.
3. There are age differences in what is regarded as the favourite possession.

---
*ACTIVITY*

Try to remember what your own favourite possession was when you were 5, 10, 15, and 20 years old.

---

On the whole young children tend to prefer cuddly toys; older children like sports equipment; adolescents prefer musical equipment, cars and jewellery and adults are interested in photographs and jewellery.

4. Males prefer action and leisure-related objects, e.g. cars. Females favour items which have more social and emotional connotations, e.g. jewellery.
5. Class differences do not seem to affect the types of possession favoured but there are differences in the reasons given for preferences. Unemployed people are more swayed by emotional and instrumental features of goods. Middle class commuters are more interested in the personal history behind items, which could lead to a preference for possessions such as antique furniture.

# TUESDAY

*Week Six*

*Implications*

- All types of products need to appeal to both the instrumental and symbolic needs of the prospective purchaser. Consumers will match their own image with that of the product.
- Different cultures will have varying preferences for products and diverse ways of interpreting symbols they present. Products need to be designed with these differences in mind.
- Consumer goods can also be used to compensate for personal inadequacies (**symbolic self-completion**). Suggesting that products will make us feel better about ourselves is one way of appealing to this need.
- Since purchasing is based on perceived needs, such needs must be activated or created in the first instance, e.g. in-store displays and advertising may boost sales of flagging products which people are not bothering to renew. New product lines may have to be

# Week Six
# TUESDAY

> more pro-active: Reebok trainers created the need for adolescents to have new-style footwear with a particular label attached.

## Psychology of purchasing

*Definitions/issues*

The complexity of consumer behaviour is evident in this section as well. There are several different types of consumption and different psychological theories about the purchasing process. They both have implications for marketing strategies.

*Important points*

1 The first type of consumption involves important purchases which are usually novel or infrequent. They are described as **high involvement** and include houses, cars and pension schemes.
2 Repetitive consumption is when items are bought frequently. Little conscious thought occurs when making such purchases so they are often described as **low involvement**, e.g. grocery shopping.
3 **Involuntary consumption** occurs when we have little choice about the purchase or when changing to another source is inconvenient. This includes petrol and banking services.
4 **Group consumption** is defined as being the result of group decisions. For example, the views of different family members may be taken into account when purchasing a holiday.
5 The **cognitive** approach views purchase as being the outcome of a decision-making process involving seeking

# TUESDAY

Week Six

*Anne felt a spot of involuntary consumption coming on...*

and sifting information, evaluation of costs and benefits of the product, consideration of alternatives and a rational choice between them. This is more likely with high involvement products. Most purchases are replacements (e.g. cars) or additions (e.g. televisions) so the brand last bought is often the most important determinant of purchase.

6 The **learning theory** approach views purchase as a learned response based on previous rewards in the form of satisfactory outcomes. Pleasant experiences also create good associations with products; a wine associated with a pleasant evening out may well be chosen again. Repeated purchase may then lead to the formation of habits whereby the same choices are made without thinking when confronted with the same situation. This is more likely with repetitive consumption.

7 The **social** approach sees consumption as determined by the influence of other people. This includes beliefs about what 'important' people think about the purchase, the effect of sales staff on behaviour and the notion of fairness in social exchanges making rewards appropriate to costs.

Week Six
# TUESDAY

> **ACTIVITY**
>
> Identify some important purchases you have made and some habitual purchases. Which of the three approaches outlined above (cognitive, learning and social) provides the best explanation for your behaviour in each case?

*Implications*

- First purchasers are a key group because the purchase may establish a habit and determine later purchases even for high involvement products.
- Establishing brand loyalty has important consequences for later buying behaviour (more about this on Thursday).
- Information search may well be curtailed when an adequate option is found in order to save time. Known as **satisficing**, this implies that the order in which options are evaluated is crucial since those considered first have a better chance of being accepted. Products which are more in the public eye are likely to be in this category.
- Distinctive logos and packaging make it more likely that consumers will be cued to purchase by the sight of a product.
- Advertisements, like any reinforcer, lose their ability to affect behaviour after repetition (known as '**wearout**'). They need to be 'rested' for a while to avoid this happening.
- Unpleasant experiences with products (such as odd taste or faults in manufacture) may have a strong

# TUESDAY

> deterrent effect on behaviour for a long period. This can be very costly to the manufacturer.
> - The retailing environment can also contribute towards the rewards experienced by purchasing. This can be done through the provision of pleasure (e.g. free videos on flights) or information (e.g. about the journey).
> - Sales staff can significantly contribute to rewards experienced by consumers and can shape their behaviour in the direction of purchasing; the opinions of others are important reinforcers.
> - The notion of a fair exchange means that if consumers are not making large purchases, or are not very committed to a particular purchase, if it is made difficult for them they may readily change their minds. Thus supermarkets which allow those with only a few items to use a 'baskets only' till will have more chance of retaining their custom.

## Decision-making

*Definitions/issues*

If decision-making is a rational process, marketing managers should simply need to focus on providing products which meet the criteria specified by consumers and ensuring that the information about those products is readily available in an understandable form. If it cannot be explained rationally, awareness of biases and emotional and social influences become more relevant to attempts to influence consumer decisions.

*Important points*

1 Once a need has been recognised, the first stage of decision-making is the **pre-purchase information search**.

## Week Six
# TUESDAY

This may be based on previous knowledge and experiences, advertisements, consumer reports and talking to others. There is also **ongoing search**, such as browsing, which is carried out regardless of any needs to purchase. Some information-gathering may also be accidental as a result of simple exposure to advertisements.

2 Search varies in terms of how many alternatives are considered, which alternatives are considered (and in which order) and which information sources are consulted.

3 Search is increased when there is high consumer involvement and when the information is readily available. Grocery shopping involves on average only 12 seconds decision-making time for each purchase.

4 Different groups of consumers have been identified who search for varying lengths of time. A study of car purchasers revealed that 32% were moderate searchers, 26% were low and only 5% were high searchers, the remainder being in between. More educated consumers generally have more confidence in their ability to use information effectively. Very knowledgeable and very inexperienced product users are likely to search the least. Search is also dependent on whether shopping is regarded as a pleasure or a chore and the perceived costs and benefits of searching. Older, higher-income groups usually search less.

5 Significant sources of information during search are advertisements (TV advertisements are especially important for information about style and design of outdoor products and small electrical goods); in-store information (including packaging labels, which are particularly important to women and older consumers), salespeople and family/friends.

# TUESDAY

Week Six

6  If brands are perceived to be similar and stores are geographically spread out then search will be reduced.
7  The **consideration set** is the set of alternatives from which the consumer will make a choice. This will depend on memory and what is available at the point of purchase. The size of the set varies according to product, one study finding 6.9 for beer and only 2.2 for air freshener.
8  **Evaluative criteria** used to assess alternative brands will include price (often considered to indicate quality), brand name (which can indicate quality or status, as in designer labels) and country of origin (which may have ideological implications to indicate quality). The importance of each will vary according to product and consumer.

*Implications*

- Since information about products is often acquired passively and then made use of in the pre-purchase search, 'low-dose' advertising over a period of time may prove to have beneficial long-term effects.
- Knowing which brands consumers consider as alternative purchases provides useful information about the competition faced by a given product.
- Information about which stores are visited can be useful when planning distribution and promotional displays.
- Understanding the differences between segments of the populace regarding search can be useful when planning promotion. If high-search segments are more likely to purchase the product then encouraging search by providing information is likely to prove beneficial. Labelling and advertising

> may well pay off. Low search groups may be better targeted by free samples and price cuts.
> - Choice of advertising medium depends on the nature of the product and the consumer. Salespeople often play an essential role in explaining information to the consumer and indicating which characteristics of products are important when making a decision.
> - It is essential to ensure that a product is part of the consumer's consideration set or it will not stand a chance of being purchased. This can be done by advertising (e.g. Saab's slogan: 'Most car accidents happen in a showroom') or by offering incentives such as discounts.
> - Understanding the product attributes that are key evaluative criteria can provide a basis for product development and promotion. Cutoffs (e.g. acceptable price ranges) and priorities for different attributes must also be established.

## Purchasing behaviour

*Definitions/issues*

The process of purchasing involves decisions about whether to buy, what, when and where to buy and how to pay for the item. The purchasing process may be aborted at any stage as a result of new information or changing circumstances. There are also many factors which can promote purchase and this is where good marketing strategies pay off.

# TUESDAY

*Important points*

1 Many purchases are fully planned. This includes high-involvement items e.g. personal computers (88% of shoppers make planned purchases in this category) and low-involvement items e.g. groceries (61% of purchases are based on planning in the form of lists and 80% of items on shopping lists are actually purchased). Planned purchases mostly consist of items which are needed and items which there are financial incentives – such as coupons – to purchase. Partially planned purchases involve plans to buy a product but choice of brand is left until the time of purchase. Unplanned purchases may account for up to 50% of purchases in some categories and can be either the result of memory being triggered or true impulse buying where consumers yield to a sudden urge to buy a product.

> ### ACTIVITY
>
> Think about how many of your purchases were planned, partly planned or unplanned on your last shopping trip.

2 **Shopping orientation** (attitude towards shopping) varies. Although shopping has been a key leisure activity in the recent past (serving social, informational and other purposes as well as purchasing) it seems that it is now decreasing. This may be due to lack of time, stress or economic considerations: around 20% of the populace actively dislike shopping. General mood at the time of shopping may affect purchase decisions.

# Week Six
## TUESDAY

3 Price comparisons between stores ('shopping around') are now less frequent. Stores which offer 'Everyday Low Prices' such as Toys 'R' Us are preferred instead. Service and atmosphere are also important features of their success.

4 Store choice depends on the store's **image** (including carpeting, lighting, aisle width, music and clientele); location; assortment and quality of goods; efficiency of sales personnel; and services offered (e.g. cash machines, restaurants).

5 Successful sales staff are those who are high in expertise and trustworthiness, knowledgeable about customers and their needs, and able to adapt their interaction styles to suit the customer they are dealing with. They can be additionally motivated by salary and/or commission for sales.

6 Sales can be promoted by eye-level displays and displays located at the end of aisles and near check-outs. Price reductions, coupons, free samples and offers of other goods at reduced prices can also boost sales. These are all known as **point-of-purchase stimuli.**

7 Direct sales via mail-order, telephone, newspapers and electronic media (cable TV and internet) are increasing rapidly. This is due to the greater availability of credit cards and lifestyle changes such as less time, more traffic and queues. Such shoppers tend to be younger, higher income, better educated and live in small towns or rural areas although there will be variation according to the mode of purchase. Internet shoppers (or 'fast laners') now consitute 14% of the population in America and tend to be in their early twenties. Direct sales purchasers buy mainly clothing, home and office equipment and magazines.

Week Six

# TUESDAY

*Implications*

- Planned purchases can be encouraged by creating needs and offering financial incentives such as coupons.
- Since unplanned purchases account for a significant proportion of sales it is important to trigger needs at the point of purchase with displays and information rather than just relying on consumers' existing plans. Partially planned purchases may also be swayed at this time by special displays and promotions.
- Stores need to establish a good image to prevent customers from shopping around. We will return to this topic in more detail on Thursday as there are many aspects to consider. One option is the provision of facilties such as restrooms (rated as influencing store choice by 51% of women).
- Sales staff need to be well-trained and motivated by incentive schemes. These schemes need to be carefully designed to ensure that they attend to customer satisfaction as well as volume of sales. **Relationship marketing** is a term for the process of building up a relationship with customers in order to keep them using the service/product offered.
- Prime in-store displays and price incentives can boost sales considerably, but they can be expensive. Price cuts in particular can lead to retaliation from competitors or stocking up by consumers, which interrupts projected cash flow.
- Many successful marketers are now using some form of direct sales in addition to the traditional

# Week Six
# TUESDAY

> methods. In France vending machines are a popular way of buying Levis, since they can be sold for £6 less than in the shops. Shopping malls sometimes provide some form of entertainment in order to improve the attitude of consumers towards shopping as an experience.

## Summary

Today we have established that:

- Products and services must appeal to both the instrumental and symbolic needs of consumers; and that marketing strategy must activate those needs at the time of purchase.
- Habitual behaviour when purchasing can be developed through establishing brand loyalty; where behaviour is not habitual the perceived rewards and costs of purchasing one product rather than another will determine purchase decisions.
- Provision of product information through advertisements, incentives and trial offers plus point-of-purchase stimuli is an essential part of marketing success.
- Choice of retailing method needs to take account of store image, the importance of relationships in marketing and various forms of direct sales.

Tomorrow we will be exploring different types of consumer and how understanding these differences can be put to good use.

Week Six

# WEDNESDAY

# Different types of consumer

We have already seen that all consumers do not behave in the same way. An awareness of these differences – **'market segmentation'** – is essential for effective product development and marketing. The differences we will be exploring today are:

- age
- social class
- culture
- family and gender
- lifestyle and attitudes

## Age

*Definitions/issues*

Here we will be concentrating on young people and the elderly as consumers. Young people are defined as those aged up to the mid- to late teens. They are an important market segment because in some countries they account for as much as 50% of the population and they have more spending power than ever before. In 1994 the average 14 year-old had an income of £9.57 per week. Older ('grey') consumers can be defined as those over 50. Their numbers are increasing as people in general live longer (20% of Europeans will be 62+ by the year 2010). They too have more disposable income and more time to spend it as generous pensions and early retirement are available to many.

Week Six

# WEDNESDAY

*Important points*

1. Children go shopping with their mothers from a very early age and by five they have a good understanding of money. Parents and families are a significant source of consumer information for children.
2. Children primarily buy sweets, snacks, toys, clothes, videos and sports equipment. By the age of seven 90% will have made purchases without parental supervision. Their favourite purchases change from cuddly toys and sports equipment when younger to more clothing, jewellery and music centres when adolescent.
3. Children also have indirect purchasing power as a result of the influence they exert over their parents (often referred to as '**product pestering**'). This may be the result of seeing advertisements or point-of-sale stimuli in the store. Their requests will be met 50% of the time. They may also show preferences for particular retail outlets.

Jim's son soon learnt the art of product pestering

# WEDNESDAY

*Week Six*

4 By the age of eight most children can distinguish advertisements from TV programmes and have a moderate understanding of the content of advertisements although they can be easily misled. Memory for advertisements improves with age and is enhanced by the use of visually vivid material and slogans.

5 After the 30–49 year-olds, the 50–64 year-olds have the highest weekly expenditure of any age group. Older consumers tend to spend more on drugs and health care, fuel, household supplies, food to be consumed at home, cars and travel.

6 Older consumers may be less mobile than younger, prefer to shop close to home, less inclined to shop around and like shops where they are recognised by staff. They are also keen to buy particular brands especially goods that come with money-back guarantees.

7 They are less inclined to use credit cards and loans than other groups, preferring to keep their excess money in government securities or accounts that yield interest.

8 Older consumers seem to be less willing to complain about products and services, although there is some variation according to the product. They complain the most about cars, groceries, mail order services and appliances.

9 Self-perceived or 'cognitive age' can be a more important determinant of consumer behaviour than actual chronological age. People generally see themselves as being younger than they really are.

10 Negative stereotypes of the elderly in the media and advertisements may lead to their having a negative self-image and being treated in an offensive way by others – e.g. speaking slowly and loudly on the assumption that they cannot hear well. In one study one third of those

## Week Six
# WEDNESDAY

aged 55+ claimed that they did not buy a product because of the stereotyping in the advertisement.

*Implications*

- Shops can influence budding consumers by providing play facilities, eye-level displays that children can readily see, window displays that they find interesting, sales staff trained to deal with children, and attending to ethical and legal worries of parents, e.g. not selling tobacco to underage children.
- Advertisements aimed at children can influence requests for products but they need to be memorable for the child (using action, heroes and slogans) and repeated frequently. Humour, novelty, fast pace and careful selection of music, language and images are all essential if they are to appeal to this age group. Care must be taken that the advertisement is not misleading to younger children.
- Products aimed at children need to be thoroughly tested on children to ensure that they are appealing; such testing rejected the idea of a Batman lollipop because children thought that sucking Batman would not be appropriate.
- Older consumers have different interests to younger ones but it is better to focus on their cognitive age rather than their chronological age. Older women who have a younger cognitive age will prefer younger fashions.
- Older consumers need to feel confident about what they purchase and where they purchase it. Relationship marketing may be particularly important with this group, as is providing transport and safe comfortable environments in which to

Week Six
# WEDNESDAY

> shop. This will pay off in terms of brand or store loyalty as older people are more loyal customers.
> - Encouraging complaints and feedback from this group may be particularly important, given that they will not always complain spontaneously.
> - Advertisements aimed at older people are few and far between. They can be effective provided that they avoid stereotyping (ideally avoid portraying older people and focusing instead on the issue concerned) and stress quality, security and independence. Since information is processsed more slowly, the pace of the presentation needs to be slower than that for younger groups. Nostalgia can often be put to good use, as in advertisements for Hovis.
> - Product developers need to consult potential users. Heinz blundered by introducing 'senior food' after finding that older people were buying jars of baby food because it did not require chewing. Older people would not buy it because of the image although they continued to buy the baby food!

## Social class

*Definitions/issues*

Social status is position in society relative to others. A social class is a group of individuals who have a similar status. It is measured by a number of indicators including education, occupation and income. In some societies (described as 'open'), movement between classes is easy; in closed societies it is difficult or impossible. It is relevant to consumer behaviour because it indicates both purchasing power and purchasing preferences.

# WEDNESDAY

> **ACTIVITY**
>
> Which products and activities would you associate with the upper, middle and working classes?

*Important points*

1 Certain products, services and stores are associated with particular social classes. Social class seems to be a good predictor of purchasing goods such as cosmetics and alcohol – and items associated with 'taste' such as homes, cars and furnishings. Some items, like Rolex watches, may be bought as indicators of class.

2 Leisure activities also vary according to class. Jogging, swimming and tennis may be favoured by the upper classes and team sports by the lower classes. The middle classes are more likely to use public facilities as the rich have their own (although high-status health clubs and golf clubs are an exception). The lower classes may not be able to afford them at all. Tastes in music and reading material also vary.

3 The reasons for valuing different possessions have been found to vary with class. Sentimental or aesthetic reasons were given by business people far more than by unemployed people, who were more likely to refer to economic value and usefulness.

4 Purchasing can be affected by the desire to 'buy up' into a particular social class. The idea is that by making the right purchases, a person can be accepted as being from a higher social class. The ultimate extension of this idea can be seen in the form of **conspicuous consumption** where wealth is displayed through lavish entertaining or **conspicuous waste** where resources are not properly used

or thrown away when still useful.
5 **Parody display** is another way of displaying status. In this case it is done through conspicuous avoidance of status symbols and fashionable items as in the fashion for ex-military vehicles instead of luxury motors.

6 Product information-search varies with social class. The working class may have fewer sources available and may rely more on word of mouth. Particular newspapers and magazines are read by particular social classes as well. Use of language by classes differs, with more complex linguistic forms being used by the upper classes and simpler sentence forms and vocabulary by the lower classes.

*Implications*

- Analysis of product usage by social class allows the product itself, pricing, advertising and retailing to be adapted to market it appropriately.
- Offering a complete service to those attempting to 'buy up' but unsure of their own taste may well

# Week Six
# WEDNESDAY

> prove to be successful – e.g. many home builders now provide a furnishing service.
> - Products must be accepted as suitable status symbols and their acceptability reviewed regularly to keep pace with changes in fashion.
> - Advertising needs to make it clear which social class the product is aimed at. Working class-oriented advertisements tend to use more slang, powerful imagery rather than words to emphasise physical qualities and uses of the product, and are placed in appropriate publications.

## Culture

*Definitions/issues*

Culture refers to the values, attitudes, ways of communicating and material objects (including works of art and everyday artifacts) shared by a group of people. It is an important source of self-identity and ideas about acceptable behaviour. Within any culture there are also smaller subcultural groups which vary in distinctive ways; these may be regional (as in the different parts of the UK), religious or ethnic. It is essential to understand the values and traditions of different groups if marketing is to be done successfully. This is known as **ethnoconsumerism**.

*Important points*

1 Culturally appropriate behaviour regarding choice and use of products is embodied in **consumption values**. These dictate the product's function (and consumer expectations of quality), form (e.g. whether washing machines have to be front or top-loading), and meaning (e.g. certain food may have religious connotations in some societies).

# WEDNESDAY

2 Cultures produce their own myths – often stories about the triumph of good over evil; Superman can be regarded as a modern myth.

3 Cultures also have rituals such as the observance of Christmas Day and birthdays, taking holidays, weddings and gift-giving.

4 Some events, people and objects are given special significance in a culture and are described as being **sacred.** They may then be collected or indulged in for their own sake.

5 Many countries (such as Britain and the USA) are multicultural and need to take account of the sizeable minority group market. African Americans, for example, comprise 12% of the population and have distinctive lifestyles, family structures, dietary practices, fashion preferences and cosmetic needs.

6 Although the core values of a culture remain relatively constant, changes in society are occurring all the time; for example, there are changes in divorce rates and gender roles. Particular generations may also have specific experiences (e.g. living through a period of social protest) which give them unique characteristics. Political and social conditions can thus lead to certain products being more acceptable than others.

7 Popular culture involves changes in fashion being accepted by large numbers of people at the same time because they express relevant meanings and needs. This can affect a wide range of products from clothing to foods, music, leisure activities, holiday destinations etc. Fashions may be long-lived, in which case they are known as 'classics' (e.g. court shoes for women) or short-term 'fads' such as yo-yos.

Week Six
# WEDNESDAY

8 Marketing itself is part of modern culture. **Product placement** (paying film and televison producers to include products such as in the use of BMW cars in James Bond films) has become big business. Theme parks represent an extreme form of **reality engineering** where an entire cultural environment is constructed by the marketers.

*Implications*

- Violation of cultural expectations will have an adverse impact on product success. The Spice Girls did not go down too well in New Zealand when they performed a Maori war dance meant to be performed only by men! In Japan, the word for the number '4' also means death, and Japanese people are very superstitious about buying items in fours.
- Consumption values need to be researched before products are marketed in specific cultures. For example, expensive high-quality washing machines have not proved to be succcessful in the USA although they are sought after in Germany.
- Advertisements based on mythological figures or popular themes (e.g. the alien from outer space/ET) will be easy for consumers to understand and relate to.
- Rituals can be used to marketing advantage, as in Christmas and birthday presents. Self-gifts ('because you're worth it') can be used to boost sales.
- Items which are sacred take on a value that far exceeds their worth and therefore present a good marketing opportunity. Consider the success of Pokemon cards, for example.
- Using advertisements directed at minority groups could be beneficial where the product is of interest

# WEDNESDAY
Week Six

> to them and advertisements are placed in appropriate media.
> - Cultural change can indicate important new marketing opportunities e.g. as family structures and working life have changed, ready meals have become more acceptable to consumers. As well as cultural change the values of different generations need to be taken into account when devising advertising campaigns.
> - Marketers have an ethical responsibility to consider the way that products can shape society.

## Family and gender roles

*Definitions/issues*
A family is generally defined as a group of two or more persons who live together and are related by blood, marriage or adoption. A household is a group of persons who share a housing unit and have common housekeeping arrangements. Both groups are important to marketers since they purchase items jointly and influence one another's decisions about what to buy.

*Important points*
1 A family goes through changes over time: this is known as the **Family Life Cycle (FLC)**. Young couples have children who eventually leave home and the family then consists of two older adults. At each stage there will be changes in income and in expenditure on leisure, food, durables and services according to family requirements. After the birth of a child a young couple may have less money available for leisure activities and for eating out.

Week Six

# WEDNESDAY

2 Family members also have different roles to play in purchasing decisions. One person may originate an idea and others may provide information, make financial decisions and carry out the purchasing.

> *ACTIVITY*
>
> Think about who makes the purchasing decisions for different types of goods in one household with which you are familiar.

In most families women tend to dominate where groceries and clothing are concerned while men dominate when purchasing hardware and lawnmowers. Holidays, televisions, refrigerators and furniture are joint decisions. Autonomy tends to be the rule for decisions about jewellery, mens' clothing, painting/decorating supplies, luggage, sports equipment and toys/games. Since 1980 consumer research has shown that changes in family structures are leading to changes in gender roles within the family. There is now far more joint decision-making about purchases.

3 Gender roles within the family may also differ; such differences may extend to product preferences (e.g. men prefer meat and women fruit) and expected behaviours (e.g. women are traditionally the gift-givers and organisers of social events such as parties). Particular products (such as toys) are often associated with masculinity or femininity (e.g. Barbie dolls and Action men).
4 The nature of the family has always been variable according to culture; some cultures have extended family units which include grandparents. Recent cultural

# WEDNESDAY

changes have introduced a variety of new family forms such as single parents, cohabiting couples, reconstituted families (e.g. remarried couples with step-children) as well as single-person and multiple-person households.

5 Societal changes in gender roles, based on the rise of feminism and the 'new man', have led to rejection of the sex-typed product by many consumers. The increase in women's employment has created new strains for women who feel they have to cope with two 'jobs'.

New Man    Two Jobs Woman

6 As well as defining the typical behaviours of men and women, society portrays ideal images of how they should look – what is regarded as 'beautiful'. This differs according to culture and era, as shown by the fact that Miss World winners are getting thinner and thinner.

*Implications*

- FLC affects consumption and marketers can target different groups accordingly. Alcohol consumption and leisure activities are more relevant to young couples,

# Week Six
## WEDNESDAY

   child care facilities to those with young children and home maintenance services to older couples.
- Understanding of roles played in decision-making can help marketers to target the correct family member. Decision-makers and buyers may be more important to marketers than users are for some items.
- Advertisers have traditionally portrayed certain gender roles in advertisements and sex-typed their products. As a result of public concern with the effects of such communications, this is no longer acceptable to most consumers. Women are increasingly being portrayed as independent and responsible and men as sharing in domestic work.
- New types of family unit present new opportunities for market segmentation. Gay and lesbian couples, single parents and cohabiting couples and the divorced can all be focused on by advertisers for different purposes. For example, divorced persons may need an entire set of household equipment. Similarly, changing gender roles offer scope for new marketing strategies. Unisex toys, and new depictions of men and women in advertisements are all responses to societal changes which in turn act to socialise the next generation into their roles.
- Ideals of beauty are used by advertisers to heighten the insecurity that many people feel about their appearance and to promote the wish to use particular products to change themselves. Clothing, cosmetics, dietary aids, plastic surgery, body piercing and tattooing are all promoted with this in mind and provide lucrative markets.

# WEDNESDAY

## Summary

Today we have been looking at different types of consumer and we have seen that:

- Children and the elderly present different types of challenges to marketers.
- Social class is associated with differences in product usage and therefore 'buying up' can be encouraged.
- An awareness of cultural values and cultural changes is essential for effective product development and marketing.
- Marketing opportunities are presented by changing gender roles and different stages of family life.

Tomorrow we will be looking at product branding and advertising, to explore how this information can be put to good use.

Week Six

# T H U R S D A Y

# Product advertising

Today we will be examining the process of communicating with potential consumers. The success of a product is dependent on this and in turn depends on the knowledge about consumers that you have already acquired from previous chapters of this week.

*Definitions/issues*
The process of persuasion involves a source of information (e.g. the company which is marketing the product or the person who appears for them in the advertisement), a message (e.g. that butter substitutes are better for your health), a medium of communication (e.g. newspapers), and a receiver (the consumers who interpret the information). Examining the process in terms of these elements demonstrates that a variety of factors can influence how persuasive the process is.

---

*ACTIVITY*

Think about four advertisements that you can recall well. What has made them memorable?

---

*Important points*
1 The effectiveness of the source depends primarily on communicator credibility (including expertise and trustworthiness) and attractiveness (which can include physical appearance as well as status).
2 Messages are more effective if they use both rational and

emotional appeals and avoid excessive use of fear. Sex and humour attract attention but may not improve attitudes towards the product. The way that information is presented and the words used to describe the product (including its name) will influence the way that it is perceived. For example, the colour orange is perceived as cheap, and dark-coloured objects are perceived as heavier than identical ones in lighter colours. Big Mac or Whopper burgers will be perceived as bigger than burgers of an identical size which are described as singles.

Big                    Supergianthumungousburger

3 The nature of the target group will also determine the content of the advertisement; better-educated consumers prefer two-sided arguments and those low in self-esteem will respond to products which offer to increase this.
4 The **elaboration likelihood model** of persuasion suggests that an important factor in advertisement design is the degree of involvement of the consumer with the product. Highly involved consumers will be more influenced by the message content, and low-involvement consumers by the message source.

Week Six
# THURSDAY

5 The nature of the product (whether it is utilitarian or purely for enjoyment, whether it is a new product, what kind of image is desired for it, whether it is better than its competitors) will also influence the nature of the advertisement.

6 Finally, the attention, interest and desire that have been generated by the advertisement need to be translated into action in the form of purchase.

*Implications*

- It is essential to determine the nature of the target consumer group before an advertising campaign can be mounted since it affects choice of source, message content and medium.
- Use of celebrities can enhance source effectiveness provided that their image and that of the product are well-matched. Gary Lineker's 'Mr Nice Guy' reputation was used appropriately by Walkers to increase awareness of their product from 40 to 60%, for example. On the other hand, Pepsi had to abandon Michael Jackson after he was accused of child abuse. The credibility of celebrities is not always high, especially if they endorse too many products.
- Advertisements need to be carefully designed to interest the target consumers, and will need to be regularly changed to prevent them losing interest.
- Advertisements must take existing levels of knowledge of consumers into account and understanding and interpretation must be checked at an early stage in the campaign; it cannot be

# THURSDAY

assumed that the perception will be as intended.
- In order to gain acceptance, advertisements must evoke positive thoughts and feelings. Pictures which have this effect – even if irrelevant to the product – can improve acceptance of the product.
- Information which is well organised, repeated, makes good use of visual images, and is relevant to needs will be better remembered.
- Both source and content ('how' and 'what') are important elements of advertising since they appeal to different types of consumer (high vs low involvement).
- Utilitarian products may be better promoted by informational than by emotional appeals. Where there is no clear difference in performance that the advert can capitalise on, sales may be promoted by peripheral cues such as the use of attractive pictures.
- Information needs to be presented using media that will be observed by the target group of consumers e.g. the 'Sun' or the 'Independent'.
- The product must be readily available and appropriately priced to encourage purchase. Indicating where it can be bought may be a useful part of the advertising process.

## Direct behaviour shaping

*Definitions/issues*

Advertising has limitations in producing behaviour change as there is no guaranteee that consumers will see advertisements or respond to them. Behaviour shaping

## THURSDAY

approaches have therefore been developed which involve requests being made directly to consumers.

*Important points*

1 Prompts to buy something related can be given when consumers are making a purchase. For example, a waitress in a restaurant may ask consumers if they would like anything to drink with the meal.
2 A large request can be preceded by a smaller one (known as the 'foot-in-the-door' technique). Research has shown that asking homeowners to display a large road safety sign in their gardens was successful only 17% of the time; if they were asked first of all to display a smaller poster in the window on the same theme, 76% agreed to the larger request when it was made later.

3 The 'door-in-the-face' technique involves making an initial large request in the hope that a smaller one will then prove to be more acceptable – which it generally is.
4 Reciprocity is the idea that if a consumer is given something as a gift they will then feel obliged to

# THURSDAY

reciprocate by making a purchase.
5 Making a public commitment to an action has been found to increase the chances that people will stick to it. This can apply to agreeing to give something a try or to writing something down for future reference.
6 Incentives can be used to increase purchases or interest in the product. Coupons have been found to lead to double the number of purchases in households which received them compared with no-coupon households. Price discounts and competitions are other incentive schemes.

*Implications*

- Prompts can be an effective way of encouraging consumers to consider purchases they may otherwise have overlooked.
- The foot-in-the-door technique is generally more effective than a simple request though its effectiveness is dependent on the amount of time delay between the two requests, the similarity of the two requests and whether or not the first one is actually carried out in practice.
- Door-in-the-face is used by sales staff to encourage more expensive purchases, by offering the top of the range products first and then working down to the lower. The average sale has been found to be considerably more than if the reverse is done.
- Offering tasters of foods in supermarkets can lead to consumers feeling obliged to make purchases; similarly charities often include free gifts (such as pens) in letters requesting donations.
- If consumers fill in agreement forms themselves

> they are more likely to feel committed to the purchase. Research has shown that they are then less likely to cancel the agreement.
> - Although incentives increase purchases, they are costly and may therefore be unwise unless the increased sales compensate for the reduced profits on each sale. Consumers may also become so used to incentives that they will not purchase without them. Ford cars tried to remove incentives only to find that sales fell dramatically, obliging them to reintroduce the schemes.

## Summary

Today you have seen that:

- Message content and source are equally important when designing advertisements and must be tailored to the product and the target consumer.
- Advertising may often need to be supplemented by direct requests and offers in order to bring about behaviour change.

Tomorrow we shall move on to retailing which is hopefully the final stage of selling your product.

Week Six

**F R I D A Y**

# Product retailing

Today we will be looking at the process of matching consumers with products so that purchases can be made. Even when they have decided to make a purchase, consumers may be put off if there are obstacles in their way, so anything that can be done to make the shopping process easier will obviously boost sales. Important areas to consider include:

- shoppers
- store preferences
- store loyalty
- shopping locations and shopping trends

## Shoppers

*Definitions/issues*
It is important to consider the reasons why people go shopping and the influences on them when they do shop. If the retail environment can be set up to appeal to their needs more fully, they may be encouraged to spend more time there and/or spend more money during their trip.

> *ACTIVITY*
>
> How much time each week do you spend shopping? How many trips do you make? Why do you go shopping?

*Important points*
1 People are spending less time shopping than they used to. Most make one main trip each week – often on the same

# FRIDAY

day – and sometimes secondary trips. Shopping no longer rates as a popular leisure activity having been replaced by relaxing at home, spending time with families and outdoor activities.

2 Several different shopping types have been identified including economic consumers (concern with value), personalised consumers (concern with relationships), ethical consumers (wanting to help the underdog), recreational shoppers (shopping as a leisure activity) and apathetic consumers (who dislike shopping).

3 Frequent shoppers are motivated by personal motives such as dispelling boredom, beating the system, relieving depression and fulfilling fantasies as well as social motives such as alleviating loneliness and providing for others.

4 The number and type of other shoppers in a retail outlet influences the way shoppers see their surroundings and how they feel. Places which are too crowded or too empty are generally unpopular. Crowding in particular reduces shopping time, non-essential purchases and interaction with sales staff, and generally leads to a negative evaluation of the shopping experience. The appearance of other shoppers gives important clues to the status of the establishment.

5 Lack of time is expressed by many shoppers as a problem; however, this may be a matter of perception since modern society has more time free of work and housework than ever before.

6 People who are stimulated or aroused and have pleasant experiences will be in a better mood and evaluate goods and services more positively. Shopping is not just a utilitarian exercise.

## FRIDAY

*Implications*

- As time for shopping is limited to one weekly trip in many cases, goods and services must be available from a fairly compact area. If it can be made family-friendly and relaxing, shoppers may be able to combine their needs to spend time with families and relax with shopping. Many supermarkets now have cafes and children's areas for this reason.
- Retail outlets need to cater for a range of motives as well as simply providing products and services. This includes giving good value, doing so in an ethical way, providing a personal touch and creating an enjoyable leisure experience.
- Design of the retail area can go a long way towards reducing the impression of crowding; high ceilings create a feeling of spaciousness. Offering discounts at off-peak times (at the beginning of the week, around lunch-times and in the afternoon) or simply advertising so that consumers know when those quiet times are, may also reduce crowding.
- For some types of product or service it may be necessary to restrict access to consumers who have the right appearance. Hence many restaurants and clubs will have dress codes.
- Time spent waiting in queues needs to be reduced. This can be done by changing the layout of the outlet as in an airport where baggage reclaims were moved further away, making travellers spend more time walking but less time queueing. Or it can be done by providing a diversion, such as a mirror placed by a lift, which decreases reported waiting times.

Week Six

## FRIDAY

- Happy music, attention to store design (including colour, smells, etc.) and cheerful staff can be used to improve mood and hence evaluation of products.

## Store preferences

*Definitions/issues*

Since most consumers will visit a limited range of shops, it is important to identify what determines their choices. Choice and design of outlet from which to sell products has become a key feature of successful marketing. It has been found that a store can improve its sales by up to 300% by changing colours, lighting and signs.

*ACTIVITY*

Which stores do you prefer to shop in and why?

# FRIDAY

Week Six

*Important points*

1 Availability of information about products may influence preference; if it is readily available, in an easily understandable form, consumers will be more likely to make use of the store.
2 Music contributes considerably to store atmospherics. Slow music increases both shopping time and expenditure, compared to fast music. Loud music reduces shopping time but not expenditure.
3 Layout of stores can be manipulated to ensure that consumers can move around the store easily (even when other shoppers and trolleys may be around) and to ensure that they come into contact with particular products.
4 Studies of the effects of colour are not always reliable, but it has been suggested that using bright, warm colours outside helps to draw consumers in. Inside, cool colours like blue and green may be more relaxing. Green in particular may be calming where queueing takes place and red may stimulate impulse-buying and perceptions that goods are up-to-date.
5 Stores are also chosen for their image which represents a general view about the range, quality, value and service that the store provides.
6 Other important determinants of supermarket preference have been found to be cleanliness, well-stocked shelves, range of products, number of checkouts, helpful staff, disabled access, wide aisles, car parking, range of different checkouts (e.g. express), free bags and environmentally friendly goods.

## Week Six

# FRIDAY

*Implications*

- Information must be available in the appropriate form. Consumers prefer number ratings or figures (e.g. 30mpg) to written evaluation (excellent, good, etc.).
- Choice of music needs to be adapted to the nature of the store; where consumers need to be encouraged to pass through quickly, louder music may be beneficial. Music can be used to manipulate perceptions of the store's image – classical music may give the store a more up-market image and has been found to be associated with the purchase of more expensive wines when played in a wine store. Music also needs to be matched to the demographic characteristics of the consumers as can be seen in fashion shops. Studies have shown that when it is, shopping time and purchases can rise by around 18%.
- Placing bakery departments near entrances to provide good smells and impulse buy products near the check-outs are two examples of how location can be utilised within-store to promote purchases. Areas where a lot of people will pass (e.g. the ends of aisles) can be used for special promotions. Placing popular lines – such as the delicatessen – at the back of the store means that people will have to go past all of the other products in order to reach them.
- Cueing can be done by placing products near those that they may be associated with eg placing dips near crisps. Items at eye level sell twice as well as those at low levels.

# FRIDAY

**Week Six**

## Good Smells

- Although the effects are more variable, the colour of both the exterior and the interior of a store needs careful thought. The general colour scheme may contribute to store image but it may also be necessary to change the colour in different parts of the store. As well as colour, materials used can convey particular impressions; Laura Ashley use wood to convey quality and solidity. Aromas can also be used, as they are in the Body Shop.
- Because the image of a store is slow to change, it is important to make use of corporate advertising to ensure that this is a good one. Tesco are still thought of as relatively cheap and cheerful despite having improved their range of products in recent years.
- Consumer surveys indicate that a wide range of features to do with the social and physical aspects of the store need to be considered when trying to increase the store's share of the market.

Week Six

# FRIDAY

## Store loyalty

*Definitions/issues*

Store loyalty is usually defined as the proportion of expenditure that occurs in the store most used for any particular type of purchase. This need not necessarily be the largest proportion – it is possible to spend more money in a store that is less often used. Therefore it is important to understand the reasons for store loyalty.

*Important points*

1 Levels of loyalty appear to be quite high – around 75% over one month and 65% over a year for supermarkets. 75% of expenditure occurs in the favourite store.
2 Store loyalty may be the outcome of limited resources in terms of choice, time, transport or money, or it may simply reflect lack of interest in shopping around.
3 High loyalty is most common in the 25–44 age group, particularly where there are several school age children in the family and the mother works. This indicates that loyalty may be a form of efficiency reflecting a preference for 'one-stop' shopping in those people who have busy lives.

*Implications*

- Since loyalty levels are generally quite high it would seem to be the preferred way to shop where the right stores are available.
- High loyalty shoppers have been shown to spend up to 70% more in their preferred store than low loyalty shoppers, making them useful people to recruit.
- Increasing the efficiency with which shopping can

# Week Six
## FRIDAY

> be carried out may well appeal to high loyalty shoppers and encourage them to use the store.
> - Loyalty cards have been introduced by many stores to try to keep customers, offering dividends or discounts in return for repeated purchases. Sainsbury's managed to increase their share of the market by 1% following the introduction of such a card.

## Shopping locations and shopping trends

*Definitions/issues*

Shopping has changed a great deal in recent years – in terms of both where the main shops are located in a town or city and what kind of shops there are. There have also been changes in the method of retailing so that shopping can be done through other channels. These changes can have implications for marketers as well as for consumers.

*Important points*

1 Location is a key determinant of store preference and can affect sales dramatically. E.g., McDonald's makes twice as many sales as its two main rivals combined.
2 Out-of-town shopping complexes, such as Lakeside and Bluewater, offer easy parking and a large number of different retail outlets, as well as entertainment centres and recreational facilities. They have proved to be popular with shoppers who see shopping as a leisure activity.
3 City-centre shopping is often concentrated in shopping malls. The largest of these is the West Edmonton Mall in Canada which has 800 stores, 19 cinemas, a hotel, 110 food outlets, a 5-acre indoor waterpark, a golf course, a

chapel and a zoo. These pedestrianised zones tend to have a large number of smaller specialist shops such as newsagents.
4 Mail order shopping has changed from providing cheap fashion and household goods on credit to the working classes to selling a wide range of specialist and high-quality goods (e.g. Laura Ashley's 'Home' catalogue) to the middle and upper classes. The availability of credit cards, telephones and the internet has boosted this type of retailing in recent years.
5 Internet shopping is particularly popular with younger shoppers (in their teens and twenties). Danish figures for the year 2000 estimated that 60% of companies would have a website and 20% of households internet access.

*Implications*

- When planning to expand into new locations it is important to analyse the demographic characteristics of the consumers in that area as well as the competition from other retailers. This is known as market selection and should help to identify key cities that could be targeted. Then area analysis can be carried out to narrow down the choice to certain areas within those cities. Finally choice of specific site can be made based on size, cost, parking, public transport, ease of access, visibility, etc. A few hundred yards difference can be crucial in determining the success of the store.
- Very large complexes and stores can suffer from impersonality, and loyalty may be reduced because of this. Therefore it is all the more important to

# FRIDAY

Week Six

emphasise the relationship aspects of selling when training staff.
- Leisure facilities are essential in some types of outlet but will not be cost-effective in others, as shoppers are there for functional reasons only.
- Smaller shops may be making a come-back. Planning authorities are now less prepared to give permission for out-of-town stores because city centres are becoming deserted. Smaller local shops are also more convenient and personal. Hence Sainsbury's have introduced the 'Sainsbury's Local', a smaller version shop with a good range of popular items that remains open for long hours.

# Week Six
## FRIDAY

- Many retailers are trying out a variety of retail forms so that they do not lose customers to the new non-store retailers. Next have mail order and internet strategies as well as their own shops.
- Solving the problems of internet shopping (e.g. lack of security) is an important issue. However it requires consumers to take the initiative and many still prefer the experience of visiting shops.

## Summary

Today we have seen that:

- Shoppers are motivated by pleasure and practicality; stores must cater for both aspects of the shopping experience.
- Shoppers also prefer stores that have a particular image and are influenced by physical aspects of the environment such as layout, design, music, smells and form in which information is presented.
- Encouraging store loyalty boosts sales a great deal.
- Careful consideration also needs to be given to store size and location as well as alternative retailing strategies.

Tomorrow we will finish our exploration of consumer behaviour by looking at some of the negative effects of a 'consumer society'.

Week Six

## SATURDAY

# Negative effects and implications

Today we are going to look at difficulties that may arise as a result of living in a consumer society and being subjected to some of the marketing strategies we have been discussing. This chapter is divided into three sections, as follows:

- individual effects
- environmental effects
- socio-cultural effects

## Individual effects

*Definitions/issues*
Encouraging consumption may have detrimental consequences for individuals which can lead to behaviour disorders. Consumption can become a compulsion, often carried out in order to boost the self-esteem of the person concerned. It becomes disruptive both socially and financially and is associated with guilt and depression. In this section we will consider the following: compulsive shopping, hoarding and collecting; shoplifting and kleptomania; gambling; eating disorders; and other disorders of body image.

*Important points*
1 Compulsive shoppers ('shopaholics') are driven by the impulse to buy; in many cases they never use the things that they acquire. It has been estimated that 15 million Americans may be compulsive shoppers. Up to 92% of these may be younger women who have problems with self-esteem and disturbed relationships with partners.

# SATURDAY

Those with partners who work excessively, control or ignore them, are more likely to be compulsive shoppers. Making purchases lifts their mood temporarily.

2 Collecting and hoarding behaviour differs from compulsive shopping in that it is the objects themselves that are valued, not the act of purchase. It has been reported that two-thirds of American households have collections of some kind. It is problematic when it becomes single-minded, when debts are incurred and when space becomes limited because sufferers refuse to part with anything, even old newspapers. This in turn impairs social life because they cannot receive visitors.

3 Shoplifting occurs in as many as 5% of shoppers at some point in time – though up to 50% of thefts from shops are in fact carried out by staff. Having open shelves (as in supermarkets) promotes sales and reduces the need for staff but promotes shoplifting. Although traditionally seen as a female behaviour, most shoplifters in recent years have been males aged 10–18. It may be done for gain and excitement (particularly in poorer groups) or it may be associated with depression (especially likely in isolated or bereaved women), or the absent-mindedness associated with early dementia.

4 **Kleptomania** is defined as repeated failure to resist impulses to steal objects that are not required for personal use or for monetary gain. The items stolen may even be thrown away. The act of stealing provides a momentary thrill that relieves tension. Fewer than 5% of arrested shoplifters have this disorder and it is more prevalent in females. Relationships, both childhood and marital, are often unhappy.

5 Pathological gambling occurs when people become

# SATURDAY

*Week Six*

John is training to be a shoplifter

unable to resist the impulse to gamble despite often being financially ruined. In America, it has been estimated to affect 3% of the adult population, most of whom are men. Heavy lottery players have been found to be low income but with high levels of fantasy about winning. Gamblers may also be motivated by the excitement associated with taking risks, and may be prone to mood disorders.

6 The gambling situation is also set up to increase gambling behaviour: advertising levels are high (e.g. National Lottery and scratchcards); the behaviour is quick to carry out (some American states have lottery draws every hour); it can be repeated as often as the gambler can afford to do it (e.g. scratchcards); payouts are large and unpredictable; and many near misses are built into the system (e.g. with fruit machines). Casinos often have minimum bets, low light levels and no clocks so that people lose track of time, stay longer and spend more.

7 Motivating consumers to aspire to an ideal physical

# Week Six
## SATURDAY

appearance can lead to a variety of mental disorders. The most obvious of these are the eating disorders anorexia nervosa and bulimia nervosa. Anorexics are mainly young girls (as many as 90% of whom report being dissatisfied with their weight) and they have a perception of themselves as being overweight which leads them to starve themselves. Bulimics are not neccessarily underweight but are prone to massive food binges (up to 5000 calories) followed by guilt and purging in the form of induced vomiting or use of laxatives. This can lead to physical problems such as constipation, or even burst stomachs, and to social isolation as a result of their guilt feelings and the cost of all the food needed to maintain the behaviour.

8  Bodily dysmorphophobia is a general term for body image distortions. Sufferers may feel that their breasts are too small or their noses too large though objectively they are normal. This may lead to their seeking plastic surgery (which can in itself be hazardous, as in silicone breast implants), or to self-mutilation.

*Implications*

- Therapy for compulsive shopping, hoarding and collecting starts with investigating upbringing and attitudes to money and possessions, followed by an examination of the functions that the behaviour serves at present for the client. Changes in lifestyles and self-concept may be necessary to reduce these needs.
- Surveillance of open shelves is particularly important and most shops now have CCTV and store detectives. Limiting the number of young people allowed in a shop at one time has also been used as

# SATURDAY
Week Six

a way of increasing their visibility to staff. Most shoplifters are unlikely to re-offend and would benefit from therapeutic interventions to treat their emotional problems which courts will often arrange.
- Very little has been done to assist people with kleptomania as it is rarely seen. It may respond to treatment with antidepressant drugs such as Prozac and to psychotherapy.
- Gamblers require psychotherapy to treat their problems. They may need to develop other outlets for their need for excitement, and family problems will also need to be dealt with. It has been suggested that organisations such as Camelot should be required to fund treatment centres.
- Regulation of gambling can also be achieved through restriction of advertising, reducing the number of outlets and locating them away from vulnerable members of the populace. The frequency of lottery draws can also be reduced so that there is less chance of habits forming.
- Disorders of bodily image have been blamed on the excessive use of advertising that promotes unattainable ideals, especially for young women, and the use of extremely thin models. Recently, advertisers and fashion houses have been encouraged to use women who are average-sized, and there have been more campaigns in support of fat people.
- Many people who suffer from disorders of body image have other difficulties, such as low self-esteem, depression and family problems which have been found to respond to treatment using antidepressant drugs and psychotherapy.

Week Six
# SATURDAY

## Environmental effects

*Definitions/issues*

The relationship between people and the environment they inhabit is a complex one and it has many implications for consumer behaviour. Consumption of resources and disposal of waste are key issues. The attitudes of consumers have changed in recent years with respect to green issues and health, affecting their choice of products and their attitudes towards the companies that manufacture them.

*Important points*

1 Private households, industry and service/commercial users contribute roughly equally to energy consumption which in turn depletes resources and adds to the greenhouse effect and pollution levels.
2 A typical American has been estimated to generate 25lb of solid waste in a week. This causes problems when considering where to dispose of it – landfill sites, incinerators, disposal at sea and littering being the obvious choices. Not only is this dangerous and polluting, it simply adds to the problem of inadequate resources.
3 As many as 80% of consumers – 'green consumers' – want to buy environmentally responsible products. In the UK, around 10% of these are heavily committed to doing so. This extends to the means of production (is the company responsible for pollution?), resources used (is timber from sustainable forests?), packaging (is it recyclable?), product development (is it tested on animals?), and effects on health of consumers.

# SATURDAY

Week Six

## *ACTIVITY*

What do you feel about environmental issues? Give yourself a rating on a scale from 1 (not at all interested) to 10 (very concerned). Now think about your shopping behaviour. Do concerns about the environment affect your product choices? Does this fit in with your general level of concern for the environment as noted above? If there is a discrepancy, why do you think this is?

*Implications*

- Consumers can be encouraged to use products which are themselves energy-saving. For example, it has been estimated that in 1970, if the most efficient refrigerator had been chosen by all purchasers in the USA, 17 million tons of coal and 26,000 acres of land from which it would have been mined could have been saved. At some point it may even be necessary

# Week Six
# SATURDAY

to consider demarketing of some products – encouraging consumers to buy them less often if at all – the motor car being the obvious example.

- Littering (disposing of waste in the wrong place) can be reduced by around 15% by the provision of more bins on the street; these are most effective if they are bright and colourful. A more direct way of reducing littering would be to reduce the excess packaging of products or offer incentives for disposing of it correctly.
- The amount of waste generated can also be reduced by introducing recycling (recovery of materials, as in bottle banks), re-use (using things for different purposes as in the use of worn tyres for sileage clamps), remarketing (e.g. second hand sales), and reclamation (remanufacture of materials e.g. making plastic drinks bottles into insulation). Some manufacturers, such as BMW, have introduced incentives for recycling components from their cars. The easier it is made for consumers to comply with such schemes, the more likely it is that they will do so.
- Green concerns present new marketing opportunities. The Belgian company Ecover has produced a range of cleaning products which are enzyme and phosphate-free; CFC-free pump-action sprays; and Body Shop cosmetics are all products designed with the environment in mind. Recent food products which cater for consumers' health concerns include vegetarian and organic foods, sugar, salt and fat-free foods and alcohol-free beers and wines.

Week Six

# SATURDAY

- Some companies have responded to environmental concerns by representing themselves as green: BP has now presented a new image of being 'Beyond Petroleum'.

## Social/cultural effects

*Definitions/issues*
Consumer rights have been an issue since early campaigners (such as Ralph Nader in 1950s America) first made people aware that they were not always being treated ethically by companies. With the rise of global marketing in recent years, it has now extended to ethical concerns about the way that companies behave in other parts of the world.

*Important points*
1 Consumer rights in America include: the right to safety; to be (accurately) informed; to have a choice of products; to be heard (redress); to enjoy a healthy environment; and (for minority groups) to have their interests protected.
2 In the UK similar rights are upheld by the Office of Fair Trading, the Health and Safety Executive, the Consumer Association and the Advertising Standards Authority.
3 The rights of children has become a particular issue in recent years as children are felt to be more persuadable and more companies are targeting child consumers. There is also concern about the amount of conflict between parent and child that may be promoted by child-focused advertising.
4 Finally, given that people in the West seem to be suffering from increasing levels of unhappiness due to the erosion of community and family life, it has been suggested that

# Week Six
## SATURDAY

marketing our lifestyle to other cultures may be ethically unsound.

*Implications*

- Product safety is a major issue and products which are unsafe – such as DDT, some children's toys and certain vehicles – have been withdrawn from the market or recalled for expensive modifications. Other products which raise health concerns – such as silicone breast implants and cigarettes – may go unnoticed for many years but eventually result in costly legal action against the company.
- Labelling of products, listing ingredients and identifying additives and sell-by dates for foods, has now become mandatory. Provision of accurate information extends to advertising, which is required to be 'honest'. Deception is difficult to prove, given that material is often misunderstood by consumers anyway. Volvo cars in North America have been reported for using reinforcement in the cars used for crash tests in their advertisements. Cosmetic surgery clinics have recently been ordered not to play down the risks of surgery in their advertisements and not to claim to be 'leading' establishments unless they have some evidence to back this up.
- The right to choice of products means that companies cannot be allowed to develop monopolies. Education about how to make choices has been advocated in order to improve the quality of choices made by consumers.

# SATURDAY

Week Six

- The right to redress means that many more products are accompanied by guarantees these days.
- In 1996, the Advertising Standards Authority in the UK received 12,055 complaints about advertisements. Of these, 846 were complaints about the sexist portrayal of women, which is more than double the number in the previous year. In 17 cases the adverts were withdrawn. Sexist portrayal of men has also been criticised as in the Micra 'Ask before you borrow it' advert which portrays a man clutching his crotch after taking his wife's car without permission. Another example is the Wallis 'Dressed to kill' slogan showing women distracting male motorists so that they have fatal accidents.
- The extent to which global marketing should show respect for the customs of other cultures needs to be carefully considered. Producers of the TV programme 'Blind Date' were subjected to death threats from Muslim fundamentalists when the programme was exported to Turkey.
- On a more sinister level some tobacco companies are now concentrating their sales drives on Third World countries where awareness of the dangers is less and there are fewer restriction on sales (e.g. to children).

# SATURDAY

Week Six

## Summary

In this final chapter we have seen that:

- Encouraging excessive consumption and conveying particular images of the ideal person can affect some individuals detrimentally in the form of compulsive shopping, hoarding, shoplifting, kleptomania, eating disorders and bodily dysmorphophobia.
- Such individuals often have problems with self-esteem and relationships, and need psychotherapy.
- Environmental issues can be addressed by encouraging conservation, use of energy-saving products and recycling, reuse and remarketing.
- Green consumers present new marketing opportunities but also demand environmentally responsible behaviours from companies.
- The rights of consumers to safety, information, choice, redress and a healthy environment must be met.
- The rights of minority groups and members of other cultures must also be respected.

This brief survey of consumer behaviour has attempted to introduce you to some of the key areas of interest to researchers and practitioners as well as addressing the concerns of consumers themselves.

For information

on other

**IN A WEEK** titles

go to

www.inaweek.co.uk